THE CIVIL WAR
IN THE UNITED STATES

MARXIST LIBRARY
Works of Marxism – Leninism
VOLUME XXX

THE

CIVIL WAR

IN THE

UNITED STATES

BY

KARL MARX

AND

FREDERICK ENGELS

NEW YORK
INTERNATIONAL PUBLISHERS

This volume was edited by
MR. RICHARD ENMALE
who supplied the explanatory
notes and the introduction

CONTENTS

PART III

CORRESPONDENCE BETWEEN KARL MARX AND FREDERICK ENGELS (1861-1866)

APPENDIX

EDITOR'S INTRODUCTION

THE struggle between revolution and counter-revolution which agitated the American scene from 1861 to 1865 was followed with great interest by Karl Marx and Frederick Engels. Their appraisal of the "first grand war of contemporaneous history," contained within the present volume in the form of newspaper articles and extracts from a voluminous correspondence, clearly shows the progressive and revolutionary character of the American conflict.

The articles appeared originally in the New York *Daily Tribune* and the Vienna *Presse* in 1861 and 1862. Though essentially the work of Marx, they were written in close collaboration with Engels. Marx's connection with the *Daily Tribune* dates back to the close of 1851 when Charles Dana, hoping to recruit new readers, especially from the ranks of the German immigrant element, invited Marx to write a series of articles on conditions in Germany. Marx eagerly accepted the offer for two reasons. In the first place, the New York newspaper with its 200,000 readers was one of the most influential periodicals in America and as such, could be used as an excellent medium for the dissemination of his views. Secondly, the American journal offered the German revolutionary emigré the prospect of a steady source of income, a prospect especially pleasing because Marx at that time was in such dire financial straits that he did not have enough money to meet the expenses entailed in the running of a household.

It was therefore with high hopes that Marx began to work for the *Daily Tribune*. Yet, if he expected to gain economic security in his new position, he was quickly disillusioned. Paid as he was for each article accepted, the editors of the New York newspaper were not remiss to throw out whole columns whose tone they did not approve or to use those which they liked as leading editorials. It is interesting to note in passing that when Marx first began to write for the American periodical, he turned to Engels for help. The latter, knowing that his friend was at the time finding it difficult to write English easily and in addition was busily engaged in other matters, responded by writing a number of articles which were later collected into a separate volume called *Germany: Revolution and Counter-revolution*. This work, though written by Engels, was for a long time attributed to Marx. However, ideologically it represented the combined expression of their views.

For over a decade Marx kept the *Daily Tribune* readers informed of European developments, especially as they affected the United States. Consequently when the Civil War broke out, Marx continued his past work and wrote a series of articles on that momentous conflict. Designed for American consumption, his contributions emphasized the attitude of Europe in general and England in particular to the Union cause. Subjects such as the cotton crisis in Great Britain, the threatened invasion of Mexico, the *Trent* case and British public opinion were discussed. Finally, in the early part of 1862, all connections between the American paper and Marx were severed. In April of that year, Dana informed the latter that the English correspondence would have to be discontinued because the internal American situation took up all the room there was in the paper.

In the meantime, Marx became the English correspondent of *Die Presse,* one of the leading newspapers in Vienna. He was promised a pound for every article accepted and ten shillings for every report. Unfortunately for Marx many of his articles were given "the honors of the waste-paper basket" because Max Friedländer, a cousin of Lassalle and the editor of *Die Presse,* felt that they were not in harmony with the tastes of his readers. On January 7, 1862, Friedländer wrote to Marx asking him "to take into account an Austrian bourgeois public." Yet, in spite of these obstacles, Marx's Vienna *Presse* contributions stand as testimonials to his ability to anticipate future events. For example, as early as November 7, 1861, Marx wrote that American developments were driving the North to promulgate the decisive slogan, *"the emancipation of the slaves."* On August 9, 1862, he informed his readers that "Negro slavery [would] not long outlive the Civil War."

Unlike the articles, the correspondence between Marx and Engels, contained in the present volume, goes beyond the year 1862 and consequently treats not only of the constitutional but also of the revolutionary phase of the struggle. Of particular interest to American readers will be those letters dealing with the relative advantages enjoyed by the North over the South, the character of the Secessionist movement, the significance of the Northwest in bringing matters to a head, the estimate of Lincoln, the military collapse of the Confederacy, and the reconstruction plans of Johnson. After the Civil War, Marx and Engels continued to correspond with each other, as well as with American friends of theirs, on conditions in the United States.

From the articles and letters included herein a panoramic picture of the Civil War is unfolded and its significance clearly shown. The clashing interests of divergent social systems, the inevitable recourse to arms, the offensive taken by the slave power, and the *coup d'état* spirit of the Secessionist conspiracy are graphically developed. Similarly, the relationship of the West to the question of slavery is indicated. Some thirty years before Turner, Marx informed Engels that the more he studied this "American business," the more he became convinced that the struggle "was brought to a head by the weight thrown into the scales by the extraordinary development of the Northwestern States."

In a like fashion, Marx practically anticipated by half a century the "discovery" of Schmidt and other bourgeois historians that Northern wheat played an important role in shaping Anglo-American relations during the Civil War. In his articles Marx made frequent references to England's growing need of American wheat, a need which he recognized as a factor of prime importance in preventing the British ruling classes from intervening on behalf of the Confederacy. The ever-present implication behind these references is that if Great Britain was ever forced to choose between a cotton and a wheat shortage, she would risk her future on the former rather than on the latter.[*]

Marx's power of acute observation is further displayed in his dismissal of the theory that the question of a high protective tariff was responsible for the outbreak of the Civil War. He clearly demonstrated that secession "did not take place because the Morrill tariff had gone through

[*] On this point compare Marx with L. B. Schmidt. See the latter's article on "The Influence of Wheat and Cotton on Anglo-American Relations during the Civil War" in *Iowa Journal of History and Politics*, vol. xvi, no. 3 (July, 1918), pp. 400-439. See also E. D. Fite, *Social and Industrial Conditions in the North during the Civil War* (New York, 1910), p. 21.

Congress, but at most the Morrill tariff went through Congress because secession had taken place."

Marx and Engels followed the military aspects of the American conflict with great interest. No pacifist illusions caused them to shut their eyes to the historical importance of war, especially in respect to revolution and counter-revolution. Engels, a keen student of military science, helped Marx considerably in the latter's evaluation of the campaigns in America. The interest of Engels in military matters was not purely theoretical; it arose out of the concrete events of 1849 in Germany when he participated as an adjutant in the unsuccessful Baden insurrection. From that time on, he devoted himself to the study of military science on the assumption that if the working class was to overcome the bourgeoisie, it would first have to master the art and strategy of war. By 1861, Engels was thoroughly versed in military science, and was thus in an excellent position to help Marx evaluate military developments in America. Marx very often incorporated into his articles whole portions of the letters of Engels, especially those dealing with the military situation in the United States. The result is an admirable military appraisal of the American conflict. Especially praiseworthy are those articles dealing with a criticism of the Confederate defense of Kentucky and of McClellan's "anaconda" plan. It is interesting to note that two years before the Union high command decided to conquer Georgia and thereby cut the Confederacy in two, this plan was suggested in the Vienna *Presse*. On March 27, 1862, after a careful analysis of the military situation, such a procedure was advanced on the ground that Georgia was *"the key to Secessia."*

During the early part of the Civil War, Engels entertained reasonable doubts as to a Northern victory. Discouraged by the blunders of the Union generals and

disgusted by the hesitancy of the North to wage a revolutionary war, Engels asked Marx on September 9, 1862
whether he still believed that "the gentlemen in the
North [would] crush the 'rebellion.'" Marx, taking into
account the economic and social advantages enjoyed by
the North, answered in the affirmative and then went on
to chide his friend for allowing himself to be "swayed a
little too much by the military aspect of things." As the
war progressed, Engels became less pessimistic and finally
agreed fully with Marx as to the ultimate outcome of the
struggle.

Marx and Engels were essentially interested in the
revolutionary implications of the Civil War. From the
very beginning of the conflict, they clearly perceived that
the objective purpose of the struggle was the destruction
of the slave power and with it the South's "peculiar institution." They therefore urged the bourgeois republic
to wage a revolutionary war: to arm the Negroes and to
abolish slavery. Consequently, they greeted with satisfaction the efforts of the Union government during the last
two years of the war to smash the counter-revolution and
to free the slaves.

It was evident to Marx that the eventual emancipation
of the American working class depended upon the preliminary destruction of Negro slavery. "Labor cannot
emancipate itself in the white skin," wrote Marx in
Capital, "where in the black it is branded." Moreover,
he justly observed that the development of any sort of
"independent movement of the workers" would be greatly
hindered "so long as slavery disfigured a part of the Republic." The validity of this observation is obvious once
the devastating effects of chattel labor are realized. So
far as the South was concerned, slavery definitely im-
peded the development of a militant labor movement by
throwing into disrepute the dignity of manual work and

by hindering the growth of manufacturing. The rise of the latter was inconceivable so long as ante-bellum planters preferred to invest their surplus capital in chattels and lands, rather than in factories and railroads. Under these conditions the emergence of a strong independent labor movement in the South was practically impossible. Slavery likewise threatened the rise of a vigorous proletarian movement in the North by menacing the industrial expansion of that section through limiting its market possibilities in the South, impeding its opportunities for exploitation in the West, and preventing the passage of favorable legislation at Washington.

Convinced that the germ of the future revolution lay in the North, Marx supported the bourgeois republic in its struggle against the slave oligarchy. In this respect he had the wholehearted aid of the British proletariat. When in the latter part of 1861, the reactionary Palmerston government attempted to use the *Trent* affair as a pretext for a war against the North, English workers held protest meetings in Brighton and elsewhere. These demonstrations were called in spite of the fact that the British ruling classes did everything in their power to make the workers believe that an alliance with the Confederacy would result in the breaking of the Northern blockade of Southern ports, which in turn, would mean the importation of greater quantities of cotton with consequent re-employment and prosperity. Yet, the British workers could not be so easily fooled; despite widespread misery and starvation, they showed their "indestructible excellence" by opposing the war-mongers and by demanding peace. Their pro-Union demonstrations forced the Palmerston government to adopt a more conciliatory tone throughout the entire *Trent* affair. Marx, in reporting these meetings to his American readers, requested them never to forget that "at least the *working classes* of England" were on their side.

Similarly, the international proletariat supported the American Republic against the slave power. In 1864, Marx, carrying out the instructions of the First International, sent a message to the people of the United States congratulating them upon the re-election of Lincoln. In this address (to be found in the Appendix of the present volume), Marx pointed out that from the beginning of the struggle European workers had made the Northern cause their own and that "the fanatic partisanship of the upper classes for the Confederate gentry had given its dismal warning, that the slaveholders' rebellion was to sound the tocsin for the general holy crusade of property against labor. . . ." In conclusion, Marx asserted that just as the "American War of Independence initiated a new era of ascendancy for the middle class, so the American anti-slavery war will for the working classes."

From the foregoing, it is obvious that the articles and letters, included herein, come as a refreshing antidote to much that has been written on the Civil War. On the whole, the American conflict has been analyzed in such simple and idealistic terms that historical actualities have been sacrificed for preconceived notions based on fantastic premises.

Among these the most unrealistic is the one propounded by Alexander H. Stephens and Jefferson Davis, leading exponents of the Southern Bourbon school. Faced by "the brutal fact of defeat," these two politicians sought to defend the "lost cause" and at the same time to obscure the historic problem of Negro slavery by discovering the cause of the conflict in the convenient American doctrine of states' rights. In his *Constitutional View of the Late War between the States* (1868-70), Stephens set forth the thesis that the civil strife was occasioned by "opposing ideas as to the nature of what is known as the General Government. The contest was between those who held it to be strictly Federal in character and those who maintained it to be thoroughly National." To the former Vice-President of the Confederacy, slavery was merely the spark that brought these "antagonistic principles" in actual collision "on the field of battle." Jefferson Davis, President of the Confederate States, put it even more simply. "The question of slavery," he wrote in his *Rise and Fall of the Confederate Government* (1881) "served as an *occasion*, it was far from being the *cause* of the conflict." Moreover, Stephens and Davis both agreed that the Civil War was inevitable. To them it was inconceivable to imagine the North and South living peacefully side by side so long as one accepted the Hamiltonian concept of government and the other the Jeffersonian.

The traditional Northern thesis was formulated by James F. Rhodes, a retired business man and brother-in-law of Mark Hanna, the Republican leader who helped "make" McKinley president. In his seven-volume *History of the United States* (1893-1906), he set forth the theory that the Civil War was the result of clashing ideas as to the moral justification of slavery. Throughout his work, Rhodes adopted a tolerant attitude toward the South and was of course in entire sympathy with the prevalent Northern disposition to let bygones be bygones.

At present most historians reject the traditional Northern and Southern thesis as to the cause of the Civil War. Even such conservatives of the South as George F. Milton have so modified the time-honored Stephens-Davis apology that it can hardly be recognized. In his *Eve of the Conflict* (1934), Milton, repudiating the old Southern theory of the inevitability of the struggle, holds that the civil strife was a "needless war." He maintains that the conflict could have been avoided if the people had followed the dictates of reason and intelligence exemplified in the attitude of Douglas and had repudiated the promptings of emotion and passion aroused by "inflamed minorities." In essence the Civil War was a "battle between rational and mystic democracy...."

Unlike Milton, Edward Channing, late professor of history at Harvard, does not belittle the force of Northern anti-slavery sentiment, nor does he deny the fact that the anti-slavery struggle, especially as it affected the territories, was tangible and material. Moreover, his designation of the Civil War as the War for Southern Independence is a step in the right direction * and is distinctly superior to the old title of the War between the States, a title used by Stephens and other reactionaries to establish the legitimacy of the Secessionist conspiracy.

Probably the best description of the Civil War is the one given by Charles A. Beard in his *Rise of American Civilization* (1927). His title, the Second American Revolution, conceals nothing and suggests a great deal. In his discussion, the leader of the liberal bourgeois school shows that the conflict was a struggle between two divergent economic and social systems, one a mono-agricultural order based upon slavery and the other a diversified system of agrarian and industrial productivity built upon free labor. He shows how the Civil War was the inevitable outcome of these clashing forces and how it represented a revolutionary occurrence of prime importance. A similar position is taken by Arthur C. Cole whose *Irrepressible Conflict* (1934) is a more complete study of the period.

The work of Beard and Cole, though containing much useful material, suffers from certain limitations inherent in the liberal bourgeois approach. These restrictions become evident when examined in the light of the articles and letters contained in the present volume. Failing to

* E. Channing, *History of the United States* (New York, 1925), vol. vi.

appreciate fully the class dynamics of historical development, liberal bourgeois historians do not clearly distinguish between the class forces at work. This leads them
to ignore some of the most significant revolutionary
phenomena of the period. Not least is the part played by
the American working class in bringing the Civil War to
a successful conclusion. This subject, worthy of extended
treatment, is either completely disregarded or quickly
disposed of.

On the eve of the Civil War, the American working
class, fully cognizant of the dangers inherent in the Secessionist movement, vigorously declared itself for the
preservation of the Union. Labor organizations in the
South joined with those in the North in passing resolutions favoring the unity of the American Republic. These
resolutions, though fundamentally directed against the
Secessionist movement, were nevertheless for the most
part animated by a desire to prevent war if that was at
all possible. As such, they reflected the attitude of a
number of prominent labor leaders whose pacifistic
tendencies and political immaturity blinded them to the
full significance of the impending conflict. Among these
leaders was William H. Sylvis, head of the Iron Molders
Union, who was later to distinguish himself as the guiding spirit behind the National Labor Union and as a
friend of the First International. The desire of Sylvis
to avert the coming struggle did not prevent him from
standing in strong opposition to the Secessionist movement, an opposition amply demonstrated by his activities
prior to and during the war. On February 12, 1861, Sylvis,
writing in a workingman's newspaper, the *Mechanics'
Own*, proposed that the wage-earners of the country hold
demonstrations in which the unity of the Republic should
be made the dominant note. When hostilities actually
broke out, Sylvis recruited a detachment of iron molders

which helped protect Washington from Lee's threatened invasion.

A considerable number of unorganized workers adopted a pacifistic attitude on the eve of the Civil War. Their outlook, however, was largely manufactured by powerful pro-slavery interests located in such large Eastern mercantile centers as Boston, New York and Philadelphia. These elements, connected with the slave barons of the South in the capacity of financiers, merchants and politicians, played upon the working-class fear of unemployment to such an extent that they were able to stampede many unorganized wage-earners into the anti-war camp.

However, once "the irrepressible conflict" began, the working class as a whole came to the defense of the Union and workers "vied with farmers in furnishing [the Lincoln administration] with volunteers." Writing many years later, Powderly, head of the Knights of Labor, stated, "... It is true that men in other walks of life enlisted and did good service in the Union cause, but the great bulk of the army was made up of working men." In the front rank of those who volunteered were trade union officials who actively recruited military companies in the factories where they worked. In some cases labor organizations joined the army in a body; for instance, one in Philadelphia passed the following resolution: "It having been resolved to enlist with Uncle Sam for the war, this union stands adjourned until either the Union is saved or we are whipped."

An even more advanced position than this was taken by some German-American working-class leaders, such as, for instance, Joseph Weydemeyer, loyal friend of Karl Marx. This Socialist fighter, along with many other leaders, fought on the side of the North not only to preserve the Union, but also to abolish slavery. The eradication of the latter was held essential to the ultimate emancipation of the proletariat. As the war progressed, American wage-earners began to exhibit a similar orientation. Their desire "to secure freedom for all the inhabitants of the United States" gave them, as Powderly puts it, "renewed zeal in the work of emancipation."

The working class of America did yeomen service not only at the front but behind the lines. Here in the factories of the nation wage-earners toiled unceasingly to produce the sinews of war. While capitalists were reaping millions as a result of fat war contracts, the laboring classes were working at pitifully inadequate wages. Yet, they worked on and on in order to bring the war to a successful conclusion. Their devotion to the Union government is well illustrated in a testimonial drawn up by the sewing women of Cincinnati on February 20, 1865, and addressed to Lincoln. In this memorial, these "wives, widows, sisters and friends of the soldiers in the army of the United States" contrasted their wretched conditions with those of the war-profiteers "who fatten on their contracts by grinding immense profits out of the labor of their operatives." Yet, despite this example of upper class selfishness, these women assured Lincoln of their sympathy with and loyalty to the government, a government they were still "desirous of aiding."

With the war won and the Southern slavocracy crushed, the wage-earners of America served notice on the ruling classes that they intended to secure in the very near future a more equitable distribution of wealth and a more equal share in those democratic institutions which they had defended with their blood. On November 2, 1865, Ira Steward, prominent leader of the eight-hour-day movement, proposed a number of resolutions at a mass meeting of Boston workers held at Faneuil Hall. Among those adopted was the following:

...we rejoice that the rebel aristocracy of the South has been crushed, that...beneath the glorious shadow of our victorious flag men of every clime, lineage and color are recognized as free. But while we will bear with patient endurance the burden of the public debt, we yet want it to be known that the workingmen of America will demand in future a more equal share in the wealth their industry creates...and a more equal participation in the privileges and blessings of those free institutions, defended by their manhood on many a bloody field of battle.

Within a short time after the passage of this resolution, an eight-hour-day movement was running, as Marx so aptly put it, "with express speed from the Atlantic to the Pacific," and a national federation of labor—the National Labor Union—was being launched.

Thus, the American working class played a significant role in the winning of the Civil War. Its splendid response to Lincoln's continuous plea for troops together with the heroic sacrifices of the British proletariat and the magnificent work of Marx and the First International form one of the most inspiring chapters in the history of the working-class movement.

Liberal historians likewise ignore or at best gloss over the part played by the Negro people in helping the North win the Civil War. The arming of Negroes (the necessity of which Marx realized and the revolutionary implications of which he was cognizant) is given scant notice despite the fact that, according to official figures, 186,017 colored troops served in the Northern armies during the struggle. Of these 123,156 were still in service on July 16, 1865. Drawn from working-class and petty bourgeois circles in the North and from free Negro and fugitive slave elements in the South, Negro soldiers participated in 198 battles and skirmishes and lost some 68,178 men. These statistics tell only part of the story; they do not disclose the heroism exhibited by Union Negro troops in battle nor their caliber as fighting men. These can be appreciated only through an examination of testimonials still available. For instance, there is the communication of Colonel Thomas Wentworth Higginson who commanded a Federal detachment of Negroes in Florida. "It would have been madness," he wrote in February, 1863, "to attempt with the bravest white troops what [I] successfully accomplished with black ones." The excellence of the Negro as a soldier was matched only by his eagerness to enlist and fight for freedom. Despite petty discriminations of all kinds (for example, colored troops received less pay in the Union army than white ones), Negroes flocked to the colors; pay or no pay, they did not hesitate to volunteer. Negroes served in the Northern armies not only as privates but as officers. Without previous military experience and solely on the basis of ability, Negro fighters rose from the ranks to become commissioned officers, some even attaining the rank of Major and Lieutenant-Colonel.

In addition to officers and soldiers, the Negro people furnished the Union armies with servants, helpers and laborers. These were mainly drawn from the ranks of fugitive slaves who deserted their plantations in ever-increasing numbers as the war went on. Serving within the Federal lines, these runaway Negroes helped build roads and fortifications which, in turn, permitted tens of thousands of white troops to take up their guns and return to the ranks, thereby increasing the military strength and efficiency of the Northern armies.

The present volume serves not only to disclose the limitations inherent in the liberal bourgeois approach to the Civil War and the shallowness of the traditional idealistic interpretations of the subject, but also preserves the revolutionary traditions of that struggle from reactionary and conservative distortions. The years 1861-65

marked the defeat of the armed insurrection of the slave
power and the unleashing of a revolutionary movement
of vast potentialities. In its Civil War phase, the revolution abolished chattel slavery and destroyed the old
plantocracy. At the same time it insured the continuance
of democracy, freedom and progress by putting an end to
the rule of an oligarchy, by preventing the further suppression of civil liberties in the interests of chattel slavery
and by paving the way for the forward movement of
American labor. The revolution during the Civil War was
essentially the work of a broad and progressive coalition
of wage-earners and farmers who after four years of bitter
struggle crushed the counter-revolution and brushed aside
an antiquated social order. In their fight for freedom, the
workers and farmers of the nation were aided, as were
their forefathers during the first American Revolution
and their spiritual descendants in Spain today, by European revolutionaries. Particularly conspicuous in this
connection were the German refugees of 1848-49, bourgeois liberals like Schurz and Kapp and working-class
radicals like Weydemeyer and Anneke. The revolutionary
character of the American conflict was fully appreciated
by contemporary observers. On December 30, 1860, one
of these, a militant abolitionist connected with the
Chicago *Tribune,* Horace White by name, wrote, "We live
in revolutionary times and I say God bless the revolution!" Some fifty-eight years later, Lenin in his *Letter to
American Workers* reminded the people of the United
States that their revolutionary tradition went back to
"the war of liberation against the English in the 18th
and the Civil War in the 19th century." The latter
he described as "world-historic, progressive and revolutionary. . . ."

Today, ultra-reactionary political groups, professional
patriots and big business Bourbons are attempting to ex-

ploit this great revolutionary and democratic heritage of the people for the purpose of maintaining and increasing their stranglehold upon the nation. Using the same tactics as the slavocracy did on the eve of the second American revolution, these present-day reactionary elements vigorously defend the Supreme Court as "the bulwark of the nation's liberties," assiduously advance states' rights arguments for the purpose of thwarting the will of a national majority and hypocritically profess a devotion for Jeffersonian democracy (as in the case of the Liberty League). But, as in the 'sixties, so now the progressive forces of the nation will not be deceived into perpetuating a corrupt and decadent social order. Led by the working class, they will accept the challenge of the present by repeating the only true and genuine tradition of American history—the revolutionary solution of deep-seated social antagonisms.

The present volume consists of a text, appendix, explanatory notes and biographical index. The text, composed of newspaper articles and correspondence, contains footnotes designed for the purpose of explaining foreign expressions and in some cases literary allusions and historic events. It should be noted in passing that all titles appearing at the head of newspaper articles are similar to those in the original and are therefore in the first instance the work of the editors of the periodicals involved. The appendix is made up of the Addresses of the First International to Abraham Lincoln and Andrew Johnson, and the reply of the former through the American Legation in London. In addition to the above-mentioned source material, the present work includes explanatory notes intended to acquaint the reader with important events and legislative acts as well as biographical sketches dealing with most of the figures referred to in the text.

RICHARD ENMALE.

PART ONE

ARTICLES FROM THE
NEW YORK DAILY TRIBUNE
(1861-1862)

By KARL MARX

1.

THE AMERICAN QUESTION IN ENGLAND

London, September 18, 1861.

MRS. BEECHER STOWE's letter to Lord Shaftesbury, whatever its intrinsic merit may be, has done a great deal of good by forcing the anti-Northern organs of the London press to speak out and lay before the general public the ostensible reasons for their hostile tone against the North and their ill-concealed sympathies with the South, which looks rather strange on the part of people affecting an utter horror of slavery. Their first main grievance is that the present American war is "not one for the abolition of slavery," and that, therefore, the high-minded Britisher, used to undertake wars of his own and interest himself in other people's wars only on the basis of "broad humanitarian principles," cannot be expected to feel any sympathy with his Northern cousins. "In the first place," says *The Economist*, "the assumption that the quarrel between the North and South is a quarrel between Negro freedom on the one side and Negro slavery on the other is as impudent as it is untrue." "The North," says *The Saturday Review*, "does not proclaim Abolition, and never pretended to fight for anti-slavery. The North has not hoisted for its oriflamme the sacred symbol of justice to the Negro; its *cri de guerre* * is not unconditional

* War cry.—*Ed.*

3

abolition." "If," says *The Examiner*, "we have been deceived about the real significance of the sublime movement, who but the Federalists themselves have to answer for the deception?"

Now, in the first instance, the premise must be conceded. The war has not been undertaken with a view to put down slavery, and the United States authorities themselves have taken the greatest pains to protest against any such idea. But then, it ought to be remembered that it was not the North, but the South, which undertook this war; the former acting only on the defense. If it be true, that the North, after long hesitations, and an exhibition of forbearance unknown in the annals of European history, drew at last the sword, not for crushing slavery, but for saving the Union, the South, on its part, inaugurated the war by loudly proclaiming "the peculiar institution" as the only and main end of the rebellion. It confessed to fight for the liberty of enslaving other people, a liberty which, despite the Northern protests, it asserted to be put in danger by the victory of the Republican Party and the election of Mr. Lincoln to the Presidential chair. The Confederate Congress boasted that its new-fangled Constitution, as distinguished from the Constitution of the Washingtons, Jeffersons and Adamses, had recognized for the first time slavery as a thing good in itself, a bulwark of civilization, and a divine institution. If the North professed to fight but for the Union, the South gloried in rebellion for the supremacy of slavery. If anti-slavery and idealistic England felt not attracted by the profession of the North, how came it to pass that it was not violently repulsed by the cynical confessions of the South?

The Saturday Review helps itself out of this ugly dilemma by disbelieving the declarations of the seceders themselves. It sees deeper than this, and discovers *"that slavery had very little to do with secession,"* the declarations of Jeff[erson] Davis and company to the contrary being mere "conventionalisms" with "about as much meaning as the conventionalisms about violated altars and desecrated hearths, which always occur in such proclamations."

The staple of argument on the part of the anti-Northern papers is very scanty, and throughout all of them we find almost the same sentences recurring, like the formulas of a mathematical series, at certain intervals, with very little art of variation or combination. "Why," exclaims *The Economist,* "it is only yesterday, when the secession movement first gained serious head, on the first announcement of Mr. Lincoln's election, that the Northerners offered to the South, if they would remain in the Union, every conceivable security for the performance and inviolability of the obnoxious institution—that they disavowed in the most solemn manner all intention of interfering with it—that their leaders proposed compromise after compromise in Congress, all based upon the concession that slavery should not be meddled with." "How happens it," says *The Examiner,* "that the North was ready to compromise matters by the largest concessions to the South as to slavery? How was it that a certain geographical line was proposed in Congress within which slavery was to be recognized as an essential institution? The Southern states were not content with this."

What *The Economist* and *The Examiner* had to ask was not only why the Crittenden and other compromise measures were *proposed* in Congress, but why they were not *passed.*[1] They affect to consider those compromise proposals as accepted by the North and rejected by the South, while, in point of fact, they were baffled by the Northern party that had carried the Lincoln election. Proposals never matured into resolutions, but always

remaining in the embryo of *pia desideria,** the South had
of course, never any occasion either of rejecting or
acquiescing. We come nearer to the pith of the question
by the following remark of *The Examiner:*

Mrs. Stowe says, "The slave party, finding they could no
longer use the Union for their purposes, resolved to destroy it."
There is here an admission that up to that time the slave
party had used the Union for their purposes, and it would have
been well if Mrs. Stowe could have distinctly shown where
it was that the North began to make its stand against slavery.

One might suppose that *The Examiner* and the other
oracles of public opinion in England had made themselves sufficiently familiar with contemporaneous history
to not need Mrs. Stowe's information on such all-impor-
tant points. The progressive abuse of the Union by the
slave power, working through its alliance with the Northern Democratic Party, is, so to say, the general formula
of United States history since the beginning of this century. The successive compromise measures mark the successive degrees of the encroachment by which the Union
became more and more transformed into the slave of the
slaveowner. Each of these compromises denotes a new
encroachment of the South, a new concession of the
North. At the same time none of the successive victories
of the South was carried but after a hot contest with an
antagonistic force in the North, appearing under different party names with different watchwords and under
different colors. If the positive and final result of each
single contest told in favor of the South, the attentive observer of history could not but see that every new advance of the slave power was a step forward to its
ultimate defeat. Even at the time of the Missouri Compromise the contending forces were so evenly balanced

* Pious wishes.—*Ed.*

that Jefferson, as we see from his memoirs, apprehended the Union to be in danger of splitting on that deadly antagonism.[2] The encroachments of the slaveholding power reached their maximum point, when, by the Kansas-Nebraska Bill,[3] for the first time in the history of the United States, as Mr. Douglas himself confessed, every legal barrier to the diffusion of slavery within the United States territories was broken down, when afterward, a Northern candidate [4] bought his presidential nomination by pledging the Union to conquer or purchase in Cuba a new field of dominion for the slaveholder; when later on, by the Dred Scott decision,[5] diffusion of slavery by the Federal power was proclaimed as the law of the American Constitution, and lastly, when the African slave trade [6] was *de facto* reopened on a larger scale than during the times of its legal existence. But, concurrently with this climax of Southern encroachments, carried by the connivance of the Northern Democratic Party, there were unmistakable signs of Northern antagonistic agencies having gathered such strength as must soon turn the balance of power. The Kansas war,[7] the formation of the Republican Party,[8] and the large vote cast for Mr. Frémont during the presidential election of 1856,[9] were so many palpable proofs that the North had accumulated sufficient energies to rectify the aberrations which United States history, under the slaveowners' pressure, had undergone, for half a century, and to make it return to the true principles of its development. Apart from those political phenomena, there was one broad statistical and economical fact indicating that the abuse of the Federal Union by the slave interest had approached the point from which it would have to recede forcibly, or *de bonne grace.** That fact was the growth of the Northwest, the immense strides its population had made from 1850 to

* With good grace.—*Ed.*

1860,[10] and the new and reinvigorating influence it could not but bear on the destinies of the United States.

Now, was all this a secret chapter of history? Was "the admission" of Mrs. Beecher Stowe wanted to reveal to *The Examiner* and the other political *illuminati* of the London press the carefully hidden truth that "up to that time the slave party had used the Union for their purposes"? Is it the fault of the American North that the English pressmen were taken quite unawares by the violent clash of the antagonistic forces, the friction of which was the moving power of its history for half a century? Is it the fault of the Americans that the English press mistake for the fanciful crotchet hatched in a single day what was in the reality the matured result of long years of struggle? The very fact that the formation and the progress of the Republican Party in America have hardly been noticed by the London press, speaks volumes as to the hollowness of its anti-slavery tirades. Take, for instance, the two antipodes of the London press, the London *Times* and *Reynolds's Weekly Newspaper,* the one the great organ of the respectable classes, and the other the only remaining organ of the working class. The former, not long before Mr. Buchanan's career drew to an end, published an elaborate apology for his administration and a defamatory libel against the Republican movement. Reynolds, on his part, was, during Mr. Buchanan's stay at London,[11] one of his minions, and since that time never missed an occasion to write him up and to write his adversaries down. How did it come to pass that the Republican Party, whose platform was drawn up on the avowed antagonism to the encroachments of the slavocracy and the abuse of the Union by the slave interest, carried the day in the North? How, in the second instance, did it come to pass that the great bulk of the Northern Democratic Party, flinging aside its old connections with the leaders of slavocracy, setting at naught its traditions of half a century, sacrificing great commercial interests and greater political prejudices, rushed to the support of the present Republican administration and offered it men and money with an unsparing hand?

Instead of answering these questions *The Economist* exclaims:

Can we forget that Abolitionists have habitually been as ferociously persecuted and maltreated in the North and West as in the South? Can it be denied that the testiness and half-heartedness, not to say insincerity, of the government at Washington have for years supplied the chief impediment which has thwarted our efforts for the effectual suppression of the slave trade on the coast of Africa; while a vast proportion of the clippers actually engaged in that trade have been built with Northern capital, owned by Northern merchants and manned by Northern seamen?

This is, in fact, a masterly piece of logic. Anti-slavery England cannot sympathize with the North breaking down the withering influence of slavocracy, because she cannot forget that the North, while bound by that influence, supported the slave trade, mobbed the Abolitionists, and had its democratic institutions tainted by the slavedriver's prejudices. She cannot sympathize with Mr. Lincoln's administration, because she had to find fault with Mr. Buchanan's administration. She must needs sullenly cavil at the present movement of the Northern resurrection, cheer up the Northern sympathizers with the slave trade, branded in the Republican platform; [12] and coquet with the Southern slavocracy, setting up an empire of its own, because she cannot forget that the North of yesterday was not the North of today. The necessity of justifying its attitude by such pettifogging Old Bailey * pleas proves more than anything else that the

* Seat of the Central Criminal Court in London.—*Ed.*

anti-Northern part of the English press is instigated by hidden motives, too mean and dastardly to be openly avowed.

As it is one of its pet maneuvers to taunt the present Republican administration with the doings of its pro-slavery predecessors, so it tries hard to persuade the English people that *The New York Herald* ought to be considered the only authentic expositor of Northern opinion. The London *Times* having given out the cue in this direction the *servum pecus* * of the other anti-Northern organs, great and small, persist in beating the same bush. So says *The Economist:* "In the light of the strife, New York papers and New York politicians were not wanting who exhorted the combatants, now that they had large armies in the field, to employ them, not against each other, but against Great Britain—to compromise the internal quarrel, the slave question included, and invade the British territory without notice and with overwhelming force." *The Economist* knows perfectly well that *The New York Herald's* efforts, which were eagerly supported by the London *Times*, at embroiling the United States into a war with England, only intended securing the success of secession and thwarting the movement of Northern regeneration.

Still there is one concession made by the anti-Northern English press. *The Saturday [Review]* snob tells us: "What was at issue in Lincoln's election, and what has precipitated the convulsion, was merely *the limitation of the institution of slavery to states where that institution already exists.*" And *The Economist* remarks: "It is true enough that it was the aim of the Republican Party which elected Mr. Lincoln to prevent slavery from spreading into the unsettled Territories. . . . It may be

* Slavish herd.—*Ed.*

true that the success of the North, if complete and unconditional, would enable them to confine slavery within the fifteen states which have already adopted it, and might thus lead to its eventual extinction—though this is rather probable than certain."

In 1859, on the occasion of John Brown's Harper's Ferry expedition,[13] the very same *Economist* published a series of elaborate articles with a view to prove that, by dint of an *economical law,* American slavery was doomed to gradual extinction from the moment it should be deprived of its power of expansion. That "economical law" was perfectly understood by the slavocracy. "In 15 years more," said Toombs, "without a great increase in slave territory, either the slaves must be permitted to flee from the whites, or the whites must flee from the slaves." The limitation of slavery to its constitutional area, as proclaimed by the Republicans, was the distinct ground upon which the menace of secession was first uttered in the House of Representatives on December 19, 1859. Mr. Singleton (Mississippi) having asked Mr. Curtis (Iowa), if the Republican Party would never let the South have another foot of slave territory while it remained in the Union, and Mr. Curtis having responded in the affirmative, Mr. Singleton said *this would dissolve the Union.* His advice to Mississippi was the sooner it got out of the Union the better—"gentlemen should recollect that Jefferson Davis led our forces in Mexico, and still he lives, perhaps to lead the Southern army." *
Quite apart from the *economical law* which makes the diffusion of slavery a vital condition for its maintenance within its constitutional areas, the leaders of the South had never deceived themselves as to the necessity for keeping up their *political* sway over the United States.

* For Singleton's speech of December 19, 1859, see Appendix to the *Congressional Globe, First Session 36th Congress, Part IV* (Washington, 1860), pp. 47-54.—*Ed.*

John Calhoun, in the defense of his propositions to the
Senate, stated distinctly on February 19, 1847, "that the
Senate was the only balance of power left to the South
in the government," and that the creation of new slave
states had become necessary "for the retention of the
equipoise of power in the Senate." [14] Moreover, the
oligarchy of the 300,000 slaveowners could not even maintain their sway at home save by constantly throwing out
to their white plebeians the bait of prospective conquests
within and without the frontiers of the United States.
If, then, according to the oracles of the English press, the
North had arrived at the fixed resolution of circumscrib-
ing slavery within its present limits, and of thus
extinguishing it in a constitutional way, was this not sufficient to enlist the sympathies of anti-slavery England?

But the English Puritans seem indeed not to be contented save by an explicit Abolitionist war. "This," says
The Economist, "therefore, not being a war for the
emancipation of the Negro race, on what other ground
can we be fairly called upon to sympathize so warmly
with the Federal cause?" "There was a time," says *The
Examiner,* "when our sympathies were with the North,
thinking that it was really in earnest in making a stand
against the encroachments of the slave states, and in
adopting emancipation as a measure of justice to the
black race."

However, in the very same number in which these
papers tell us that they cannot sympathize with the
North because its war is no Abolitionist war, we are informed that "the desperate expedient" of proclaiming
Negro emancipation and summoning the slaves to a general insurrection, is a thing "the mere conception of which
is repulsive and dreadful," and that "a compromise"
would be "far preferable to success purchased at such a
cost and *stained by such a crime.*"

Thus the English eagerness for the Abolitionist war is all cant. The cloven foot peeps out in the following sentences: "Lastly," says *The Economist,* "is the *Morrill tariff* a title to our gratitude and to our sympathy, or is the certainty that, in case of Northern triumph, that tariff should be extended over the whole republic, a reason why we ought to be clamorously anxious for their success?" "The North Americans," says *The Examiner,* "are in earnest about nothing but a selfish protective tariff.... The Southern states were tired of being robbed of the fruits of their slave labor by the protective tariff of the North."

The Examiner and *The Economist* complement each other. The latter is honest enough to confess at last that with it and its followers sympathy is a mere question of tariff, while the former reduces the war between North and South to a tariff war, to a war between protection and free trade. *The Examiner* is perhaps not aware that even the South Carolina Nullifiers of 1832, as General Jackson testified, used protection only as a pretext for secession; [15] but even *The Examiner* ought to know that the present rebellion did not wait upon the passing of the Morrill tariff for breaking out.[16] In point of fact, the Southerners could not have been tired of being robbed of the fruits of their slave labor by the protective tariff of the North, considering that from 1846-1861 a free trade tariff had obtained.

The Spectator characterizes in its last number the secret thought of some of the anti-Northern organs in the following striking manner:

What, then, do the anti-Northern organs really profess to think desirable, under the justification of this plea of deferring to the inexorable logic of facts? They argue that disunion is desirable, just because, as we have said, it is the only possible

step to a conclusion of this "causeless and fratricidal strife";
and next, of course, only as an afterthought, and as an humble
apology for Providence and "justification of the ways of God
to man," now that the inevitable necessity stands revealed—
for further reasons discovered as beautiful adaptations to the
moral exigencies of the country, when once the issue is dis-
cerned. It is discovered that it will be very much for the
advantage of the states to be dissolved into rival groups.
They will mutually check each other's ambition; they will
neutralize each other's power, and if ever England should
get into a dispute with one or more of them, mere jealousy will
bring the antagonistic groups to our aid. This will be, it is
urged, a very wholesome state of things, for it will relieve us
from anxiety and it will encourage political "competition,"
that great safeguard of honesty and purity, among the states
themselves.

Such is the case—very gravely urged—of the numerous class
of Southern sympathizers now springing up among us. Trans-
lated into English—and we grieve that an English argument
on such a subject should be of a nature that requires trans-
lating it—it means that we deplore the present great scale of
this "fratricidal" war, because it may concentrate in one
fearful spasm a series of chronic petty wars and passions and
jealousies among groups of rival states in times to come. The
real truth is, and this very un-English feeling distinctly discerns
this truth, though it cloaks it in decent phrases, that rival
groups of American states could not live together in peace or
harmony. The chronic condition would be one of malignant
hostility rising out of the very causes which have produced
the present contest. It is asserted that the different groups of
states have different tariff interests. These different tariff interests would be sources of constant petty wars if the states
were once dissolved, and slavery, the root of all the strife,
would be the spring of innumerable animosities, discords and
campaigns. No stable equilibrium could ever again be established among the rival states. And yet it is maintained that this
long future of incessant strife is the providential solution of
the great question now at issue, the only real reason why it is
looked upon favorably being this, that whereas the present
great-scale conflict may issue in a restored and stronger political unity, the alternative of infinitely multiplied small-scale

quarrels will issue in a weak and divided continent, that England cannot fear.

Now we do not deny that the Americans themselves sowed the seeds of this petty and contemptible state of feeling by the unfriendly and bullying attitude they have so often manifested to England, but we do say that the state of feeling on our part is petty and contemptible. We see that in a deferred issue there is no hope of a deep and enduring tranquillity for America, that it means a decline and fall of the American nation into quarrelsome clans and tribes, and yet hold up our hands in horror at the present "fratricidal" strife because it holds out hopes of finality. We exhort them to look favorably on the indefinite future of small strifes, equally fratricidal and probably far more demoralizing, because the latter would draw out of our side the thorn of American rivalry.

New York Daily Tribune, October 11, 1861.

2.

THE BRITISH COTTON TRADE

London, September 21, 1861.

THE CONTINUAL rise in the price of raw cotton begins at last to seriously react upon the cotton factories, their consumption of cotton being now 25 per cent less than the full consumption. This result has been brought about by a daily lessening rate of production, many mills working only four or three days per week, part of the machinery being stopped, both in those establishments where short time has been commenced and in those which are still running full time, and some mills being temporarily altogether closed.

In some places, as at Blackburn, for instance, short time has been coupled with a reduction of wages. However, the short-time movement is only in its incipient state and we may predict with perfect security that some weeks later the trade will have generally resorted to three days' working per week, concurrently with a large stoppage of machinery in most establishments. On the whole, English manufacturers and merchants were extremely slow and reluctant in acknowledging the awkward position of their cotton supplies. "The whole of the last American crop," they said, "has long since been forwarded to Europe. The picking of the new crop has barely commenced. Not a bale of cotton could have reached us more than has reached us, even if the war and the blockade had never been heard of. The shipping season does not commence till far in November, and it is usually the end of December before any large exportations take place. Till then, it is of little consequence whether the cotton is retained on the plantations or is forwarded to the ports as fast as it is bagged. If the blockade ceases any time *before the end of this year,* the probability is that by March or April we shall have received just as full a supply of cotton as if the blockade had never been declared."

In the innermost recesses of the mercantile mind the notion was cherished that the whole American crisis, and, consequently the blockade, would have ceased before the end of the year, or that Lord Palmerston would forcibly break through the blockade. The latter idea has been altogether abandoned, since, beside all other circumstances, Manchester * became aware that two vast interests, the monetary interest having sunk an immense capital in the industrial enterprises of Northern America, and the corn trade, relying on Northern America as its principal source of supply, would combine to check any unprovoked aggression on the part of the British government. The hopes of the blockade being raised in due time,

* The center of the textile industry in England.—*Ed.*

for the requirements of Liverpool* or Manchester, or the American war being wound up by a compromise with the secessionists, have given way before a feature hitherto unknown in the English cotton market, *viz.*, American operations in cotton at Liverpool, partly on speculation, partly for reshipment to America. Consequently, for the last two weeks the Liverpool cotton market has been feverishly excited, the speculative investments in cotton on the part of the Liverpool merchants being backed by speculative investments on the part of the Manchester and other manufacturers eager to provide themselves with stocks of raw material for the winter. The extent of the latter transactions is sufficiently shown by the fact that a considerable portion of the spare warehouse room in Manchester is already occupied by such stocks, and that throughout the week beginning with September 15 and ending with September 22, Middling Americans** had increased ⅜d. per lb., and fair ones ⅝d.

From the outbreak of the American war the prices of cotton were steadily rising, but the ruinous disproportion between the prices of the raw material and the prices of yarns and cloth was not declared until the last weeks of August. Till then, any serious decline in the prices of cotton manufactures, which might have been anticipated from the considerable decrease of the American demand, had been balanced by an accumulation of stocks in first hands, and by speculative consignments to China and India. Those Asiatic markets, however, were soon overdone. "Stocks," says *The Calcutta Price Current* of August 7, 1861, "are accumulating, the arrivals since our last being no less than 24,000,000 yards of plain cottons. Home advices show a continuation of shipments in ex-

* The center of the cotton trade.—*Ed.*
** A quality of cotton.—*Ed.*

cess of our requirements, and so long as this is the case, improvement cannot be looked for...."

The Bombay market, also, has been greatly over-supplied. Some other circumstances contributed to contract the Indian market. The late famine in the north-western provinces has been succeeded by the ravages of the cholera, while throughout Lower Bengal an excessive fall of rain, laying the country under water, seriously damaged the rice crops. In letters from Calcutta, which reached England last week, sales were reported giving a net return of 9¼d. per pound for 40s twist, which cannot be bought at Manchester for less than 11⅜d., while sales of 4C-inch shirtings, compared with present rates at Manchester, yield losses at 7½d., 9d. and 12d. per piece. In the China market, prices were also forced down by the accumulation of the stocks imported. Under these circumstances, the demand for the British cotton manufactures decreasing, their prices can, of course, not keep pace with the progressive rise in the price of the raw material; but, on the contrary, the spinning, weaving, and printing of cotton must, in many instances, cease to pay the costs of production. Take, as an example, the following case, stated by one of the greatest Manchester manufacturers, in reference to coarse spinning:

			Cost of Spinning
Sept. 17, 1860	*Per lb.*	*Margin*	*per lb.*
Cost of cotton	6¼d.	4d.	3d.
16s warp sold for	10¼d.	—	—
Profit, 1d. per lb.			
Sept. 17, 1861			
Cost of cotton	9d.	2d.	3½d.
16s warp sold for	11d.	—	—
Loss, 1½d. per lb.			

The consumption of Indian cotton is rapidly growing, and with a further rise in prices, the Indian supply will come forward at increasing ratios; but still it remains impossible to change, at a few months' notice, all the conditions of production and turn the current of commerce. England pays now, in fact, the penalty for her protracted misrule of that vast Indian empire. The two main obstacles she has now to grapple with in her attempts at supplanting American cotton by Indian cotton are the want of means of communication and transport throughout India, and the miserable state of the Indian peasant, disabling him from improving favorable circumstances. Both these difficulties the English have themselves to thank for. English modern industry, in general, relied upon two pivots equally monstrous. The one was the potato as the only means of feeding Ireland and a great part of the English working class. This pivot was swept away by the potato disease and the subsequent Irish catastrophe.[17] A larger basis for the reproduction and maintenance of the toiling millions had then to be adopted. The second pivot of English industry was the slave-grown cotton of the United States. The present American crisis forces them to enlarge their field of supply and emancipate cotton from slave-breeding and slave-consuming oligarchies. As long as the English cotton manufacturers depended on slave-grown cotton, it could be truthfully asserted that they rested on a twofold slavery, the indirect slavery of the white man in England and the direct slavery of the black man on the other side of the Atlantic.

New York Daily Tribune, October 14, 1861.

3.

THE LONDON *TIMES* ON THE ORLEANS PRINCES IN AMERICA

London, October 12, 1861.

ON THE occasion of the King of Prussia's visit at Compiègne,[18] the London *Times* published some racy articles, giving great offense on the other side of the Channel. The *Pays, Journal de l'Empire*, in its turn characterized *The Times* writers as people whose heads were poisoned by gin, and whose pens were dipped into mud. Such occasional exchanges of invective are only intended to mislead public opinion as to the intimate relations connecting Printing House Square to the Tuileries.* There exists beyond the French frontiers no greater sycophant of the Man of December ** than the London *Times,* and its services are the more invaluable, the more that paper now and then assumes the tone and the air of a Cato censor towards its Cæsar.***

The Times had for months heaped insult upon Prussia. Improving the miserable MacDonald affair, it had told Prussia that England would feel glad to see a transfer of the Rhenish provinces from the barbarous sway of the Hohenzollern to the enlightened despotism of a Bonaparte. It had not only exasperated the Prussian dynasty, but the Prussian people. It had written down the idea of an Anglo-Prussian alliance in case of a Prussian conflict with France. It had strained all its powers to con-

---

* Editorial offices of *The Times* situated in Printing House Square and Napoleon III whose residence was the Palace of the Tuileries in Paris.—*Ed.*

** Napoleon III, Louis Bonaparte.—*Ed.*

*** The adoption of a critically moralistic tone towards the ruler of a state. The phrase is based on the historical character of Cato the Censor (234-149 B.C.), a Roman noted for the severity of his manners and for his supervision of public morals.—*Ed.*

vince Prussia that she had nothing to hope from England, and that the next best thing she could do would be to come to some understanding with France. When at last the weak and trimming monarch of Prussia resolved upon the visit at Compiègne, *The Times* could proudly exclaim: *"quorum magna pars fui,"* * but now the time had also arrived for obliterating from the memory of the British the fact that *The Times* had been the pathfinder of the Prussian monarch. Hence the roar of its theatrical thunders. Hence the counter roars of the *Pays, Journal de l'Empire.*

The Times had now recovered its position of the deadly antagonist of Bonapartism, and, therefore, the power of lending its aid to the Man of December. An occasion soon offered. Louis Bonaparte is, of course, most touchy whenever the renown of rival pretenders to the French crown is concerned. He had covered himself with ridicule in the affair of the Duc d'Aumale's pamphlet against Plon-Plon,[19] and, by his proceedings, had done more in furtherance of the Orleanist cause than all the Orleanist partisans combined. Again, in these latter days, the French people were called upon to draw a parallel between Plon-Plon and the Orleans princes. When Plon-Plon set out for America, there were caricatures circulated in the Faubourg St. Antoine ** representing him as a fat man in search of a crown, but professing at the same time to be a most inoffensive traveler, with a peculiar aversion to the smell of powder. While Plon-Plon is returning to France with no more laurels than he gathered in the Crimea and in Italy, the Princes of Orleans cross the Atlantic to take service in the ranks of the national army.[20] Hence a great stir in the Bonapartist camp. It would not do to give vent to Bonapartist anger through

* In which I had a large share.—*Ed.*
** A district in Paris.—*Ed.*

the venal press of Paris. The imperialist fears would thus only be betrayed, the pamphlet scandal renewed, and odious comparisons provoked between exiled princes who fight under the republican banner against the enslavers of working millions, with another exiled prince, who had himself sworn in as an English special constable to share in the glory of putting down an English workingmen's movement.[21]

Who should extricate the Man of December out of this dilemma? Who but the London *Times?* If the same London *Times,* which on the 6th, 8th and 9th of October, 1861, had roused the furies of the *Pays, Journal de l'Empire,* by its rather cynical strictures on the visit at Compiègne—if that very same paper should come out on the 12th of October, with a merciless onslaught on the Orleans princes, because of their enlistment in the ranks of the national army of the United States, would Louis Bonaparte not have proved his case against the Orleans princes? Would *The Times* article not be done into French, commented upon by the Paris papers, sent by the *Prefect de Police* * to all the journals of all the departments,** and circulated throughout the whole of France, as the impartial sentence passed by the London *Times,* the personal foe of Louis Bonaparte, upon the last proceedings of the Orleans princes? Consequently, *The Times* of today has come out with a most scurrilous onslaught on these princes.

Louis Bonaparte is, of course, too much of a business man to share the judicial blindness in regard to the American war of the official public opinion-mongers. He knows that the true people of England, of France, of Germany, of Europe, consider the cause of the United States as their own cause, as the cause of liberty, and

* Chief of Police.—*Ed.*
** Provinces.—*Ed.*

that, despite all paid sophistry, they consider the soil of the United States as the free soil of the landless millions of Europe, as their land of promise, now to be defended sword in hand, from the sordid grasp of the slaveholder. Louis Napoleon knows, moreover, that in France the masses connect the fight for the maintenance of the Union with the fight of their forefathers for the foundation of American independence, and that with them every Frenchman drawing his sword for the national government appears only to execute the bequest of Lafayette. Bonaparte, therefore, knows that if anything is able to win the Orleans princes good opinions from the French people, it will be their enlistment in the ranks of the national army of the United States. He shudders at this very notion, and consequently the London *Times,* his censorious sycophant, today tells the Orleans princes that "they will derive no increase of popularity with the French nation from stooping to serve on this *ignoble field of action.*" Louis Napoleon knows that all the wars waged in Europe between hostile nations since his *coup d'état,** have been mock wars, groundless, wanton, and carried on on false pretenses. The Russian war,** and the Italian war [1859], not to speak of the piratical expeditions against China, Cochin-China,[22] and so forth, never enlisted the sympathies of the French people, instinctively aware that both wars were carried on only with the view to strengthening the chains forged by the *coup d'état.* The first grand war of contemporaneous history is the American war.

The people of Europe know that the Southern slavocracy commenced that war with the declaration that the continuance of slavocracy was no longer compatible with the continuance of the Union. Consequently, the people

---

* That is, since December 2, 1851. By a *coup d'état* is meant a sudden decisive blow in politics.—*Ed.*
** Crimean War, 1853-56.—*Ed.*

of Europe know that a fight for the continuance of the
Union is a fight against the continuance of the slavocracy
—that in this contest the highest form of popular self-
government till now realized is giving battle to the mean-
est and most shameless form of man's enslaving recorded
in the annals of history.

Louis Bonaparte feels, of course, extremely sorry that
the Orleans princes should embark in just such a war, so
distinguished, by the vastness of its dimensions and the
grandeur of its ends, from the groundless, wanton and
diminutive wars Europe has passed through since 1849.
Consequently, the London *Times* must needs declare:
"To overlook the difference between a war waged by
hostile nations, and this most groundless and wanton civil
conflict of which history gives us any account, is a species
of offense against public morals."

The Times is, of course, bound to wind up its onslaught
on the Orleans princes because of their "stooping to serve
on such an ignoble field of action," with a deep bow
before the victor of Sebastopol and Solferino. "It is un-
wise," says the London *Times*, "to challenge a comparison between such actions as Springfield and Manassas,[23]
and the exploits of Sebastopol and Solferino." [24] The next
mail will testify to the premeditated use made of *The
Times* article by the imperialist organs. A friend in times
of need is proverbially worth a thousand friends in times
of prosperity, and the secret ally of the London *Times*
is just now very badly off.

A dearth of cotton, backed by a dearth of grain; a
commercial crisis coupled with an agricultural distress,
and both of them combined with a reduction of customs
revenues and a monetary embarrassment compelling the
Bank of France to screw its rate of discount to six per
cent, to enter into transactions with Rothschilds and
Baring for a loan of two millions sterling on the London

market, to pawn abroad French government stock, and
with all that to show but a reserve of 12,000,000 against
liabilities amounting to more than 40,000,000. Such a
state of economical affairs prepares just the situation for
rival pretenders to stake double. Already there have
been bread-riots in the Faubourg St. Antoine, and this
of all times is therefore the most inappropriate time for
allowing Orleans princes to catch popularity. Hence the
fierce forward rush of the London *Times*.

New York Daily Tribune, November 7, 1861.

4.

THE INTERVENTION IN MEXICO

London, November 8, 1861.

THE CONTEMPLATED intervention in Mexico by England,
France and Spain, is, in my opinion one of the most
monstrous enterprises ever chronicled in the annals of
international history. It is a contrivance of the true
Palmerston make, astounding the uninitiated by an
insanity of purpose and imbecility of the means employed
which appear quite incompatible with the known capacity
of the old schemer.

It is probable that, among the many irons which, to
amuse the French public, Louis Bonaparte is compelled
to always keep in the fire, a Mexican expedition may
have figured. It is sure that Spain, whose never over-
strong head has been quite turned by her recent cheap
successes in Morocco and St. Domingo,[25] dreams of a
restoration in Mexico, but nevertheless, it is certain that
the French plan was far from being matured, and that
both France and Spain strove hard against a joint expedition to Mexico under English leadership.

On September 24, Palmerston's private *Moniteur*,* the London *Morning Post,* first announced in detail the scheme for the joint intervention, according to the terms of a treaty just concluded, as it said, between England, France, and Spain. This statement had hardly crossed the channel, when the French government, through the columns of the Paris *Patrie* gave it the direct lie. On September 27, the London *Times,* Palmerston's national organ, first broke its silence on the scheme in a leader ** contradicting, but not quoting, the *Patrie. The Times* even stated that Earl Russel had communicated to the French government the resolution arrived at on the part of England of interfering in Mexico, and that M. de Thouvenel replied that the Emperor of the French had come to a similar conclusion. Now it was the turn of Spain. A semi-official paper of Madrid, while affirming Spain's intention to meddle with Mexico, repudiated at the same time the idea of a joint intervention with England. The *dementis* *** were not yet exhausted. *The Times* had categorically asserted that "the full assent of the American President had been given to the expedition." All the American papers taking notice of *The Times* article, have long since contradicted its assertion.

It is, therefore, certain, and has even been expressly admitted by *The Times,* that the joint intervention in its present form is of English—*i.e.,* Palmerstonian—make. Spain was cowed into adherence by the pressure of France; and France was brought round by concessions made to her in the field of European policy. In this respect, it is a significant coincidence that *The Times* of November 6, in the very number in which it announces

* *"Moniteur"* is used by Marx to designate the *Morning Post* as the official paper of Palmerston, comparing its function to that of *Le Moniteur Universal,* which was the official organ of the French government from 1789 to 1868.—*Ed.*
** Chief editorial article of a newspaper.—*Ed.*
*** Official denials.—*Ed.*

the conclusion at Paris of a convention for the joint interference in Mexico, simultaneously published a leader pooh-poohing and treating with exquisite contumely the protest of Switzerland against the recent invasion of her territory—*viz.*, the Dappenthal by a French military force. In return for his fellowship in the Mexican expedition, Louis Bonaparte had obtained *carte blanche* * for his contemplated encroachments on Switzerland, and, perhaps, on other parts of the European continent. The transactions on these points between England and France have lasted throughout the whole of the months of September and October.

There exist in England no people desirous of an intervention in Mexico save the Mexican bondholders, who, however, had never to boast the least sway over the national mind. Hence the difficulty of breaking to the public the Palmerstonian scheme. The next best means was to bewilder the British elephant by contradictory statements, proceeding from the same laboratory, compounded of the same materials, but varying in the doses administered to the animal.

The *Morning Post,* in its print of September 24, announced there would be "no territorial war in Mexico," that the only point at issue was the monetary claims on the Mexican exchequer; that "it would be impossible to deal with Mexico as an organized and established government," and that, consequently, "the principal Mexican ports would be temporarily occupied and their customs revenues sequestered."

The Times of September 27 declared, on the contrary, that "to dishonesty, to repudiation, to the legal and irremediable plunder of our countrymen by the default of a bankrupt community, we were steeled by long endurance," and that, consequently, "the private robbery

* A free hand.—*Ed.*

of the English bondholders" lay not, as the [*Morning*] *Post* had it, at the bottom of the intervention. While remarking, *en passant*,* that "the City of Mexico was sufficiently healthy, should it be necessary to penetrate so far," *The Times* hoped, however, that "the mere presence of a combined squadron in the Gulf, and the seizure of certain ports, will urge the Mexican government to *new* exertions in keeping the peace, and will convince the malcontents that they must confine themselves to some form of opposition more constitutional than brigandage." If, then, according to the [*Morning*] *Post*, the expedition was to start because there "exists no government in Mexico," it was, according to *The Times*, only intended as encouraging and supporting the *existing* Mexican government. To be sure! The oddest means ever hit upon for the consolidation of a government consists in the seizure of its territory and the sequestration of its revenue.

The Times and the *Morning Post*, having once given out the cue, John Bull was then handed over to the minor ministerial oracles, systematically belaboring him in the same contradictory style for four weeks, until public opinion had at last become sufficiently trained to the idea of a joint intervention in Mexico, although kept in deliberate ignorance of the aim and purpose of that intervention. At last, the transactions with France had drawn to an end; the *Moniteur* announced that the convention between the three interfering powers had been concluded on October 31; and the *Journal des Débats*, one of whose co-proprietors is appointed to the command of one of the vessels of the French squadron, informed the world that no permanent territorial conquest was intended; that Vera Cruz and other points on the coast were to be seized, an advance to the capital being agreed upon in

* In passing.—*Ed.*

case of non-compliance by the constituted authorities in
Mexico with the demands of the intervention; that, moreover, a strong government was to be imported into the
republic.

The Times, which ever since its first announcement on
September 27, seemed to have forgotten the very existence of Mexico, had now again to step forward. Everybody ignorant of its connection with Palmerston, and the
original introduction in its columns of his scheme, would
be induced to consider the today's leader of *The Times*
as the most cutting and merciless satire on the whole ad-
venture. It sets out by stating that "the expedition is a
very remarkable one (later on it says a curious one).
Three States are combining to coerce a fourth into good
behavior, *not so much by way of war as by authoritative
interference in behalf of order.*"

Authoritative interference in behalf of order! This is
literally the Holy Alliance[26] slang, and sounds very
remarkable indeed on the part of England, glorying in the
non-intervention principle! And why is "the way of war,
and of declaration of war, and all other behests of international law," supplanted by "an authoritative interference in behalf of order"? Because, says *The Times,* there
"exists no government in Mexico." And what is the professed aim of the expedition? "To address demands to
the constituted authorities at Mexico."

The only grievances complained of by the intervening Powers, the only causes which might give to their
hostile procedure the slightest shade of justification, are
easily to be summed up. They are the monetary claims of
the bondholders and a series of personal outrages said to
have been committed upon subjects of England, France
and Spain. These were also the reasons of the intervention as originally put forth by the *Morning Post,* and as
some time ago officially endorsed by Lord John Russell

in an interview with some representatives of the Mexican bondholders in England. Today's *Times* states: "England, France, and Spain have concerted an expedition to bring Mexico to the *performance of her specific engagements, and to give protection to the subjects of the respective crowns.*" However, in the progress of its article, *The Times* veers round, and exclaims:

We shall, no doubt, succeed *in obtaining* at least a *recognition of our pecuniary claims,* in fact, *a single British frigate could have obtained that amount of satisfaction at any moment.* We may trust, too, that the more scandalous of the outrages committed will be expiated by more immediate and substantial atonements; but *it is clear that, if only this much was to be brought about we need not have resorted to such extremities as are now proposed.*

The Times, then, confesses in so many words that the reasons originally given out for the expedition are shallow pretexts; that for the attainment of redress nothing like the present procedure was needed; and that, in point of fact, the "recognition of monetary claims, and the protection of European subjects" have nothing at all to do with the present joint intervention in Mexico. What, then, is its real aim and purpose?

Before following *The Times* in its further explanations, we will, *en passant,* note some more *"curiosities"* which it has taken good care not to touch upon. In the first instance, it is a real "curiosity" to see Spain—Spain out of all other countries—turn crusader for the sanctity of foreign debts! Last Sunday's *Courrier des Dimanches* already summons the French government to improve the opportunity, and compel Spain, "into the eternally delayed performance of her old standing engagements to French bondholders."

The second still greater "curiosity" is, that the very same Palmerston who, according to Lord John Russell's recent declaration, is about invading Mexico to make its government pay the English bondholders, has himself, voluntarily, and despite the Mexican government, *sacrificed* the treaty rights of England and the security mortgaged by Mexico to her British creditors.

By the treaty concluded with England in 1826, Mexico became bound to not allow the establishment of slavery in any of the territories constituting her then empire. By another clause of the same treaty, she tendered England, as a security for the loans obtained from British capitalists, the mortgage of 45,000,000 acres of the public lands in Texas. It was Palmerston who, ten or twelve years later, interfered as the mediator for Texas against Mexico. In the treaty then concluded by him with Texas, he sacrificed not only *the anti-slavery cause,* but also the *mortgage on the public lands,* thus robbing the English bondholders of the security. The Mexican government protested at the time, but meanwhile, later on Secretary John C. Calhoun could permit himself the jest of informing the Cabinet of St. James * that its desire "of seeing slavery abolished in Texas would be" best realized by annexing Texas to the United States. The English bondholders lost, in fact, any claim upon Mexico, by the voluntary sacrifice on the part of Palmerston of the mortgage secured to them in the treaty of 1826.

But, since the London *Times* avows that the present intervention has nothing to do either with monetary claims or with personal outrages, what, then, in all the world, is its real or pretended aim?

"An authoritative interference in behalf of order." England, France and Spain, planning a new Holy Alliance, and having formed themselves into an armed areopagus for the restoration of order all over the world.

* St. James Palace is the King's residence in London.—*Ed.*

"Mexico," says *The Times, "must be rescued from anarchy,* and put in the way of self-government and peace. A strong and stable government must be established" there by the invaders, and that government is to be extracted from "some Mexican party."

Now, does any one imagine that Palmerston and his mouthpiece, *The Times,* really consider the joint intervention as a means to the professed end, *viz.:* the extinction of anarchy, and the establishment in Mexico of a strong and stable government? So far from cherishing any such chimerical creed, *The Times* states expressly in its first leader of September 27: "The only point on which there may possibly be a difference between ourselves and our allies, regards *the government of the Republic.* England will be content to see it *remain* in the hands of the *Liberal Party which is now in power,* while France and Spain are suspected of a partiality for the *ecclesiastical rule which has recently been overthrown....*[27] It would, indeed, be strange, if France were, in both the old and new world, to make herself the protector of priests and bandits." In today's leader, *The Times* goes on reasoning in the same strain, and resumes its scruples in the sentence: "It is *hard to suppose* that the intervening powers could all concur in the absolute preference of either of the two parties between which Mexico is divided, and *equally hard* to imagine that a compromise would be found practicable between enemies so determined."

Palmerston and *The Times,* then, are fully aware that there "exists a government in Mexico"; that the Liberal Party, "ostensibly favored by England, is now in power"; that "the ecclesiastical rule has been overthrown"; that Spanish intervention was the last forlorn hope of the priests and bandits; and finally, that Mexican anarchy was dying away. They know, then, that the joint intervention, with no other avowed end save the rescue of

Mexico from anarchy, will produce just the opposite effect, weaken the constitutional government, strengthen the priestly party by a supply of French and Spanish bayonets, rekindle the embers of civil war, and, instead of extinguishing, *restore* anarchy to its bloom.

The inference *The Times* itself draws from those premises is really "remarkable" and "curious." "Although," it says, "the considerations may induce us to look with some anxiety to the results of the expedition, they do not militate against *the expediency of the expedition itself*."

It does, consequently, not militate against the expediency of the expedition itself, that the expedition militates against the only ostensible purpose. It does not militate against the means that it baffles its own avowed end.

The greatest "curiosity" pointed out by *The Times*, I have, however, still kept *in petto*.* "If," says it, "President Lincoln should accept the invitation, which is provided for by the convention, to participate in the approaching operations, *the character of the work would become more curious still*."

It would, indeed, be the greatest "curiosity" of all if the United States, living in amity with Mexico, should associate with the European order-mongers, and, by participating in their acts, sanction the interference of a European armed areopagi with the internal affairs of American states. The first scheme of such a transplantation of the Holy Alliance to the other side of the Atlantic was, at the time of the restoration, drawn up for the French and Spanish Bourbons by Chateaubriand. The attempt was baffled by an English Minister, Mr. Canning, and an American President, Mr. Monroe. The present convulsion in the United States appeared to Palmerston an opportune moment for taking up the

* Secret.—*Ed.*

old project in a modified form. Since the United States, for the present, must allow no foreign complication to interfere with their war for the Union, all they can do is to *protest*. Their best well-wishers in Europe hope that they will protest, and thus, before the eyes of the world, firmly repudiate any complicity in one of the most nefarious schemes.

This military expedition of Palmerston's carried out by a coalition with two other European powers, is started during the prorogation, without the sanction, and against the will of the British Parliament. The first extra-parliamentary war of Palmerston's was the Afghan war, softened and justified by the production of *forged papers*. Another war of that [kind] was his Persian war of 1857-1858. He defended it at the time on the plea that "the principle of the previous sanction of the House did not apply to *Asiatic* wars." It seems that neither does it apply to *American* wars. With the control of the foreign wars, Parliament will lose all control over the national exchequer, and parliamentary government turn to a mere farce.

New York Daily Tribune, November 23, 1861.

5.

THE NEWS AND ITS EFFECT IN LONDON

London, November 30, 1861.

SINCE the declaration of war against Russia I never witnessed an excitement throughout all the strata of English society equal to that produced by the news of the *Trent* affair,[28] conveyed to Southampton by the *La Plata* on the 27th inst. At about 2 o'clock P.M., by means of the electric telegraph, the announcement of the "untoward event" was posted in the newsrooms of all the British exchanges. All commercial securities went down, while the price of saltpeter went up. Consols * declined three-quarters of one per cent, while at Lloyd's [29] war risks of five guineas were demanded on vessels from New York. Late in the evening the wildest rumors circulated in London, to the effect that the American Minister ** had forthwith been sent his passports, that orders had been issued for the immediate seizure of all American ships in the ports of the United Kingdom, and so forth. The cotton friends of secession at Liverpool improved the opportunity for holding, at ten minutes' notice, in the cotton salesroom of the Stock Exchange, an indignation meeting, under the presidency of Mr. Spence, the author of some obscure pamphlet in the interest of the Southern Confederacy.[30] Commodore Williams, the Admiralty Agent on board the *Trent,* who had arrived with the *La Plata,* was at once summoned to London.

On the following day, the 28th of November, the London press exhibited, on the whole, a tone of moderation strangely contrasting with the tremendous political and mercantile excitement of the previous evening. The Palmerston papers, *The Times, Morning Post, Daily Telegraph, Morning Advertiser,* and *Sun,* had received orders to calm down rather than to exasperate. *The Daily News,* by its strictures on the conduct of the *San Jacinto,* evidently aimed less at hitting the Federal government than clearing itself of the suspicion of "Yankee prejudices," while *The Morning Star,* John Bright's organ, without passing any judgment on the policy and wisdom of the "act," pleaded its lawfulness. There were only two exceptions to the general tenor of the London press. The Tory-scribblers of *The Morning Herald* and

* A contraction for "consolidated annuities," a British governmental security.—*Ed.*
** Charles F. Adams. See biographical notes.—*Ed.*

The Standard, forming in fact one paper under different names, gave full vent to their savage satisfaction of having at last caught the "republicans" in a trap, and finding a *casus belli,** ready cut out. They were supported by but one other journal, *The Morning Chronicle,* which for years had tried to prolong its checkered existence by alternately selling itself to the poisoner Palmer ** and the Tuileries. The excitement of the Exchange greatly subsided in consequence of the pacific tone of the leading London papers. On the same 28th of November, Commander Williams attended at the Admiralty, and reported the circumstances of the occurrence in the Old Bahama Channel. His report, together with the written depositions of the officers on board the *Trent,* were at once submitted to the law officers of the Crown, whose opinion, late in the evening, was officially brought to the notice of Lord Palmerston, Earl Russell and other members of the government.

On the 29th of November there was to be remarked some slight change in the tone of the ministerial press. It became known that the law officers of the Crown, on a technical ground, had declared the proceedings of the frigate *San Jacinto illegal,* and that later in the day, the Cabinet summoned to a general council, had decided to send by next steamer to Lord Lyons instructions to conform to the opinion of the English law officers. Hence the excitement in the principal places of business, such as the Stock Exchange, Lloyd's, the Jerusalem, the Baltic, etc., set in with redoubled force, and was further stimulated by the news, that the projected shipments to America of saltpeter had been stopped on the previous day, and that on the 29th a general order was received at the

---

* A cause justifying a war.—*Ed.*
** William Palmer (1824-56) poisoned his wife and brother in order to inherit their property; defended by the *Morning Chronicle* as "being of unsound mind."—*Ed.*

Customs House prohibiting the exportation of this article to any country except under certain stringent conditions. The English funds further fell three-quarters, and at one time a real panic prevailed in all the stock markets, it having become impossible to transact any business in some securities, while in all descriptions a severe depression of prices occurred. In the afternoon a recovery in the stock market was due to several rumors, but principally to the report that Mr. Adams had expressed his opinion, that the act of the *San Jacinto* would be disavowed by the Washington Cabinet.

On the 30th of November (today) all the London papers, with the single exception of *The Morning Star,* put the alternative of reparation by the Washington Cabinet or—war.

Having summed up the history of the events from the arrival of the *La Plata* to the present day, I shall now proceed to recording opinions. There were, of course, two points to be considered—on the one hand the law, on the other hand the policy of the seizure of the Southern Commissioners on board an English mail steamer.

As to the legal aspect of the affair, the first difficulty mooted by the Tory press and *The Morning Chronicle* was that the United States had never recognized the Southern secessionists as belligerents, and consequently, could not claim belligerent rights in regard to them.

This quibble was at once disposed of by the Ministerial press itself. "We," said *The Times,* "have already recognized these Confederate States as a belligerent power, and we shall, when the time comes, recognize their government. Therefore we have imposed on ourselves all the duties and inconveniences of a power neutral between two belligerents." Hence whether or not the United States recognize the Confederates as belligerents, they have the right to insist upon England submitting to all the duties and inconveniences of a neutral in maritime warfare.

Consequently, with the exceptions mentioned, the whole London press acknowledges the right of the *San Jacinto* to overhaul, visit, and search the *Trent,* in order to ascertain whether she carried goods or persons belonging to the category of "contraband of war." *The Times* insinuation that the English law of decisions "was given *under circumstances very different from* those which now occur"; that "steamers did not then exist, and mail vessels, carrying letters wherein all the nations of the world have immediate interest, were unknown"; that "we (the English) were *fighting for existence,* and did in those days *what we should not* allow others to *do,*" was not seriously thrown out. Palmerston's private *Moniteur,* the *Morning Post,* declared on the same day that mail steamers were simple merchantmen, not sharing the exemption from the right of search of men-of-war and transports. The *right of search,* on the part of the *San Jacinto,* was in point of fact conceded by the London press as well as the law officers of the Crown. The objection that the *Trent,* instead of sailing from a belligerent to a belligerent port, was, on the contrary, bound from a neutral to a neutral port, fell to the ground by Lord Stowell's decision that the right of search is intended to ascertain the destination of a ship.

In the second instance, the question arose whether by firing a round shot across the bows of the *Trent,* and subsequently throwing a shell, bursting close to her, the *San Jacinto* had not violated the usage and courtesies appurtenant to the exercise of the right of visitation and search. It was generally conceded by the London press that, since the details of the event have till now been only ascertained by the depositions of one of the parties concerned, no such minor question could influence the decision to be arrived at by the British government.

The right of search, exercised by the *San Jacinto,* thus being conceded, what had she to look for? For *contraband of war,* presumed to be conveyed by the *Trent.* What is contraband of war? Are the *dispatches* of the belligerent government contraband of war? Are the persons carrying those dispatches contraband of war? And, both questions being answered in the affirmative, do those dispatches and the bearers of them continue to be contraband of war, if found on a merchant ship bound from a neutral port to a neutral port? The London press admits that the decisions of the highest legal authorities on both sides of the Atlantic are so contradictory, and may be claimed with such appearance of justice for both the affirmative and the negative, that, at all events, a *prima facie* case * is made out for the *San Jacinto.*

Concurrently with this prevalent opinion of the English press, the English Crown lawyers have altogether dropped the material question, and only taken up the formal question. They assert that the law of nations was not violated in *substance* but in *form* only. They have arrived at the conclusion that the *San Jacinto* failed in seizing, on her own responsibility, the Southern Commissioners, instead of taking the *Trent* to a Federal port and submitting the question to a Federal Prize Court, no armed cruiser having a right to make itself a judge at sea. A violation in the *procedure* of the *San Jacinto* is, therefore, all that is imputed to her by the English Crown lawyers, who, in my opinion, are right in their conclusion. It might be easy to unearth precedents, showing England to have similarly trespassed on the formalities of mari-

* A case established by evidence sufficient to raise a presumption of fact or to establish the fact in question unless successfully opposed.—*Ed.*

time law; but violations of law can never be allowed to
supplant the law itself.

The question may now be mooted, whether the reparation demanded by the English government—that is, the
restitution of the Southern Commissioners—be warranted
by an injury which the English themselves avow to be
of *form* rather than of *substance?* A lawyer of the
Temple,* in today's *Times,* remarks, in respect to this
point:

If the case is not so clearly in our favor as that a decision
in the American Court condemning the vessel would have
been liable to be questioned by us as manifestly contrary to the
laws of nations, then the irregularity of the American captain
in allowing the *Trent* to proceed to Southampton, clearly re-
dounded to the advantage of the British owners and the British
passengers. Could we in such case find a ground of international quarrel in an error of procedure which in effect told
in our own favor?

Still, if the American government must concede, as it
seems to me, that Captain Wilkes has committed a violation of maritime law, whether formal or material, their
fair fame and their interest ought alike to prevent them
from nibbling at the terms of the satisfaction to be given
to the injured party. They ought to remember that they
do the work of the secessionists in embroiling the United
States in a war with England, that such a war would
be a godsend to Louis Bonaparte in his present difficulties, and would, consequently, be supported by all the
official weight of France; and, lastly, that, what with
the actual force under the command of the British on
the North American and West Indian stations, what
with the forces of the Mexican expedition, the English

* A building in London formerly the dwelling of the Knights Tem-
plars now used for two groups of buildings consisting of two Inns of
Court which have the right of calling persons to the degree of bar-
rister.—*Ed.*

government would have at its disposal an overwhelming maritime power.[81]

As to the policy of the seizure in the Bahama Channel, the voice not only of the English, but of the European press is unanimous in expressions of bewilderment at the strange conduct of the American government, provoking such tremendous international dangers, for gaining the bodies of Messrs. Mason, Slidell & Co., while Messrs. Yancey and Mann are strutting in London. *The Times* is certainly right in saying: "Even Mr. Seward himself must know that the voices of these Southern Commissioners, sounding from their captivity, are a thousand times more eloquent in London and in Paris than they would have been if they had been heard at St. James and the Tuileries." The people of the United States, having magnanimously submitted to a curtailment of their own liberties in order to save their country, will certainly be no less ready to turn the tide of popular opinion in England by openly avowing, and carefully making up for, an international blunder the vindication of which might realize the boldest hopes of the rebels.

New York Daily Tribune, December 19, 1861.

6.

PROGRESS OF FEELING IN ENGLAND

London, December 7, 1861.

THE FRIENDS of the United States on this side of the Atlantic anxiously hope that conciliatory steps will be taken by the Federal government. They do so not from a concurrence in the frantic crowing of the British press over a war incident, which, according to the English Crown lawyers themselves, resolves itself into a mere error of procedure, and may be summed up in the words that there has been a breach of international law, because Captain Wilkes, instead of taking the *Trent,* her cargo, her passengers and the Commissioners, did only take the Commissioners. Nor springs the anxiety of the well-wishers of the Great Republic from an apprehension lest, in the long run, it should not prove able to cope with England, although backed by the civil war; and, least of all, do they expect the United States to abdicate, even for a moment, and in a dark hour of trial, the proud position held by them in the council of nations. The motives that prompt them are of quite a different nature.

In the first instance, the business next in hand for the United States is to crush the rebellion and to restore the Union. The wish uppermost in the minds of the slavocracy and their Northern tools was always to plunge the United States into a war with England. The first step of England as soon as hostilities broke out would be to recognize the Southern Confederacy, and the second to terminate the blockade. Secondly, no general, if not forced, will accept battle at the time and under the conditions chosen by his enemy. "A war with America," says *The Economist,* a paper deeply in Palmerston's confidence, "must always be one of the most lamentable incidents in the history of England, but if it is to happen, *the present is certainly the period at which it will do us the minimum of harm, and the only moment in our joint annals at which it would confer on us an incidental and partial compensation.*" The very reason accounting for the eagerness of England to seize upon any decent pretext for war at this "only moment" ought to withhold the United States from forwarding such a pretext at this "only moment." You go not to war with the aim to do your enemy *"the minimum of harm,"* and, even to confer upon him by the war, *"an incidental and partial compensation."* The opportunity of the moment would all be on one side, on the side of your foe.

Is there any great strain of reasoning wanted to prove that an internal war raging in a state is the least opportune time for entering upon a foreign war? At every other moment the mercantile classes of Great Britain would have looked upon the war against the United States with the utmost horror. Now, on the contrary, a large and influential party of the mercantile community has for months been urging on the government to violently break the blockade, and thus provide the main branch of British industry with its raw material. The fear of a curtailment of the English export trade to the United States has lost its sting by the curtailment of that trade having already actually occurred. "They" (the Northern States), says *The Economist,* "are wretched customers, instead of good ones." The vast credit usually given by English commerce to the United States, principally by the acceptance of bills drawn from China and India, has been already reduced to scarcely a fifth of what it was in 1857. Last, not least, Decembrist France,* bankrupt, paralyzed at home, beset with difficulty abroad, pounces upon an Anglo-American war as a real godsend, and, in order to buy English support in Europe, will strain all her power to support "Perfidious Albion" ** on the other side of the Atlantic. Read only the French newspapers. The pitch of indignation to which they have wrought themselves in their tender care for the "honor of England," their fierce diatribes as to the necessity on the part of England to revenge the outrage on the Union Jack, their vile denunciations of everything American, would be truly appalling, if they were not ridiculous and disgust-

* The France of Napoleon III, derived from date, December 2, 1851, on which Louis Napoleon carried through a successful *coup d'état.—Ed.*
** Treacherous England.—*Ed.*

ing at the same time. Lastly, if the United States give
way in this instance, they will not derogate one iota of
their dignity. England has reduced her complaint to a
mere *error of procedure,* a *technical blunder* of which she
has made herself systematically guilty in all her maritime wars, but against which the United States have
never ceased to protest, and which President Madison,
in his message inaugurating the war of 1812, expatiated
upon as one of the most shocking breaches of international law.[32] If the United States may be defended in
paying England with her own coin, will they be accused
for magnanimously disavowing, on the part of a single
American captain, acting on his own responsibility, what
they always denounced as a systematic usurpation on the
part of the British Navy! In point of fact, the gain of
such a procedure would be all on the American side.
England, on the one hand, would have acknowledged the
right of the United States to capture and bring to adjudication before an American prize court every English ship
employed in the service of the Confederacy. On the other
hand, she would, once for all, before the eyes of the whole
world, have practically resigned a claim which she was
not brought to desist from either in the Peace of Ghent
in 1814,[33] or the transactions carried on between Lord
Ashburton and Secretary Webster in 1842.[34] The question
then comes to this: Do you prefer to turn the "untoward event" to your own account, or, blinded by the
passions of the moment, turn it to the account of your
foes at home and abroad?

Since this day week, when I sent you my last letter,
British consols have again lowered, the decline, compared
with last Friday, amounting to two per cent, the present
prices being 89¾ to ⅞ for money and to 90 to ⅑ for the
new account on the 9th of January. This quotation corresponds to the quotation of the British consols during

the first two years of the Anglo-Russian War. This decline is altogether due to the warlike interpretation put upon the American papers conveyed by the last mail, to the exacerbating tone of the London press, whose moderation of two days' standing was but a feint, ordered by Palmerston, to the dispatch of troops for Canada, to the proclamation forbidding the export of arms and materials for gunpowder, and lastly, to the daily ostentatious statements concerning the formidable preparations for war in the docks and maritime arsenals.

Of one thing you may be sure, Palmerston wants a legal pretext for a war with the United States, but meets in the Cabinet councils with a most determinate opposition on the part of Messrs. Gladstone and Milner-Gibson, and, to a less degree, of Sir Cornwall Lewis. "The noble viscount" is backed by Russell, an abject tool in his hands, and the whole Whig coterie. If the Washington Cabinet should furnish the desired pretext, the present Cabinet will be sprung, to be supplanted by a Tory administration. The preliminary steps for such a change of scenery have been already settled between Palmerston and Disraeli. Hence the furious war-cry of *The Morning Herald* and *The Standard,* those hungry wolves howling at the prospect of the long missed crumbs from the public almoner.

Palmerston's designs may be shown up by calling into memory a few facts. It was he who insisted upon the proclamation, acknowledging the secessionists as belligerents, on the morning of the 14th of May, after he had been informed by telegraph from Liverpool that Mr. Adams would arrive at London on the night of the 13th May. He, after a severe struggle with his colleagues, dispatched 3,000 men to Canada, an army ridiculous, if intended to cover a frontier of 1,500 miles, but a clever sleight-of-hand if the rebellion was to be cheered, and the

Union to be irritated. He, many weeks ago, urged Bonaparte to propose a joint armed intervention "in the internecine struggle," supported that project in the Cabinet council, and failed only in carrying it by the resistance of his colleagues. He and Bonaparte then resorted to the Mexican intervention as a *pis aller*.* That operation served two purposes, by provoking just resentment on the part of the Americans, and by simultaneously furnishing a pretext for the dispatch of a squadron, ready, as the *Morning Post* has it, "to perform whatever duty the hostile conduct of the government of Washington may require us to perform in the waters of the Northern Atlantic."

At the time when that expedition was started, the *Morning Post,* together with *The Times* and the smaller fry of Palmerston's press slaves, said that it was a very fine thing, and a philanthropic thing into the bargain, because it would expose the slaveholding Confederacy to two fires—the anti-slavery North and the anti-slavery force of England and France. And what says the very same *Morning Post,* this curious compound of Jenkins ** and Rodomonte,*** of plush and swash, in its today's issue, on occasion of Jefferson Davis's address? [35] Hearken to the Palmerston oracle:

We must look to this intervention as one that may be inoperative during a considerable period of time; and while the Northern government is too distant to admit of its attitude entering materially into this question, the Southern Confederacy, on the other hand, stretches for a great distance along the frontier of Mexico, so as to render its friendly disposition to the authors of the insurrection of no slight consequence. The Northern government has invariably railed at our neutrality, but the Southern with statesmanship and moderation

* Last resource.—*Ed.*
** Popular name for a liveried footman or manservant.—*Ed.*
*** King of Algiers, a character in the poem *Orlando Furioso* of Ariosto, a personification of boastfulness.—*Ed.*

has recognized in it all that we could do for either party; and whether with a view to our transactions in Mexico, or to our relations with the Cabinet at Washington, the *friendly forbearance* of the Southern Confederacy is an important point in our favor.

I may remark that the *Nord* of December 3—a Russian paper, and consequently a paper initiated into Palmerston's designs—insinuates that the Mexican expedition was from the first set on foot, not for its ostensible purpose, but for a war against the United States.

Gen. Scott's letter [36] had produced such a beneficent reaction in public opinion, and even on the London Stock Exchange, that the conspirators of Downing Street * and the Tuileries found it necessary to let loose the *Patrie,* stating with all the airs of knowledge derived from official sources, that the seizure of the Southern Commissioners from the *Trent* was directly authorized by the Washington Cabinet.

New York Daily Tribune, December 25, 1861.

7.

ENGLISH PUBLIC OPINION

London, January 11, 1862.

THE NEWS of the pacific solution of the *Trent* conflict was, by the bulk of the English people, saluted with an exultation proving unmistakably the unpopularity of the apprehended war and the dread of its consequences. It ought never to be forgotten in the United States that at least the *working classes* of England, from the commence-

*. The street on which the residence of the Prime Minister is situated. —*Ed.*

ment to the termination of the difficulty, have never forsaken them. To them it was due that, despite the poisonous stimulants daily administered by a venal and reckless press, not one single public war meeting could be held in the United Kingdom during all the period that peace trembled in the balance. The only war meeting convened on the arrival of the *La Plata,* in the cotton salesroom of the Liverpool Stock Exchange, was a corner meeting where the cotton jobbers had it all to themselves. Even at Manchester, the temper of the working classes was so well understood that an isolated attempt at the convocation of a war meeting was almost as soon abandoned as thought of.

Wherever public meetings took place in England, Scotland or Ireland,[37] they protested against the rabid war-cries of the press, against the sinister designs of the government, and declared for a pacific settlement of the pending question. In this regard, the two last meetings held, the one at Paddington, London, the other at Newcastle-upon-Tyne, are characteristic. The former meeting applauded Mr. Washington Wilkes' argumentation that England was not warranted in finding fault with the seizure of the Southern Commissioners; while the Newcastle meeting almost unanimously carried the resolution —firstly, that the Americans had only made themselves guilty of a *lawful* exercise of the right of search and seizure; secondly, that the captain of the *Trent* ought to be punished for his violation of English neutrality, as proclaimed by the Queen. In ordinary circumstances, the conduct of the British workingmen might have been anticipated from the natural sympathy the popular classes all over the world ought to feel for the only popular government in the world.

Under the present circumstances, however, when a great portion of the British working classes directly and severely suffers under the consequences of the Southern blockade;[38] when another part is indirectly smitten by the curtailment of the American commerce, owing, as they are told, to the selfish "protective policy" of the Republicans; when the only remaining democratic weekly, Reynolds' paper,* has sold itself to Messrs. Yancey and Mann, and week after week exhausts its horse-powers of foul language in appeals to the working classes to urge the government, for their own interests, to war with the Union—under such circumstances, simple justice requires to pay a tribute to the sound attitude of the British working classes, the more so when contrasted with the hypocritical, bullying, cowardly, and stupid conduct of the official and well-to-do John Bull.

What a difference in this attitude of the people from what it had assumed at the time of the Russian complication! Then *The Times,* the [*Morning*] *Post,* and the other yellow plushes of the London press, whined for peace, to be rebuked by tremendous war meetings all over the country. Now they have howled for war, to be answered by peace meetings denouncing the liberticide schemes and the pro-slavery sympathy of the government. The grimaces cut by the augurs of public opinion at the news of the pacific solution of the *Trent* case are really amusing.

In the first place, they must needs congratulate themselves upon the dignity, common sense, good will, and moderation, daily displayed by them for the whole interval of a month. They *were* moderate for the first two days after the arrival of the *La Plata,* when Palmerston felt uneasy whether any legal pretext for a quarrel was to be picked. But hardly had the crown lawyers hit upon a legal quibble, when they opened a charivari unheard of since the anti-Jacobin war.[39] The dispatches of the Eng-

* *Reynolds's Weekly Newspaper.—Ed.*

lish government left Queenstown in the beginning of December. No official answer from Washington could possibly be looked for before the commencement of January. The new incidents arising in the interval told all in favor of the Americans. The tone of the trans-Atlantic press, although the *Nashville* affair [40] might have roused its passions, was calm. All facts ascertained concurred to show that Captain Wilkes had acted on his own hook. The position of the Washington government was delicate. If it resisted the English demands, it would complicate the civil war by a foreign war. If it gave way, it might damage its popularity at home, and appear to cede to pressure from abroad. And the government thus placed, carried, at the same time, a war which must enlist the warmest sympathies of every man, not a confessed ruffian, on its side.

Common prudence, conventional decency, ought, therefore, to have dictated to the London press, at least for the time separating the English demand from the American reply, to abstain anxiously from every word calculated to heat passion, breed ill-will, complicate the difficulty. But no! That "irrepressibly mean and groveling" press, as William Cobbett, and he was a *connoisseur*, calls it, really boasted of having, when in fear of the compact power of the United States, humbly submitted to the accumulated slights and insults of pro-slavery administration for almost half a century, while now, with the savage exultation of cowards, they panted for taking their revenge on the Republican administration, distracted by a civil war. The record of mankind chronicles no self-avowed infamy like this.

One of the yellow-plushes, Palmerston's private *Moniteur*—the *Morning Post*—finds itself arraigned on a most ugly charge from the American papers. John Bull has never been informed—on information carefully withheld

from him by the oligarchs that lord it over him—that
Mr. Seward, without awaiting Russell's dispatch, had disavowed any participation of the Washington Cabinet in
the act of Captain Wilkes. Mr. Seward's dispatch arrived
at London on December 19. On the 20th December, the
rumor of this "secret" spread on the Stock Exchange. On
the 21st, the yellow-plush of the *Morning Post* stepped
forward to herald gravely that "the dispatch in question
does not in any way whatever refer to the outrage on
our mail packet."

In *The Daily News, The Morning Star,* and other
London journals, you will find yellow-plush pretty sharply
handled, but you will not learn from them what people
out of doors say. They say that the *Morning Post* and
The Times, like the *Patrie* and the *Pays,* dupe the public
not only to mislead them politically, but to fleece them
in the monetary line on the Stock Exchange, in the interest of their patrons.

The brazen *Times,* fully aware that during the whole
crisis it had compromised nobody but itself, and given
another proof of the hollowness of its pretensions of in-
fluencing the real people of England, plays today a trick
which here, at London, only works upon the laughing
muscles, but on the other side of the Atlantic might be
misinterpreted. The "popular classes" of London, the
"mob," as the yellow-plush call them, have given unmistakable signs—have even hinted in newspapers—that
they should consider it an exceedingly seasonable joke to
treat Mason (by the by, a distant relative of Palmerston,
since the original Mason had married a daughter of Sir
W. Temple), Slidell & Co. with the same demonstrations
Hainau received on his visit at Barclay's brewery.* The
Times stands aghast at the mere idea of such a shocking

---

* In 1850, Hainau, the reactionary Austrian general, visited Barclay's
factory and was given a flogging by the angry London workers.—*Ed.*

incident, and how does it try to parry it? It admonishes
the people of England not to overwhelm Mason, Slidell
& Co. with any sort of public *ovation*. *The Times* knows
that its article of today will form the laughing-stock of
all the tap-rooms of London. But never mind! People on
the other side of the Atlantic may, perhaps, fancy that
the magnanimity of *The Times* has saved them from the
affront of public ovation to Mason, Slidell & Co., while,
in point of fact, *The Times* only intends saving those
gentlemen from public insult!

So long as the *Trent* affair was undecided, *The Times,*
the [*Morning*] *Post, The* [*Morning*] *Herald, The Economist, The Saturday Review,* in fact the whole of the
fashionable, hireling press of London, had tried its utmost to persuade John Bull that the Washington government, even if it willed, would prove unable to keep the
peace, because the Yankee mob would not allow it, and
because the Federal government was a mob government.
Facts have now given them the lie direct. Do they now
atone for their malignant slanders against the American
people? Do they at least confess the error which yellow-
plush, in presuming to judge of the acts of a free people,
could not but commit? By no means. They now unanimously discover that the American government, in not
anticipating England's demands, and not surrendering
the Southern traitors as soon as they were caught, missed
a great occasion, and deprived its present concession of
all merit. Indeed, yellow-plush! Mr. Seward disavowed
the act of Wilkes before the arrival of the English demands, and at once declared himself willing to enter upon
a conciliatory course; and what did you do on similar
occasions? When, on the pretext of impressing English
sailors on board American ships—a pretext not at all
connected with maritime belligerent rights, but a down-
right, monstrous usurpation against all international law

—the *Leopard* fired its broadside at the *Chesapeake,* killed six, wounded twenty-one of her sailors, and seized the pretended Englishmen on board the *Chesapeake,* what did the English government do? That outrage was perpetrated on the 22nd of June, 1807. The real satisfaction, the surrender of the sailors, etc., was only offered on November 8, 1812, five years later. The British government, it is true, disavowed at once the act of Admiral Berkeley, as Mr. Seward did in regard to Captain Wilkes; but, to punish the Admiral, it removed him from an inferior to a superior rank. England, in proclaiming her Orders in Council,[41] distinctly confessed that they were outrages on the rights of neutrals in general, and of the United States in particular; that they were forced upon her as measures of retaliation against Napoleon, and that she would feel but too glad to revoke them whenever Napoleon should revoke his encroachments on neutral rights. Napoleon did revoke them, as far as the United States were concerned, in the Spring of 1810. England persisted in her avowed outrage on the maritime rights of America. Her resistance lasted from 1806 to 23rd of June, 1812—after, on the 18th of June, the United States had declared war against England. England abstained, consequently, in this case for six years, not from atoning for a confessed outrage, but from discounting it. And this people talk of the magnificent occasion missed by the American government! Whether in the wrong or in the right, it was a cowardly act on the part of the British government to back a complaint grounded on pretended technical blunder, and a mere error of procedure by an ultimatum, by a demand for the surrender of the prisoners. The American government might have reasons to accede to that demand; it could have none to anticipate it.

By the present settlement of the *Trent* collision, the

question underlying the whole dispute, and likely to again occur—the belligerent rights of a maritime power against neutrals—has not been settled. I shall, with your permission, try to survey the whole question in a subsequent letter. For the present, allow me to add that, in my opinion, Messrs. Mason and Slidell have done great service to the Federal government. There was an influential war party in England, which, what for commercial, what for political reasons, showed itself eager for a fray with the United States. The *Trent* affair put that party to the test. It has failed. The war passion has been discontented on a minor issue, the steam has been let off, the vociferous fury of the oligarchy has raised the suspicions of English democracy, the large British interests connected with the United States have made a stand, the true character of the Civil War has been brought home to the working classes, and last, not least, the dangerous period when Palmerston rules single-handed without being checked by Parliament, is rapidly drawing to an end. That was the only time in which an English war for the slavocrats might have been hazarded. It is now out of question.

New York Daily Tribune, February 1, 1862.

PART TWO

ARTICLES FROM
THE VIENNA *PRESSE*
(1861-1862)

By KARL MARX
AND
FREDERICK ENGELS

1.

THE NORTH AMERICAN CIVIL WAR

The war, of which the great North American Republic has been the seat for more than half a year, already begins to react on Europe. France, which loses a market for her commodities through these troubles, and England, whose industry is threatened with partial ruin through stagnation in the export of cotton from the slave states, follow the development of the Civil War in the United States with feverish intensity. Whilst up to the most recent date Europe, indeed, the Americas themselves, still did not despair of the possibility of a peaceful solution, the war assumes ever greater dimensions, spreads more and more over the vast territories of North America and threatens, the longer it lasts, this part of the world, too, with a crisis. First England and France will be seized and shaken thereby, and the panic on the English and French markets will in like manner react on the rest of the European markets. Apart from the historical aspect, we have, therefore, a very positive interest in getting our bearings in regard to the causes, the significance and the import of the trans-Atlantic events. From London we have received a first communication on the North American Civil War from one of the most significant German publicists, who knows Anglo-American relations from long years of observation. In the measure that events on the other side of the ocean develop, we shall be in a position to present communications, deriving from the same competent pen, which will fix the events in their main points.*

* The introductory note is written by the editor of *Die Presse.—Ed.*

London, October 20, 1861.

FOR MONTHS the leading weekly and daily papers of the London press have reiterated the same litany on the American Civil War. While they insult the free states of the North, they anxiously defend themselves against the suspicion of sympathizing with the slave states of the South. In fact, they continually write two articles: one article, in which they attack the North, and another article, in which they excuse their attacks on the North. *Qui s'excuse s'accuse.**

In essence the extenuating arguments read: The war between the North and South is a tariff war. The war is, further, not for any principle, does not touch the question of slavery and in fact turns on Northern lust for sovereignty. Finally, even if justice is on the side of the North, does it not remain a vain endeavor to want to subjugate eight million Anglo-Saxons by force! Would not the separation of the South release the North from all connection with Negro slavery and assure to it, with its twenty million inhabitants and its vast territory, a higher, hitherto scarcely dreamt of, development? Accordingly must not the North welcome secession as a happy event, instead of wanting to put it down by a bloody and futile civil war?

Point by point we will probe the *plaidoyer ** * of the English press.

The war between North and South—so runs the first excuse—is a mere tariff war, a war between a protection system and a free trade system, and England naturally stands on the side of free trade. Shall the slaveowner enjoy the fruits of slave labor in their entirety or shall he be cheated of a portion of these by the protectionists of the North? That is the question which is at issue in

---

* He who excuses himself accuses himself.—*Ed.*
** Address of counsel for the defense, *i.e.,* plea.—*Ed.*

this war. It was reserved for *The Times* to make this brilliant discovery. *The Economist, The Examiner, The Saturday Review* and *tutti quanti* * expounded the theme further. It is characteristic of this discovery that it was made, not in Charleston, but in London. Naturally, in America every one knew that from 1846 to 1861 a free trade system prevailed, and that Representative Morrill carried his protectionist tariff in Congress only in 1861, after the rebellion had already broken out. Secession, therefore, did not take place because the Morrill tariff had gone through Congress, but, at most, the Morrill tariff went through Congress because secession had taken place. When South Carolina had her first attack of secession in 1831, the protectionist tariff of 1828 served her, to be sure, as a pretext, but also only as a pretext, as is known from a statement of General Jackson.[42] This time, however, the old pretext has in fact not been repeated. In the Secession Congress at Montgomery all reference to the tariff question was avoided, because the cultivation of sugar in Louisiana, one of the most influential Southern States, depends entirely on protection.

But, the London press pleads further, the war of the United States is nothing but a war for the maintenance of the Union by force. The Yankees cannot make up their minds to strike fifteen stars from their standard. They want to cut a colossal figure on the world stage. Yes, it would be different, if the war was waged for the abolition of slavery! The question of slavery, however, as, among others, *The Saturday Review* categorically declares, has absolutely nothing to do with this war.

It is above all to be remembered that the war did not emanate from the North, but from the South. The North finds itself on the defensive. For months it had quietly looked on, while the secessionists appropriated to them-

* All such.—*Ed.*

selves the Union's forts, arsenals, shipyards, customs houses, pay offices, ships and supplies of arms, insulted its flag and took prisoner bodies of its troops. Finally the secessionists resolved to force the Union government out of its passive attitude by a sensational act of war, and *solely for this reason* proceeded to the bombardment of Fort Sumter near Charleston. On April 11 (1861) their General Beauregard had learnt in a parley with Major Anderson, the commander of Fort Sumter, that the fort was only supplied with provisions for three days more and accordingly must be peacefully surrendered after this period. In order to forestall this peaceful surrender, the secessionists opened the bombardment early on the following morning (April 12), which brought about the fall of the place in a few hours. News of this had hardly been telegraphed to Montgomery, the seat of the Secession Congress, when War Minister Walter publicly declared in the name of the new Confederacy: "No man can say where *the war opened today* will end." At the same time he prophesied "that before the first of May the flag of the Southern Confederacy would wave from the dome of the old Capitol in Washington and within a short time perhaps also from the Faneuil Hall in Boston." [43] Only now ensued the proclamation in which Lincoln summoned 75,000 men to the protection of the Union. The bombardment of Fort Sumter cut off the only possible constitutional way out, namely, the summoning of a general convention of the American people, as Lincoln had proposed in his inaugural address.[44] For Lincoln there now remained only the choice of fleeing from Washington, evacuating Maryland and Delaware and surrendering Kentucky, Missouri and Virginia, or of answering war with war.

The question of the principle of the American Civil War is answered by the battle slogan with which the

South broke the peace. Stephens, the Vice-President of the Southern Confederacy, declared in the Secession Congress, that what essentially distinguished the Constitution newly hatched at Montgomery from the Constitution of the Washingtons and Jeffersons was that now for the first time slavery was recognized as an institution good in itself, and as the foundation of the whole state edifice, whereas the revolutionary fathers, men steeped in the prejudices of the eighteenth century, had treated slavery as an evil imported from England and to be eliminated in the course of time. Another matador of the South, Mr. Spratt, cried out: "For us it is a question of the foundation of a great slave republic." If, therefore, it was indeed only in defense of the Union that the North drew the sword, had not the South already declared that the continuance of slavery was no longer compatible with the continuance of the Union?

Just as the bombardment of Fort Sumter gave the signal for the opening of the war, the election victory of the Republican Party of the North, the election of Lincoln as President, gave the signal for secession. On November 6, 1860, Lincoln was elected. On November 8, 1860, it was telegraphed from South Carolina: "Secession is regarded here as an accomplished fact"; on November 10 the legislature of Georgia occupied itself with secession plans, and on November 15 a special session of the legislature of Mississippi was fixed to take secession into consideration. But Lincoln's victory was itself only the result of a split in the *Democratic* camp. During the election struggle the Democrats of the North concentrated their votes on Douglas, the Democrats of the South concentrated their votes on Breckinridge, and to this splitting of the Democratic votes the Republican Party owed its victory.[45] Whence came, on the one hand, the preponderance of the Republican Party in the North?

Whence came, on the other hand, the disunion *within* the Democratic Party, whose members, North and South, had operated in conjunction for more than half a century?

Under the presidency of Buchanan the sway that the South had gradually usurped over the Union through its alliance with the Northern Democrats, attained its zenith. The last Continental Congress of 1787 and the first Constitutional Congress of 1789-1790 had legally excluded slavery from all Territories of the republic northwest of the Ohio. (Territories, as is known, is the name given to the colonies lying within the United States themselves that have not yet attained the level of population constitutionally prescribed for the formation of autonomous states.) The so-called Missouri Compromise (1820),[46] in consequence of which Missouri entered the ranks of the United States as a slave state, excluded slavery from every remaining Territory north of 36° 30′ latitude and west of Missouri. By this compromise the slavery area was advanced several degrees of longitude, whilst, on the other hand, a geographical line setting bounds to future propaganda for it seemed quite definitely drawn. This geographical barrier, in its turn, was thrown down in 1854 by the so-called Kansas-Nebraska Bill,[47] the originator of which was St[ephen] A. Douglas, then leader of the Northern Democrats. The Bill, which passed both Houses of Congress, repealed the Missouri Compromise, placed slavery and freedom on the same footing, commanded the Union government to treat them both with equal indifference and left it to the sovereignty of the people, that is, the majority of the settlers, to decide whether or not slavery was to be introduced in a Territory. Thus, for the first time in the history of the United States, every geographical and legal limit to the extension of slavery in the Territories was removed. Under this new legislation the hitherto free Territory of

New Mexico, a Territory five times larger than the State of New York, was transformed into a slave Territory, and the area of slavery was extended from the border of the Mexican Republic to 38° north latitude. In 1859 New Mexico received a slave code that vies with the statute-books of Texas and Alabama in barbarity. Nevertheless, as the census of 1860 proves, among some hundred thousand inhabitants New Mexico does not yet number half a hundred slaves. It had therefore sufficed for the South to send some adventurers with a few slaves over the border, and then with the help of the central government, its officials and contractors to drum together a sham popular representation in New Mexico, which imposed slavery on the Territory and with it the rule of the slave-holders.

However, this convenient method did not prove applicable in other Territories. The South accordingly went a step further and appealed from Congress to the Supreme Court of the United States. This Supreme Court, which numbers nine judges, five of whom belong to the South, had been long the most willing tool of the slaveholders. It decided in 1857, in the notorious Dred Scott case,[48] that every American citizen possesses the right to take with him into any Territory any property recognized by the Constitution. The Constitution recognizes slaves as property and obliges the Union government to protect this property. Consequently, on the basis of the Constitution, slaves could be forced to labor in the Territories by their owners, and so every individual slaveholder is entitled to introduce slavery into hitherto free Territories against the will of the majority of the settlers. The right to exclude slavery was taken from the Territorial legislatures and the duty to protect pioneers of the slave system was imposed on Congress and the Union government.

If the Missouri Compromise of 1820 had extended the

geographical boundary-line of slavery in the Territories, if the Kansas-Nebraska Bill of 1854 had wiped out every geographical boundary-line and set up a political barrier instead, the will of the majority of the settlers, then the Supreme Court of the United States, by its decision of 1857, tore down even this political barrier and transformed all the Territories of the republic, present and future, from places for the cultivation of free states into places for the cultivation of slavery.

At the same time, under Buchanan's government the severer law on the surrendering of fugitive slaves enacted in 1850 [49] was ruthlessly carried out in the states of the North. To play the part of slave-catchers for the Southern slaveholders appeared to be the constitutional calling of the North. On the other hand, in order as far as possible to hinder the colonization of the Territories by free settlers, the slaveholders' party frustrated all the so-called free-soil measures, *i.e.,* measures which were to secure to the settlers a definite amount of uncultivated state land free of charge.[50]

In the foreign, as in the domestic, policy of the United States, the interest of the slaveholders served as the guiding star. Buchanan had in fact purchased the office of President through the issue of the Ostend Manifesto, in which the acquisition of Cuba, whether by robbery or by force of arms, is proclaimed as the great task of national politics.[51] Under his government northern Mexico was already divided among American land speculators, who impatiently awaited the signal to fall on Chihuahua, Coahuila and Sonora.[52] The restless, piratical expeditions of the filibusters against the states of Central America [53] were directed no less from the White House at Washington. In the closest connection with this foreign policy, whose manifest purpose was conquest of new territory for the extension of slavery and the rule of the slaveholders, stood the *reopening of the slave trade*,[54] secretly supported by the Union government. St[ephen] A. Douglas himself declared in 1859: During the last year more Negroes have been indented from Africa than ever before in any single year, even at the time when the slave trade was still legal. The number of slaves imported in the last year has amounted to fifteen thousand.

Armed propaganda of slavery abroad was the avowed aim of the national policy; the Union had in fact become the slave of the three hundred thousand slave-holders who held sway over the South. A series of com-promises, which the South owed to its alliance with the Northern Democrats, had led to this result. On this alli-ance all the attempts, periodically repeated since 1817, at resistance to the ever increasing encroachments of the slaveholders had hitherto suffered shipwreck. At length there came a turning point.

For hardly had the Kansas-Nebraska Bill gone through, which wiped out the geographical boundary-line of slavery and made its introduction into new Territories subject to the will of the majority of the settlers, when armed emissaries of the slaveholders, border rabble from Missouri and Arkansas, with bowie-knife in one hand and revolver in the other, fell upon Kansas and by the most unheard-of atrocities sought to dislodge her settlers from the Territory colonized by them. These raids were sup-ported by the central government at Washington. Hence a tremendous reaction. Throughout the North, but par-ticularly in the Northwest, a relief organization was formed to support Kansas with men, arms and money. Out of this relief organization arose the Republican Party, which therefore owes its origin to the struggle for Kansas. After the attempt to transform Kansas into a *slave Terri-tory* by force of arms had failed, the South sought to achieve the same result by way of political intrigues.

Buchanan's government, in particular, exerted its utmost efforts to relegate Kansas into the ranks of the United States as a *slave state* with a slavery constitution imposed on it. Hence renewed struggle, this time mainly conducted in Congress at Washington. Even St[ephen] A. Douglas, the chief of the Northern Democrats, now (1857-1858) entered the lists against the government and its allies of the South, because imposition of a slave constitution would contradict the principle of sovereignty of the settlers passed in the Nebraska Bill of 1854. Douglas, Senator for Illinois, a northwestern state, would naturally have lost all his influence if he wanted to concede to the South the right to steal by force of arms or through acts of Congress Territories colonized by the North.[55] As the struggle for Kansas, therefore, called the *Republican Party* into being, it occasioned at the same time the first *split within the Democratic Party* itself.

The Republican Party put forward its first platform for the presidential election in 1856. Although its candidate, John Frémont, was not victorious, the huge number of votes that were cast for him at any rate proved the rapid growth of the Party, particularly in the Northwest.[56] In their second National Convention for the presidential election (May 17, 1860), the Republicans repeated their platform of 1856, only enriched by some additions. Its principal contents were the following: Not a foot of fresh territory is further conceded to slavery. The filibustering policy abroad must cease. The reopening of the slave trade is stigmatized. Finally, free-soil laws are to be enacted for the furtherance of free colonization.

The vitally important point in this platform was that not a foot of fresh terrain was conceded to slavery; rather it was to remain once and for all confined to the limits of the states where it already legally existed.[57] Slavery was thus to be formally interned; but continual expansion of territory and continual extension of slavery beyond their old limits is a law of life for the slave states of the Union. The cultivation of the Southern export articles, cotton, tobacco, sugar, etc., carried on by slaves, is only remunerative as long as it is conducted with large gangs of slaves, on a mass scale and on wide expanses of a naturally fertile soil, that requires only simple labor. Intensive cultivation, which depends less on fertility of the soil than on investment of capital, intelligence and energy of labor, is contrary to the nature of slavery. Hence the rapid transformation of states like Maryland and Virginia, which formerly employed slaves on the production of export articles, into states which raised slaves in order to export these slaves into the deep South. Even in South Carolina, where the slaves form four-sevenths of the population, the cultivation of cotton has for years been almost completely stationary in consequence of the exhaustion of the soil. Indeed, by force of circumstances South Carolina is already transformed in part into a slave-raising state, since it already sells slaves to the states of the extreme South and Southwest for four million dollars yearly. As soon as this point is reached, the acquisition of new Territories becomes necessary, in order that one section of the slaveholders may equip new, fertile landed estates with slaves and in order that by this means a new market for slave-raising, therefore for the sale of slaves, may be created for the section left behind it. It is, for example, indubitable that without the acquisition of Louisiana, Missouri and Arkansas by the United States, slavery in Virginia and Maryland would long ago have been wiped out. In the Secessionist Congress at Montgomery, Senator Toombs, one of the spokesmen of the South, has strikingly formulated the economic law that commands the constant expansion of the territory of slavery. "In fifteen years more," said he, "without a great increase in slave territory, either the slaves must be permitted to flee from the whites, or the whites must flee from the slaves."

As is known, the representation of the individual states in Congress depends, for the House of Representatives, on the number of persons constituting their respective populations. As the populations of the free states grow far more quickly than those of the slave states, the number of the Northern Representatives was bound very rapidly to overtake that of the Southern. The real seat of the political power of the South is accordingly transferred more and more to the American Senate, where every state, be its population great or small, is represented by two Senators. In order to maintain its influence in the Senate and, through the Senate, its hegemony over the United States, the South therefore required a continual formation of new slave states. This, however, was only possible through conquest of foreign lands, as in the case of Texas, or through the transformation of the Territories belonging to the United States first into slave Territories and later into slave states, as in the case of Missouri, Arkansas, etc. John Calhoun, whom the slaveholders admire as their statesman *par excellence,** stated as early as February 19, 1847, in the Senate, that the Senate alone put a balance of power into the hands of the South, that extension of the slave territory was necessary to preserve this equilibrium between South and North in the Senate, and that the attempts of the South at the creation of new slave states by force were accordingly justified.

Finally, the number of actual slaveholders in the South of the Union does not amount to more than three hundred thousand, a narrow oligarchy that is confronted with many millions of so-called poor whites, whose numbers

* Preëminent.—*Ed.*

constantly grew through concentration of landed property and whose condition is only to be compared with that of the Roman plebeians in the period of Rome's extreme decline. Only by acquisition and the prospect of acquisition of new Territories, as well as by filibustering expeditions, is it possible to square the interests of these "poor whites" with those of the slaveholders, to give their turbulent longings for deeds a harmless direction and to tame them with the prospect of one day becoming slaveholders themselves.

A strict confinement of slavery within its old terrain, therefore, was bound according to economic law to lead to its gradual effacement, in the political sphere to annihilate the hegemony that the slave states exercised through the Senate, and finally to expose the slaveholding oligarchy within its own states to threatening perils from the side of the "poor whites." With the principle that any further extension of slave Territories was to be prohibited by law, the Republicans therefore attacked the rule of the slaveholders at its root. The Republican election victory was accordingly bound to lead to the open struggle between North and South. Meanwhile, this election victory, as already mentioned, was itself conditioned by the split in the Democratic camp.

The Kansas struggle had already called forth a split between the slave party and the Democrats of the North allied to it. With the presidential election of 1860, the same strife now broke out again in a more general form. The Democrats of the North, with Douglas as their candidate, made the introduction of slavery into Territories dependent on the will of the majority of the settlers. The slaveholders' party, with Breckinridge as their candidate, maintained that the Constitution of the United States, as the Supreme Court had also declared, brought slavery legally in its train; in and by itself slavery was already legal in all Territories and required no special naturalization. Whilst, therefore, the Republicans prohibited any increase of slave Territories, the Southern party laid claim to all Territories of the republic as legally warranted domains. What they had attempted by way of example with regard to Kansas, to force slavery on a Territory through the central government against the will of the settlers themselves, they now set up as law for all the Territories of the Union. Such a concession lay beyond the power of the Democratic leaders and would merely have occasioned the desertion of their army to the Republican camp. On the other hand, Douglas' "settlers' sovereignty" could not satisfy the slaveholders' party. What it wanted to effect had to be effected within the next four years under the new President, could only be effected by means of the central government and brooked no further delay. It did not escape the slaveholders that a new power had arisen, the *Northwest,* whose population, having almost doubled between 1850 and 1860, was already pretty well equal to the white population of the slave states [58]—a power that was not inclined either by tradition, temperament or mode of life to let itself be dragged from compromise to compromise in the manner of the old Northern states. The Union was still of value to the South only so far as it handed over the Federal power to it as the means of carrying out the slave policy. If not, then it was better to make the break now than to look on at the development of the Republican Party and the upsurge of the Northwest four years longer, and begin the struggle under more unfavorable conditions. The slaveholders' party therefore played *va banque!* * When the Democrats of the North declined to go on playing the part of the "poor whites" of the South, the South procured Lincoln the

* That is, staked all on a single card.—*Ed.*

victory by splitting the vote, and then took this victory as a pretext for drawing the sword from the scabbard.

The whole movement was and is based, as one sees, on the *slave question:* Not in the sense of whether the slaves within the existing slave states should be emancipated or not, but whether the twenty million free men of the North should subordinate themselves any longer to an oligarchy of three hundred thousand slaveholders; whether the vast Territories of the republic should be planting-places for free states or for slavery; finally, whether the national policy of the Union should take armed propaganda of slavery in Mexico, Central and South America as its device. In another article we will probe the assertion of the London press that the North must sanction secession as the most favorable and only possible solution of the conflict.

Die Presse, October 25, 1861.

2.

THE CIVIL WAR IN THE UNITED STATES

*We have received from our London correspondent a fresh communication on the events in North America, in which the motives by which the secessionist South is guided are represented in an entirely new light. We will let our informant speak for himself.** *

"LET him go, he is not worth thine ire!" ** Again and again English statesmanship—recently through the mouth of Lord John Russell—cries to the North of the United States this counsel of Leporello to Don Juan's [59] deserted love. If the North lets the South go, it then

---

* Introductory note by the editor of *Die Presse.—Ed.*
** *"Lass ihn laufen, er ist Deines Zorns nicht wert!"—Ed.*

frees itself from any admixture of slavery, from its historical original sin, and creates the basis of a new and
higher development.

In reality, if North and South formed two autonomous
countries, like, perhaps, England and Hanover, their
separation would then be no more difficult than was the
separation of England and Hanover. "The South," however, is neither a territory strictly detached from the
North geographically, nor a moral unity. It is not a country at all, but a battle slogan.

The counsel of an amicable separation presupposes
that the Southern Confederacy, although it assumed the
offensive in the Civil War, at least wages it for defensive
purposes. It is believed that the issue for the slaveholders'
party is merely one of uniting the Territories it has
hitherto dominated into an autonomous group of states
and withdrawing from the supreme authority of the
Union. Nothing could be more false: *The South needs
its entire territory. It will and must have it.*" With this
battle-cry the secessionists fell upon Kentucky. By their
"entire territory" they understand in the first place all
the so-called *border states*—Delaware, Maryland, Virginia, North Carolina, Kentucky, Tennessee, Missouri
and Arkansas. Further, they lay claim to the entire territory south of the line that runs from the northwest
corner of Missouri to the Pacific Ocean. What the slaveholders, therefore, call the South, embraces more than
three-quarters of the territory hitherto comprised by the
Union. A large part of the territory thus claimed is still
in the possession of the Union and would first have to be
conquered from it. None of the so-called border states,
however, not even those in the possession of the Confederacy, were ever *actual slave states*. Rather, they con-
stitute that area of the United States in which the system
of slavery and the system of free labor exist side by side

and contend for mastery, the actual field of battle between South and North, between slavery and freedom. The war of the Southern Confederacy is, therefore, not a war of defense, but a war of conquest, a war of conquest for the extension and perpetuation of slavery.

The chain of mountains that begins in Alabama and stretches northwards to the Hudson River—the spinal column, as it were, of the United States—cuts the so-called South into three parts. The mountainous country formed by the Alleghany Mountains with their two parallel ranges, the Cumberland Range to the west and the Blue [Ridge] Mountains to the east, divides wedge-like the lowlands along the western shores of the Atlantic Ocean from the lowlands in the southern valleys of the Mississippi. The two lowlands sundered by the mountainous country, with their vast rice swamps and far-flung cotton plantations, are the actual area of slavery. The long wedge of mountainous country driven into the heart of slavery, with its correspondingly clear atmosphere, an invigorating climate and a soil rich in coal, salt, limestone, iron ore, gold, in short, every raw material necessary for a many-sided industrial development, is already for the most part a free country. In accordance with its physical constitution, the soil here can only be cultivated with success by free small farmers. Here the slave system vegetates only sporadically and never struck roots. In the largest part of the so-called border states, the dwellers on these highlands comprise the core of the free population, which in the interests of self-preservation already sides with the Northern party.

Let us consider the contested territory in detail.

Delaware, the northeasternmost of the border states, is factually and morally in the possession of the Union. All the attempts of the secessionists at forming even one faction favorable to them have from the beginning of the war suffered shipwreck on the unanimity of the population. The slave element of this state has long been in process of dying out. From 1850 to 1860 alone the number of slaves diminished by half, so that with a total population of 112,218 Delaware now numbers only 1,700 slaves.[60] Nevertheless, Delaware is demanded by the Southern Confederacy and would in fact be militarily untenable for the North as soon as the South possesses itself of Maryland.

In Maryland itself the above-mentioned conflict between highlands and lowlands takes place. With a total population of 687,034 there are here 87,188 slaves. That the overwhelming majority of the population is on the side of the Union, the recent general elections to the Congress in Washington have again strikingly proved. The army of 30,000 Union troops, which holds Maryland at the moment, is not only to serve the army on the Potomac as a reserve, but, in particular, is also to hold the rebellious slaveowners in the interior of the state in check. For here a phenomenon manifests itself similar to what we see in other border states where the great mass of the people stands for the North and a numerically insignificant slaveholders' party for the South. What it lacks in numbers, the slaveholders' party makes up in the means of power that many years' possession of all state offices, hereditary preoccupation with political intrigue and concentration of great wealth in few hands have secured to it.

Virginia now forms the great cantonment where the main army of Secession and the main army of the Union confront one another. In the northwest highlands of Virginia the mass of slaves amounts to 15,000, whilst the twenty-times-larger free population for the greater part consists of free farmers. The eastern lowlands of Virginia, on the other hand, number well nigh half a million slaves. Raising Negroes and the sale of the Negroes in the Southern states form their principal source of income. As soon as the ringleaders of the lowlands had put through the secession ordinance by intrigues in the state legislature at Richmond and had in all haste opened the gates of Virginia to the Southern army, northwest Virginia seceded from the secession, formed a new state and under the banner of the Union now defends its territory arms in hand against the Southern invaders.

Tennessee, with 1,109,847 inhabitants, of whom 275,-784 are slaves, finds itself in the hands of the Southern Confederacy, which has subjected the whole state to martial law and to a system of proscription which recalls the days of the Roman Triumvirate. When in the winter of 1861 the slaveholders proposed a general convention of the people that should give its vote on secession or nonsecession, the majority of the people refused any convention, in order to cut off any pretext for the secession movement.[61] Later, when Tennessee was already militarily overrun and subjected to a system of terror by the Southern Confederacy, more than a third of the voters at the elections still declared themselves for the Union.[62] There, as in most of the border states, the mountainous country, east Tennessee, forms the real center of resistance to the slaveholders' party. On June 17, 1861, a General Convention of the people of east Tennessee assembled in Greenville, declared itself for the Union, deputed the former governor of the state, Andrew Johnson, one of the most ardent Unionists, to the Senate in Washington and published a "declaration of grievances," which lays bare all the means of deception, intrigue and terror by which Tennessee has been "voted out" of the Union. Since then the secessionists have held east Tennessee in check by force of arms.

Similar relationships to those in West Virginia and east

Tennessee are found in the north of Alabama, in northwest Georgia and in the north of North Carolina.

Further west, in the border state of Missouri, with
1,173,317 inhabitants and 114,985 slaves—the latter
mostly concentrated in the northwestern area of the state
—the people's convention of August 1861 decided for the
Union.[63] Jackson, the governor of the state and the tool
of the slaveholders' party, rebelled against the legislature
of Missouri, was outlawed and now takes the lead of the
armed hordes that fell upon Missouri from Texas, Arkansas and Tennessee, in order to bring her to her knees
before the Confederacy and sever her bond with the
Union by the sword. Next to Virginia, Missouri is at the
present moment the main theater of the Civil War.

New Mexico—not a State, but merely a Territory, into
which twenty-five slaves were imported during Buchanan's presidency in order to send a slave constitution
after them from Washington—has not craved the South,
as even the latter concedes. But the South craves New
Mexico and accordingly spewed an armed band of adventurers from Texas over the border. New Mexico has
implored the protection of the Union government against
these liberators.

It will have been observed that we lay particular em-
phasis on the numerical proportion of slaves to free men
in the individual border states. This proportion is in fact
decisive. It is the thermometer with which the vital fire
of the slave system must be measured. The soul of the
whole secession movement is South Carolina. It has
402,541 slaves and 301,271 free men. Mississippi, which
has given the Southern Confederacy its dictator, Jefferson Davis, comes second. It has 436,696 slaves and 354,-
699 free men. Alabama comes third, with 435,132 slaves
and 529,164 free men.

The last of the contested border states, which we have

still to mention, is Kentucky. Its recent history is particularly characteristic of the policy of the Southern Confederacy. Among 1,555,713 inhabitants Kentucky has 225,490 slaves. In three successive general elections by the people—in the winter of 1861, when elections to a congress of the border states were held; in June 1861, when the elections to the Congress at Washington took place; finally, in August 1861, in the elections to the legislature of the State of Kentucky—an ever changing majority decided for the Union. On the other hand, Magoffin, the Governor of Kentucky, and all the high officials of the state are fanatical partisans of the slaveholders' party, as is Breckinridge, representative of Kentucky in the Senate at Washington, Vice-President of the United States under Buchanan, and candidate of the slaveholders' party in the presidential election of 1860. Too weak to win Kentucky for secession, the influence of the slaveholders' party was strong enough to make it amenable to a declaration of neutrality on the outbreak of war. The Confederacy recognized the neutrality as long as it served its purposes, as long as it was preoccupied with crushing the resistance in east Tennessee. Hardly was this end attained when it knocked at the gates of Kentucky with the butt end of a gun and the cry: *"The South needs its entire territory. It will and must have it!"*

From the southwest and southeast its corps of freebooters simultaneously invaded the "neutral" state. Kentucky awoke from its dream of neutrality, its legislature openly took sides with the Union, surrounded the traitorous Governor with a committee of public safety, called the people to arms, outlawed Breckinridge and ordered the secessionists to evacuate the invaded territory. This was the signal for war. An army of the Southern Confederacy is moving on Louisville, while volunteers from

Illinois, Indiana and Ohio flock hither to save Kentucky from the armed missionaries of slavery.

The attempts of the Confederacy to annex Missouri and Kentucky, for example, against the will of these states, prove the hollowness of the pretext that it is fighting for the rights of the individual states against the encroachments of the Union. On the individual states that it counts in the "South" it confers, to be sure, the right to separate from the Union, but by no means the right to remain in the Union.

Even the actual slave states, however much external war, internal military dictatorship and slavery give them everywhere the semblance of harmony, are nevertheless not without resistant elements. A striking example is Texas, with 180,388 slaves out of 601,039 inhabitants. The law of 1845, by virtue of which Texas entered the ranks of the United States as a slave state, entitled it to form not merely one, but five states out of its territory. The South would thereby have gained ten new votes, instead of two, in the American Senate, and increase in the number of its votes in the Senate was a main object of its policy at that time. From 1845 to 1860, however, the slaveholders found it impracticable to cut up Texas, where the German population plays an important part, into even two states without giving the party of free labor the upper hand over the party of slavery in the second state.[64] This furnishes the best proof of the strength of the opposition to the slaveholding oligarchy in Texas itself.

Georgia is the largest and most populous of the slave states. It has 462,230 slaves in a total of 1,057,327 inhabitants, therefore nearly half the population. Nevertheless, the slaveholders' party has not so far succeeded in getting the Constitution imposed on the South at

Montgomery sanctioned in Georgia by a general vote of the people.[65]

In the State Convention of Louisiana, meeting on March 22, 1861, at New Orleans, Roselius, the political veteran of the State, declared: "The Montgomery Constitution is not a constitution, but a conspiracy. It does not inaugurate a government of the people, but *a detestable and unrestricted oligarchy*. The people were not permitted to play any part in this matter. The Convention of Montgomery has dug the grave of political liberty, and now we are summoned to attend its funeral."

For the oligarchy of three hundred thousand slaveholders utilized the Congress of Montgomery not only to proclaim the separation of the South from the North. It exploited it at the same time to revolutionize the internal constitutions of the slave states, to completely subjugate the section of the white population that had still maintained some independence under the protection and the democratic Constitution of the Union. Between 1856 and 1860 the political spokesmen, jurists, moralists and theologians of the slaveholders' party had already sought to prove, not so much that Negro slavery is justified, but rather that color is a matter of indifference and the working class is everywhere born to slavery.

One sees, therefore, that the war of the Southern Confederacy is in the true sense of the word a war of conquest for the extension and perpetuation of slavery. The greater part of the border states and Territories are still in the possession of the Union, whose side they have taken first through the ballot-box and then with arms. The Confederacy, however, counts them for the "South" and seeks to conquer them from the Union. In the border states which the Confederacy has occupied for the time being, it holds the relatively free highlands in check by martial law. Within the actual slave states themselves it supplants the hitherto existing democracy by the unrestricted oligarchy of three hundred thousand slaveholders.

With the relinquishment of its plans of conquest the Southern Confederacy would relinquish its capacity to live and the purpose of secession. Secession, indeed, only took place because within the Union the transformation of the border states and Territories into slave states seemed no longer attainable. On the other hand, with a peaceful cession of the contested territory to the Southern Confederacy the North would surrender to the slave republic more than three-quarters of the entire territory of the United States. The North would lose the Gulf of Mexico altogether, the Atlantic Ocean from Pensacola Bay to Delaware Bay and would even cut itself off from the Pacific Ocean. Missouri, Kansas, New Mexico, Arkansas and Texas would draw California after them. Incapable of wresting the mouth of the Mississippi from the hands of the strong, hostile slave republic in the South, the great agricultural states in the basin between the Rocky Mountains and the Alleghanies, in the valleys of the Mississippi, the Missouri and the Ohio, would be compelled by their economic interests to secede from the North and enter the Southern Confederacy. These northwestern states, in their turn, would draw after them all the Northern states lying further east, with perhaps the exception of the states of New England, into the same vortex of secession.

Thus there would in fact take place, not a dissolution of the Union, but a *reorganization* of it, a *reorganization on the basis of slavery,* under the recognized control of the slaveholding oligarchy. The plan of such a reorganization has been openly proclaimed by the principal speakers of the South at the Congress of Montgomery and explains the paragraph of the new Constitution which leaves it open to every state of the old Union to join the new Confederacy. The slave system would infect the whole Union. In the Northern states, where Negro slavery is in practice unworkable, the white working class would gradually be forced down to the level of helotry. This would accord with the loudly proclaimed principle that only certain races are capable of freedom, and as the actual labor is the lot of the Negro in the South, so in the North it is the lot of the German and the Irishman, or their direct descendants.

The present struggle between the South and North is, therefore, nothing but a struggle between two social systems, between the system of slavery and the system of free labor. The struggle has broken out because the two systems can no longer live peacefully side by side on the North American continent. It can only be ended by the victory of one system or the other.

If the border states, on the disputed areas of which the two systems have hitherto contended for mastery, are a thorn in the flesh of the South, there can, on the other hand, be no mistake that, in the course of the war up to now, they have constituted the chief weakness of the North. One section of the slaveholders in these districts simulated loyalty to the North at the bidding of the conspirators in the South; another section found that in fact it was in accordance with their real interests and traditional ideas to go with the Union. Both sections have uniformly crippled the North. Anxiety to keep the "loyal" slaveholders of the border states in good humor; fear of throwing them into the arms of secession; in a word, tender regard for the interests, prejudices and sensibilities of these ambiguous allies, has smitten the Union government with incurable weakness since the beginning of the war, driven it to half measures, forced it to dissemble away the principle of the war and to spare the foe's most vulnerable spot, the root of the evil—*slavery itself.*

When, only recently, Lincoln pusillanimously revoked Frémont's Missouri proclamation on the emancipation of Negroes belonging to the rebels,[66] this occurred merely out of regard for the loud protest of the "loyal" slaveholders of Kentucky. However, a turning point has already been reached. With Kentucky, the last border state has been pushed into the series of battlefields between South and North. With real war for the border states in the border states themselves, the question of winning or losing them is withdrawn from the sphere of diplomatic and parliamentary discussions. One section of slaveholders will throw away the mask of loyalty; the other will content itself with the prospect of compensation such as Great Britain gave the West Indian planters.[67] Events themselves drive to the promulgation of the decisive slogan—*emancipation of the slaves.*

That even the most hardened Democrats and diplomats of the North feel themselves drawn to this point, is shown by some publications of very recent date. In an open letter, General Cass, Secretary of State under Buchanan and hitherto one of the most ardent allies of the South, declares emancipation of the slaves the *conditio sine qua non* * of the Union's salvation. In his last review for October, Dr. Brownson, the spokesman of the Catholic party of the North, on his own admission the most energetic adversary of the emancipation movement from 1836 to 1860, publishes an article *for* Abolition.

"If we have opposed Abolition heretofore," he says among other things, "because we would preserve the Union, we must *a fortiori* now oppose slavery whenever, in our judgment, its continuance becomes incompatible with the maintenance of the Union, or of the nation as a

* Indispensable condition.—*Ed.*

free republican state." [68] Finally, the *World*, a New York organ of the diplomats of the Washington Cabinet, concludes one of its latest blustering articles against the Abolitionists with the words:

"On the day when it shall be decided that either slavery or the Union must go down, on that day sentence of death is passed on slavery. If the North cannot triumph *without* emancipation, it will triumph *with* emancipation."

Die Presse, November 7, 1861.

3.

THE CRISIS IN ENGLAND

TODAY, as fifteen years ago, England stands face to face with a catastrophe that threatens to strike at the root of her entire economic system. As is known, the potato formed the exclusive food of Ireland and a not inconsiderable section of the English working people when the potato blight of 1845 and 1846 struck the root of Irish life with decay. The results of this great catastrophe are known. The Irish population declined by two million, of which one part died of starvation and the other fled across the Atlantic Ocean. At the same time, this dreadful misfortune helped the English free trade party to triumph; the English landed aristocracy was compelled to sacrifice one of its most lucrative monopolies, and the abolition of the Corn Laws assured a broader and sounder basis for the reproduction and maintenance of the working millions.

What the *potato* was to Irish agriculture, *cotton* is to the dominant branch of Great Britain's industry. On its manufacture depends the subsistence of a mass of people greater than the total number of inhabitants of Scotland

and than two-thirds of the present number of inhabitants of Ireland. For according to the census of 1861, the population of Scotland consisted of 3,061,117 persons, that of Ireland still only 5,764,543, whilst more than four millions in England and Scotland live directly or indirectly by the cotton industry. Now the cotton plant is not, indeed, diseased. Just as little is its production the monopoly of a few regions of the earth. On the contrary, no other plant that yields clothing material thrives in equally extensive areas of America, Asia and Africa. The cotton monopoly of the slave states of the American Union is not a natural, but an historical monopoly. It grew and developed simultaneously with the monopoly of the English cotton industry on the world market. In the year 1793, shortly after the time of the great mechanical inventions in England, a Quaker of Connecticut, Eli Whitney, invented the cotton gin, a machine for cleaning cotton, which separates the cotton fiber from the cotton seed. Prior to this invention, a day of a Negro's most intensive labor barely sufficed to separate a pound of cotton fiber from the cotton seed. After the invention of the cotton gin, an old Negro could comfortably supply fifty pounds of cotton daily, and gradual improvements have subsequently doubled the efficiency of the machine. The fetters on the cultivation of cotton in the United States were now burst asunder. Hand in hand with the English cotton industry, it grew swiftly to a great commercial power. Now and then in the course of development, England seemed to take fright at the monopoly of American cotton, as at a specter that threatened danger. Such a moment occurred, for example, at the time when the emancipation of the Negroes in the English colonies was purchased for £20,000,000. It was a matter for misgiving that the industry in Lancashire and Yorkshire should rest on the sovereignty of the slave-whip in Georgia and Alabama, whilst the English nation imposed on itself so great a sacrifice to abolish slavery in its own colonies. Philanthropy, however, does not make history, least of all commercial history. Similar doubts arose as often as a cotton crop failure occurred in the United States and as, in addition, such a natural phenomenon was exploited by the slaveholders to artificially raise the price of cotton still higher through combination. The English cotton spinners and weavers then threatened rebellion against "King Cotton." Manifold projects for procuring cotton from Asiatic and African sources came to light. This was the case, for example, in 1850. However, the following good crop in the United States triumphantly dispelled such yearnings for emancipation. Indeed, in the last few years the American cotton monopoly attained dimensions scarcely dreamt of before, partly in consequence of the free trade legislation, which repealed the hitherto existing differential tariff on the cotton grown by slaves; partly in consequence of the simultaneous giant strides made by the English cotton industry and American cotton cultivation during the last decade. In the year 1857 the consumption of cotton in England already amounted to nearly one and a half billion pounds.

Now, all of a sudden, the American Civil War menaces this great pillar of English industry. Whilst the Union blockades the harbors of the Southern states, in order to cut off the secessionists' chief source of income by preventing the export of their cotton crop of this year, the Confederacy first lends compelling force to this blockade with the decision not to export a bale of cotton of its own accord, but rather to compel England to come and fetch her cotton from the Southern harbors herself. England is to be driven to the point of forcibly breaking through the blockade, of then declaring war on the Union and so of throwing her sword into the scale of the slave states.

From the beginning of the American Civil War the price of cotton rose continuously; for a considerable time, however, to a less degree than was to be expected. On the whole, the English commercial world appeared to look down very phlegmatically on the American crisis. The cause of this cold-blooded way of viewing things was unmistakable. The whole of the last American crop was long ago in Europe. The yield of a new crop is never shipped before the end of November, and this shipment seldom attains considerable dimensions before the end of December. Till then, therefore, it remained pretty much a matter of indifference whether the cotton bales were held back on the plantations or forwarded to the harbors of the South immediately after their packing. Should the blockade cease at any time before the end of the year, England could safely count on receiving her customary cotton imports in April or March, quite as if the blockade had never taken place. The English commercial world, in large measure misled by the English press, succumbed, however, to the delusion that a spectacle of, perchance, six months' war would end with recognition of the Confederacy by the United States. But at the end of August, North Americans appeared in the market of Liverpool to buy cotton, partly for speculation in Europe, partly for reshipment to North America. This unheard-of event opened the eyes of the English. They began to understand the seriousness of the situation. The Liverpool cotton market has since been in a state of feverish excitement; the prices of cotton were soon driven 100 per cent above their average level; the speculation in cotton assumed the same wild features that characterized the speculation in railways in 1845. The spinning and weaving mills in Lancashire and other seats of the

British cotton industry limited their labor time to three days a week; a section of the mills stopped its machines altogether; the irremediable reaction on other branches of industry was not wanting, and at this moment all England trembles at the approach of the greatest economic catastrophe that has yet threatened her.

The consumption of Indian cotton is naturally increasing, and the rising prices will ensure further increase of importation from the ancient home of cotton. Nevertheless, it remains impossible to revolutionize the conditions of production and the course of trade at, so to speak, a few months' notice. England is, in fact, now expiating her long mismanagement of India. Her present spasmodic attempts to replace American cotton by Indian encounter two great obstacles. The lack of means of communication and transport in India, and the miserable condition of the Indian peasant, which prevents him from taking advantage of the momentarily favorable circumstances. But, apart from this, apart from the process of improvement that Indian cotton has still to go through to be able to take the place of American, even under the most favorable circumstances it will be *years* before India can produce for export the requisite quantity of cotton. It is statistically established, however, that in four months the stocks of cotton in Liverpool will be exhausted. They will hold out even as long as this only if the limitation of the labor time to three days a week and the complete stoppage of a part of the machinery is effected by the British cotton spinners and weavers to a still greater extent than hitherto. Such a procedure is already exposing the factory districts to the greatest social sufferings. But if the American blockade continues over January! What then?

Die Presse, November 6, 1861.

4.

ECONOMIC NOTES

London, November 3, 1861.

AT THE present moment general politics are non-existent in England. The interest of the country is absorbed in the French financial, commercial and agricultural crisis, the British industrial crisis, the dearth of cotton and the American question.

In circles here competent to judge, people are not for a moment deceived concerning the Bank of France's bill-jobbing with a few big houses on both sides of the Channel being a palliative of the weakest sort. All that could be achieved and has been achieved thereby was a *momentary* abatement of the drain of money to England. The repeated attempts of the Bank of France to raise metallic auxiliary troops in Petersburg, Hamburg and Berlin damage its credit, without filling its coffers. The raising of the rate of interest on treasury bills, in order to keep them in currency, and the necessity of effecting a remission of the payments for the new Italian loan of Victor Emmanuel—both are held here to be serious symptoms of French financial sickness. It is known, moreover, that at the present moment two projects contend in the Tuileries for precedence. The full-blooded Bonapartists, with Persigny and Péreire (of the Crédit Mobilier [69]), at their head, want to make the Bank of France completely subject to governmental authority, to reduce it to a mere office of the Finance Ministry, and to use the institution, thus transformed, as an assignat factory.

It is known that this principle was originally at the bottom of the organization of the Crédit Mobilier. The less adventurous party, represented by Fould and other

renegades of Louis Philippe's time, propose a new national
loan, which is to amount to four hundred million francs,
according to some; to seven hundred million, according to
others. *The Times,* in a leading article today, probably
reflects the view of the City * when it states that France
is completely paralyzed by her economic crisis and robbed
of her European influence. Nevertheless, *The Times* and
the City are wrong. Should the December power succeed in outlasting the winter without great internal
storms, it will then blow the war trumpet in the spring.
The internal distress will not thereby be remedied, but
its voice will be drowned.

In an earlier letter I pointed out that the cotton swindle
in Liverpool during the last few weeks fully reminds one
of the maddest days of the railway mania of 1845.
Dentists, surgeons, barristers, cooks, widows, workers,
clerks and lords, comedians and clergymen, soldiers and
tailors, journalists and persons letting apartments, man
and wife, all speculated in cotton. Quite small quantities
of from one to four bales were bought, sold and sold
again. More considerable quantities lay for months in
the same warehouse, although they changed owners
twenty times. Whoever had bought cotton at ten o'clock,
sold it again at eleven o'clock with an addition of a half-
penny a pound. Thus the same cotton often circulated
from hand to hand six times in ten hours. This week, however, there came a lull, and for no more rational reason
than that a pound of cotton (namely, middling Orleans
cotton) had risen to a shilling, that twelve pence make
a shilling and are therefore a round figure. So every one
had purposed selling out, as soon as the maximum was
reached. Hence sudden increase of the supply, and consequent reaction. As soon as the English make themselves
conversant with the possibility that a pound of cotton

* The financial community in London.—*Ed.*

can rise *above* a shilling, the St. Vitus' dance will return more madly than ever.

The last official monthly report of the Board of Trade on British exports and imports has by no means dispelled the gloomy feeling. The export tables cover the nine months' period from January to September 1861. In comparison with the same period of 1860, they show a falling off of about £8,000,000. Of this, £5,671,730 fall to exports to the United States alone, whilst the remainder is distributed over British North America, the East Indies, Australia, Turkey and Germany. Only in Italy is an increase shown. Thus, for example, the export of British cotton commodities to Sardinia, Tuscany, Naples and Sicily has risen from £656,802 for the year 1860 to £1,204,286 for the year 1861; the export of British cotton yarn from £348,158 to £583,373; the export of iron from £120,867 to £160,912, etc. These figures are not without weight in the scale of British sympathy for Italian freedom.

Whilst the export trade of Great Britain has thus declined by nearly £8,000,000 her *import trade* has risen in still higher proportion, a circumstance that by no means [facilitates] * the adjustment of the balance, [whereas for] * the first eight months of 1860 the value of the wheat imported amounted to only £6,796,139, for the same period of the present year it totals £13,431,387.

The most remarkable phenomenon revealed by the import tables is the rapid increase of *French imports* which have now attained a volume of nearly £18,000,000 (yearly), whilst English exports to France are not much more considerable than, perhaps, those to Holland. Continental politicians have hitherto overlooked this entirely new phenomenon of modern commercial history. It proves

---

* Some words are missing from the original, and the words in square brackets have been inserted to complete the meaning.—*Ed.*

that the economic dependence of France on England is, perhaps, six times as great as the economic dependence of England on France, if, that is, one not only considers the English export and import tables, but also compares them with the French export and import tables. It then follows that England has now become the principal export market for France, whereas France has remained a quite secondary export market for England. Hence, despite all chauvinism and all Waterloo rodomontade,* the nervous dread of the conflict with "perfidious Albion."

Finally, one more important fact emerges from the latest English export and import tables. Whilst in the first nine months of this year English exports to the United States declined by more than 25 per cent in comparison with the same period of 1860, the port of New York alone has increased its exports to England by £6,000,000 during the first eight months of the present year. During this period the export of American gold to England had almost ceased, while now, on the contrary, gold has been flowing for weeks from England to New York. It is in fact England and France whose harvest deficiencies cover the American deficit, while the Morrill tariff and the economy inseparable from a civil war have simultaneously decimated the consumption of English and French manufactures in North America. And now one may compare these statistical facts with the jeremiads of *The Times* on the financial ruin of North America!

Die Presse, November 8, 1861.

* Vainglorious bluster; from Rodomonte, a boastful leader in Ariosto's *Orlando Furioso.—Ed.*

5.

INTERVENTION IN MEXICO

London, November 7, 1861.

The Times of today has a leading article in its well-known, confusedly kaleidoscopic, affectedly humorous style, on the French government's invasion of Dappenthal and on Switzerland's protest against this violation of territory. The oracle of Printing House Square recalls how, at the time of most acute struggle between English manufacturers and landowners, little children employed in the factories were led to throw needles into the most delicate parts of the machinery to upset the motion of the whole powerful automaton. The machinery is Europe, the little child is Switzerland and the needle that she throws into the smoothly running automaton is—Louis Bonaparte's invasion of her territory or, rather, her outcry at his invasion. Thus the needle is suddenly transformed into the outcry at the needle's prick and the metaphor into a piece of buffoonery at the expense of the reader who expects a metaphor. *The Times* is further enlivened by its own discovery that Dappenthal consists of a single village called Cressionières. It ends its short article with a complete contradiction of its beginning. Why, it exclaims, make so much ado about this infinitely small Swiss bagatelle, when every quarter of Europe will be ablaze next spring? One may not forget that, shortly before, Europe was a well regulated automaton. The whole article appears sheer nonsense and yet it has its sense. It is a declaration that Palmerston has given *carte blanche* in the Swiss incident to his ally on the other side of the Channel. The explanation of this declaration is found in the dry notice in the *Moniteur* that on October 31 England, France and Spain concluded a convention on joint *intervention in Mexico.*[70] The article of *The Times* on Dappenthal and the notice of the *Moniteur* on Mexico stand as close together as the Canton of Waadt * and Vera Cruz lie far apart.

It is credible that Louis Bonaparte counted on intervention in Mexico among the many possibilities which he continually has ready to divert the French people. It is sure that Spain, whose cheap successes in Morocco and St. Domingo have gone to her head, dreams of a Restoration in Mexico. But it is certain that France's project had not yet matured and that both France and Spain were opposed to a crusade against Mexico under *English* command.

On September 24, Palmerston's private *Moniteur,* the *Morning Post,* announced the details of an agreement that England, France and Spain had reached for joint intervention in Mexico. The following day the *Patrie* denied the existence of any such agreement. On September 27 *The Times* refuted the *Patrie,* without naming it. According to *The Times'* article, Lord Russell had *communicated* the English decision on intervention to the French government, whereupon M. Thouvenel had answered that the Emperor of the French had arrived at a like determination. It was now the turn of Spain. In a semi-official organ the Spanish government declared that it purposed an intervention in Mexico, but by no means an intervention alongside of England. It rained *dementis. The Times* had categorically announced that "the full assent of the American President had been given to the expedition." Hardly had the report reached the other side of the Atlantic Ocean when all the organs of the American government branded it as a lie, since [the American Union,] conjointly with President Lincoln, was going with and not against Mexico. From all

* In west central Switzerland.—*Ed.*

this it follows that the plan of intervention in its present form originated in the Cabinet of St. James.

No less puzzling and contradictory than the statements concerning the origin of the convention were the statements concerning its objects. One organ of Palmerston, the *Morning Post,* announced that Mexico was not an organized state, with an existing government, but a mere robbers' nest. It was to be treated as such. The expedition had only one object—the satisfaction of the Mexican state's creditors in England, France and Spain.[71] To this end the combined forces would occupy the principal ports of Mexico, collect the import and export duties on her coast and hold this "material guarantee" till all debt claims were satisfied.

The other organ of Palmerston, *The Times,* declared, on the contrary, that England was "steeled against plunderings on the part of bankrupt Mexico." It was not a question of the private interests of the creditors, but "they hope that the mere presence of a combined squadron in the Gulf, and the seizure of certain ports, will urge the Mexican government to new exertions in keeping the peace, and will convince the malcontents that they must confine themselves to some form of opposition more constitutional than brigandage."

According to this, the expedition would therefore take place to investigate the official government of Mexico. At the same time, however, *The Times* intimates that "the City of Mexico was sufficiently healthy, should it be necessary to penetrate so far."

The most original means of strengthening a government indisputably consist in the sequestration of its revenues and its territories by force. On the other hand, mere occupation of the ports and collection of the duties in these ports can only cause the Mexican government to set more inland-lying bounds to its domains. Import duties on foreign commodities, export duties on American commodities would in this way be doubled; the intervention would in fact satisfy the claims of European creditors by extortions from European-Mexican trade. The Mexican government can become solvent only by internal consolidation, but it can consolidate itself at home only so long as its independence is respected abroad.

If the expedition's alleged ends are contradictory, then the alleged means to these alleged ends are still more contradictory. The English government organs themselves admit that if one thing or another would be attainable by a one-sided intervention of France or England or Spain, everything becomes unattainable by a *joint* intervention of these states.

One may recall that the Liberal Party in Mexico under Juarez, the official President of the republic, has now the upper hand at almost all points; that the Catholic Party under General Márquez has suffered defeat after defeat, and that the robber band organized by it is driven back to the sierras of Queretaro and dependent on an alliance with Mejía, the Indian chief there. The last hope of the Catholic Party was Spanish intervention.

The only point—says *The Times*—on which there may possibly be a difference between ourselves and our allies, regards the *government of the republic*. England will be content to see it remain in the hands of the Liberal Party which is now in power, while France and Spain are suspected of a partiality for the ecclesiastical rule which has recently been overthrown. It would, indeed, be strange, if France were, in both the old and the new world, to make herself the protector of priests and bandits. Just as in Italy the partisans of Francis II [72] at Rome were equipped for their work of making Naples ungovernable, so in Mexico the highways, indeed, the streets of the capital, are infested with robbers, whom the church party openly declares to be its friends.

And just for this reason England strengthens the Liberal governments by undertaking a campaign against them with France and Spain; she seeks to suppress anarchy by supplying the clerical party lying *in extremis* * with fresh allied troops from Europe!

Save during the short winter months the coasts of Mexico, pestilential as they are, can only be held by conquest of the country itself. But a third English government organ, *The Economist,* declares the conquest of Mexico to be impossible.

If it is desired—says this paper—to thrust upon her a British prince with an English army, then the fiercest wrath of the United States is excited. France's jealousy would make such a conquest impossible, and a motion to this effect would be rejected almost unanimously by an English parliament the moment it was submitted to it. England, for her part, cannot entrust the government of Mexico to France. Of Spain there can be no question whatever.

The whole expedition is therefore a mystification, the key to which the *Patrie* gives in these words: "The convention recognizes the necessity of installing in Mexico a strong government, that can maintain tranquillity and order there."

The question is simply one of applying to the states of America through a new Holy Alliance the principle according to which the Holy Alliance held itself called on to interfere in the internal governmental relations of the countries of Europe. The first plan of this sort was drafted by Chateaubriand for the Bourbons of Spain and France at the time of the Restoration. It was frustrated by Canning and Monroe, the President of the United States, who declared any European interference in the internal affairs of American states to be taboo. Since then the American Union has constantly asserted the Monroe

* At the last gasp.—*Ed.*

Doctrine as an international law. The present Civil War, however, created the right situation for securing to the side of the European monarchies an intervention precedent on which they can build later. That is the real object of the English-French-Spanish intervention. Its immediate result can only be and is only intended to be the *restoration* of the anarchy just dying out in Mexico.

Apart from all standpoints of international law in general, the occurrence has the great significance for Europe that by concessions in the domain of Continental politics England has purchased the support of Louis Bonaparte in the Mexican expedition.

Die Presse, November 12, 1861.

6.

THE DISMISSAL OF FRÉMONT

FRÉMONT's dismissal from the post of Commander-in-Chief in Missouri [73] forms a turning point in the history of the development of the American Civil War. Frémont has two great sins to expiate. He was the first candidate of the Republican Party for the presidential office (1856) and he is the first general of the North to have threatened the slaveholders with emancipation of slaves (August 30, 1861). He remains, therefore, a rival of candidates for the presidency in the future and an obstacle to the makers of compromises in the present.

During the last two decades there had developed in the United States the singular practice of not electing to the presidency any man who occupied an authoritative position in his own party. The names of such men, it is true, were utilized for election demonstrations; as soon, however, as it came to actual business, they were dropped and replaced by unknown mediocrities of merely local influence. In this manner Polk, Pierce, Buchanan, etc., became Presidents. Likewise A. Lincoln. General Andrew Jackson was in fact the last President of the United States who owed his office to his personal importance, whilst all his successors owed it, on the contrary, to their personal unimportance.

In the election year, 1860, the most distinguished names of the Republican Party were Frémont and Seward. Known for his adventures during the Mexican War, for his intrepid exploration of California and his candidacy of 1856, Frémont was too striking a figure even to come under consideration, as soon as it was no longer a question of a Republican demonstration, but of a Republican success. He did not, therefore, offer himself as a candidate. It was otherwise with Seward, Republican Senator in the Congress at Washington, Governor of the State of New York and, since the rise of the Republican Party, unquestionably its leading orator. It required a series of mortifying defeats to induce Mr. Seward to renounce his own candidacy and to give his oratorical patronage to the then more or less unknown A. Lincoln. As soon, however, as he saw his attempted candidacy shipwrecked, he imposed himself as a Republican Richelieu on a man whom he took for a Republican Louis XIII. He contributed towards making Lincoln President, on condition that Lincoln make him Secretary of State, a station which is in some measure comparable with that of an English Prime Minister. As a matter of fact, Lincoln was hardly President-elect, when Seward had secured the Secretaryship of State. Straightway a singular change took place in the attitude of the Demosthenes * of the Republican Party, whom the prophesying

* An Athenian orator, born in 384 (or 383) B.C.—*Ed.*

of the "irrepressible conflict" * between the system of free labor and the system of slavery had made famous. Although elected on November 6, 1860, Lincoln had entered into office as President only on March 4, 1861. In the interval, during the winter session of Congress, Seward made himself the focus of all attempts at compromise; the Northern organs of the South, such as the *New York Herald*, for example, whose *bête noire* ** Seward had been till then, suddenly extolled him as the statesman of reconciliation and, in fact, it was not his fault that peace at any price did not come to pass. Seward manifestly regarded the Secretaryship of State as a mere preliminary step, and was less preoccupied with the "irrepressible conflict" of the present than with the presidency of the future. He has provided fresh proof that virtuosos of the lungs are dangerously inadequate statesmen. Read his state dispatches! What a repulsive mixture of greatness of phrase and smallness of mind, of mimicry of strength and acts of weakness!

For Seward, therefore, Frémont was the dangerous rival whom it was necessary to ruin; an undertaking that appeared so much the easier since Lincoln, in accordance with his legal tradition, has an aversion for all genius, anxiously clings to the letter of the Constitution and fights shy of every step that could mislead the "loyal" slaveholders of the border states. Frémont's character offered another hold. He is manifestly a man of pathos, somewhat high-stepping and haughty, and not devoid of all melodramatic flights. First the government attempted to drive him to voluntary retirement by a succession of petty chicaneries. When this did not succeed, it deprived him of his command at the very moment

* Made in a speech delivered by Seward on October 25, 1858, at Rochester. See W. H. Seward, *Works,* ed. G. E. Baker (Boston, 1884), vol. iv, pp. 289-302.—*Ed.*
** Bugbear.—*Ed.*

when the army organized by himself came face to face with the foe in southwest Missouri and a decisive battle was imminent.

Frémont is the idol of the states in the Northwest, which sing his praises as the "pathfinder." They regard his dismissal as a personal insult. Should the Union government meet with a few more mishaps like those of Bull Run and Ball's Bluff,[74] it has itself given the opposition, which will then rise up against it and smash the hitherto prevailing diplomatic system of waging war, its leader in John Frémont. To the indictment against the dismissed general which the War Board at Washington has published, we shall return later.

Die Presse, November 26, 1861.

7.

THE *TRENT* CASE

London, November 28, 1861.

THE CONFLICT of the English mail steamer *Trent* with the North American warship *San Jacinto* in the narrow passage of the Old Bahama Channel is the lion among the events of the day.[75] On the afternoon of November 8 the mail steamer *La Plata* brought information concerning the incident to Southampton, where the electric telegraph at once flashed it to all parts of Great Britain. The same evening the London Stock Exchange was the stage for stormy scenes similar to those at the time of the proclamation of the Italian war. Quotations for government stock sank three-quarters to one per cent. The wildest rumors ran through London. The American Ambassador, Adams, had received his passport, an embargo was imposed on all American ships in the Thames, etc. At the same time an indignation meeting of merchants was held at the Stock Exchange in Liverpool, to demand measures from the English government for the satisfaction of the violated honor of the British flag. Every normal Englishman went to bed with the conviction that he would go to sleep in a state of peace but wake up in a state of war.

Nevertheless, the fact is well-nigh categorically established that the conflict between the *Trent* and the *San Jacinto* brings no war in its train. The semi-official press, like *The Times* and the *Morning Post,* strikes a peaceful note and pours juridically cool deductions on the flickerings of passion. Papers like the *Daily Telegraph,* that at the faintest *mot d'ordre* * roar for the British lion, are true models of moderation. Only the Tory opposition press, *The Morning Herald* and *The Standard,* hits out. These facts force every expert to the conclusion that the ministry has already decided not to make a *casus belli* out of the "untoward event."

It must be added that the event, if not the details of its enactment, was anticipated. On October 18, Messrs. Slidell, Ambassador of the Confederacy to France, and Mason, Ambassador of the Confederacy to England, together with their secretaries Eustis and McFarland, had run the blockade from Charleston on the steamship *Theodora* and sailed for Havana, there to seek the opportunity of a passage to Europe under the English flag. In England their arrival was expected daily. North American warships had set out from Liverpool to intercept the gentlemen, with their dispatches, on this side of the Atlantic Ocean. The English ministry had already submitted the question, whether the North Americans were entitled to take such a step, to its official law counsel for their opinion. The answer of these counsel is said to have been in the affirmative.

* Word of command.—*Ed.*

The juridical question turns in a narrow circle. Since the foundation of the United States, North America has adopted English maritime law in all its rigor. A leading principle of this maritime law is that all *neutral merchantmen* are subject to *search* by the belligerent parties. "This right," said Lord Stowell in a judgment which has become famous, "offers the sole security that no contraband is carried on the neutral ships." The greatest American authority, Kent, states in the same sense: "The duty of self-preservation gives to belligerent nations this right. ... The doctrine of the *English* admiralty on the right of visitation and search ... has been recognized in its fullest extent by the courts of justice in this country." *

It was not opposition to the right of search, as is sometimes erroneously submitted, that brought about the Anglo-American War of 1812 to 1814. Rather, America declared war because England unlawfully arrogated to herself even the search of American warships, on the pretext of catching deserting English sailors.

The *San Jacinto,* therefore, had the right to search the *Trent* and to confiscate any contraband stowed aboard this ship. That *dispatches* in the possession of Mason, Slidell and Co. come under the category of contraband. even *The Times, Morning Post,* etc., admit. There remains the question whether Messrs. Mason, Slidell and Co. were themselves contraband and might consequently be confiscated! The point is a ticklish one and differences of opinion prevail among the doctors of law. Pratt, the most distinguished English authority on "Contraband," in his chapter on "Quasi-Contraband—Dispatches, Passengers" specifically refers to "communication of information and orders from the belligerent government to its

---

* J. Kent, *Commentaries on American Law* (New York, 1826), vol. 1, pp. 142, 144 (Part I).—*Ed.*

officers abroad, or the conveyance of military passengers." *
Messrs. Mason and Slidell, if not officers, were just as
little ambassadors, since their governments are recognized
neither by England nor by France. What are they, then?
In justification of the very wide conceptions of contraband asserted by England in the Anglo-French wars, Jefferson remarks in his memoirs that contraband, in the
nature of the case, excludes any conclusive definition and
necessarily leaves great scope for arbitrariness. In any
event, however, one sees that from the standpoint of
English law the legal question dwindles to a Duns Scotus
controversy,** the force of whose arguments will not go
beyond exchange of diplomatic notes.

The political side of the North American procedure was
estimated quite correctly by *The Times* in these words:
"Even Mr. Seward himself must know that the voices
of the Southern commissioners, sounding from their captivity, are a thousand times more eloquent in London
and in Paris than they would have been if they had been
heard in St. James and the Tuileries." *** And is not the
Confederacy already represented in London by Messrs.
Yancey and Mann?

We regard this latest operation of Mr. Seward as one
of the characteristic tactlessnesses of self-conscious weakness that simulates strength. If the naval exploit hastens
Seward's removal from the Washington Cabinet, the
United States will have no reason to record it as an "untoward event" in the annals of its Civil War.

The *English Correspondence* of November 28 writes
concerning the impressions produced by the news of the
incident aboard the *Trent*, as follows:

* F. T. Pratt, *Law of Contraband of War* (London, 1856), pp. liv-
lv.—*Ed.*
** Any controversy revolving about a cunningly devised or hair-split-
ting argument; derived from the name of John Duns Scotus (1265?-
1308), a scholastic philosopher described as "the Subtle Doctor."—*Ed.*
*** *The Times,* November 28, 1861.—*Ed.*

The excitement over this incident that has reigned in London and throughout the country since yesterday is extraordinary. Three hours after the arrival of the telegraphic message referred to, the merchants in Liverpool held a so-called indignation meeting. A Mr. Spence presided and a resolution was moved: "That this meeting, having learnt with indignation that a warship of the American Union has forcibly taken from a British mail steamer certain passengers who were peacefully proceeding from one neutral harbor to another under the protection of our flag, urgently calls on the government to preserve the dignity of the British flag by demanding prompt satisfaction for this affront."

Some very vehement, impassioned speeches and then, again, some conciliatory ones, were delivered. Finally, however, the resolution was carried, but with the amendment that the last words, beginning with "by," be omitted. Many of the older and more cautious merchants disapproved of the calling of the meeting and admonished it not to increase the irritation precipitately.

That there is no lack of hotheads who assert that there is here a clear *casus belli* in the event of the country's not obtaining complete satisfaction, need scarcely be mentioned: nevertheless, the more moderate will hold the field and people will await the decision of the Crown lawyers and the government with composure.

On the Stock Exchange, consols had rapidly fallen one per cent with the arrival of the news from Southampton; at closing, however, they had somewhat recovered again. In the City, as on all sides, firm confidence is placed in the self-possession and energy of Lord Palmerston. There is no lack of rumors of the worst sort, in particular that the American government had foreseen a quarrel with England; that in anticipation of this it had already bought up the entire saltpeter supply (60,000 cwt.) during the past week, and that Lord Palmerston, because he had exact knowledge of the American Cabinet's intentions, had dispatched troops to Canada and warships to the American stations in good time. Contrariwise, it is maintained by the other side that the American warship had acted quite legally and that there was no cause for complaint.

On this and other questions today's papers express themselves at sufficient length in their leading articles. Here might further be mentioned only that Earl Russell, after interrogation of the Crown lawyers through his Under-Secretary of State, Layard, has stated that he cannot give his consent to the desired search of the Confederate ship *Nashville* lying at Southampton.[76] This decision of his had reached Southampton before the new matter of the *Trent* was known there.

Die Presse, December 2, 1861.

8.

THE ANGLO-AMERICAN CONFLICT

If further proof were required that no one would be more delighted by the degeneration of the Trent *incident into a doughty Anglo-American naval war than the Paris Cabinet, then the attitude of the official and semi-official Paris press provides this proof. Hardly has the* Patrie *triumphantly recounted to its readers that the population of the Northern states is demonstrating for energetic resistance to any English demand for satisfaction, than it is already able to report from London no less warlike things. Thus it announces that at a Cabinet Council held in London on November 30 it has been decided, in the event of an unfavorable reception of the note to be handed by Lord Lyons to the Washington Cabinet, to recognize the Southern states and accredit a* chargé d'affaires *to President Jefferson Davis. Not only does the* Patrie *do its best to incite and add fuel to the fire; the* Moniteur *works in the same direction. The* Moniteur *has the following written to it from Southampton: "In Southampton the opinion is held that this incident can bring the most serious consequences in its train; moreover, this is the general opinion. Since the Southern states have gained much sympathy for themselves in England, this occurrence cannot fail further to increase the number of their supporters."*

Concerning the way in which the French government proposes to exploit a possible war between England and the American Union all positive clews are lacking up to now. But the ill-tidings broadcast from Paris prove this much: that such a war would be very suitable for the Tuileries policy, so that the latter positively desires such a misfortune. This attitude of France is a pointer for the Cabinet of St. James, and it is hardly to be supposed that it has no eye thereto. The fact also deserves to be stressed that, with the exception of the Morning Post, the attitude of the London press, and particularly The Times, is a very moderate and cautious one. From our London correspondent, who is so well-posted in Anglo-American relations, we have received a letter, dated November 29, which makes the Trent case appear in many respects much less dangerous to Western peace than, by the first dispatches from London and by the utterances of the Morning Post and the semi-official Paris papers, one was bound to suppose. The communication of our London correspondent elucidates, in the first place, the verdict of the Crown lawyers, denies that the San Jacinto forcibly apprehended Messrs. Mason, Slidell and Co. in any way on instructions from the Washington Cabinet and reduces the much discussed Liverpool indignation meeting to its true significance. We let our correspondent speak for himself. He writes: *

London, November 29.

THE counsel of the Crown had yesterday to give their opinion on the naval exploit in the Bahama Channel. Their records of the case consisted of the written reports of the English officers left behind on board the *Trent* and of the oral testimony of Commodore Williams, who was on board the *Trent* as Admiralty agent, but on November 27 disembarked from the *La Plata* at South-

* These introductory remarks are by the Editor of *Die Presse.*—*Ed.*

ampton, whence the telegraph called him at once to London. The Crown counsel acknowledged the right of the *San Jacinto* to visit and search the *Trent*. Since Queen Victoria's proclamation of neutrality on the outbreak of the American Civil War expressly counts dispatches among articles of contraband, there could be no doubt on this point either. There remained, then, the question whether Messrs. Mason, Slidell and Co. were themselves contraband and therefore confiscable. The Crown counsel appear to hold this view, for they dropped the *material* question of law entirely. According to the report of *The Times*, their opinion blames the commander of the *San Jacinto* only in respect of an *error in procedure*. Instead of Messrs. Mason, Slidell and Co., he should have taken the *Trent* herself in tow as a prize, brought her to the nearest American port and there surrendered her to the judgment of a North American prize court.[77] This is incontestably the procedure corresponding to English and therefore to North American maritime law.

It is equally incontestable that the English frequently violated this rule during the anti-Jacobin war and proceeded in the summary fashion of the *San Jacinto*. However that may be, the whole conflict is reduced by this opinion of the Crown counsel to a *technical error* and consequently robbed of any immediate import. Two circumstances make it easy for the Union government to accept this point of view and therefore to afford formal satisfaction. In the first place, Captain Wilkes, the commander of the *San Jacinto*, could have received no direct instructions from Washington. On the voyage home from Africa to New York, he touched on November 2 at Havana, which he left again on November 4, whilst his encounter with the *Trent* on the high seas took place on November 8. Captain Wilkes' stay of only two days in Havana did not permit any exchange of notes between him and his government. The consul of the Union was the sole American authority with whom he could deal. In the second place, however, he had obviously lost his head, as his failure to insist on the surrender of the dispatches proves.

The importance of the incident lies in its moral effect on the English people and in the political capital that can easily be made out of it by the English cotton friends of secession. Characteristic of the latter is the Liverpool indignation meeting organized by them and previously mentioned by me. The meeting took place on November 27 at three in the afternoon, in the cotton auction-rooms of the Liverpool Exchange, an hour after the alarming telegram from Southampton had arrived.

After vain attempts to press the chairmanship on Mr. Cunard, the owner of the Cunard steamships running between Liverpool and New York, and other high dignitaries of trade, a young merchant named Spence, notorious for a partisan treatise on behalf of the slave republic, took the chair. Contrary to the rule of English meetings, he, the chairman, himself proposed the motion to urge "the government to preserve the dignity of the British flag by demanding prompt satisfaction for this affront." Tremendous applause, handclapping and cheers upon cheers! The main argument of the opening speaker on the slave republic's behalf consisted in stating that slave ships had hitherto been protected by the American flag from the right of search claimed by England. And then this philanthropist launched a furious attack on the slave trade! He admitted that England had brought about the war of 1812 to 1814 with the United States because she insisted on searching for deserting English sailors on the warships of the Union. "But," he continued with wonderful dialectic, "but there is some difference between the right of search to take back deserters from the English navy who had escaped under the shelter of an assumed name and the right to seize passengers, men of the highest respectability, proceeding under the shadow of the English flag!" He played his highest trump, however, at the close of his diatribe.

The other day—he bellowed—while I was on the European Continent, I heard an observation made as to the course of our conduct in regard to the United States, and I was unable to reply to the allusion without a blush—that the feeling of every intelligent man upon the Continent was that we would submit to any outrage and suffer every indignity offered to us by the Government of the United States. Our patience had been exercised long enough—as long as it was possible to control it [the patience!]. At last we have arrived at facts: this is a very hard and startling fact [!] and it is the duty of every Englishman to apprise the Government of how strong and unanimous is the feeling of this great community on the outrage offered to our flag.

This senseless rigmarole was greeted with a cannonade of applause. Opposing voices were howled down and hissed down and stamped down. To the remark of a Mr. Campbell that the whole meeting was irregular, the inexorable Spence replied: "I perfectly agree with you that it is a little irregular but at the same time the fact that we have met to consider is rather an irregular fact." * To the proposal of a Mr. Turner to adjourn the meeting to the following day, in order that "the city of Liverpool can have its say and not a clique of cotton brokers usurp its name," cries of "Collar him, throw him out!" resounded from all sides. Unperturbed, Mr. Turner repeated his motion, which, however, was not put to the vote, again contrary to all the rules of English meetings. Spence triumphed. But, as a matter of fact, nothing has

* *Liverpool Daily Post,* November 28, 1861.—*Ed.*

done more to cool the temper of London than the news of Mr. Spence's triumph.

Die Presse, December 3, 1861.

9.

THE PRINCIPAL ACTORS IN THE *TRENT* DRAMA

London, December 4, 1861.

AT the present moment it is of interest to get acquainted in some measure with the leading figures in the *Trent* drama. On one side stands the active hero, Captain Wilkes, the commander of the *San Jacinto;* on the other, the passive heroes, J. M. Mason and John Slidell. Captain Charles Wilkes is a direct descendant of the brother of the celebrated English demagogue, John Wilkes, who threatened for a moment to shake the throne of George III. The struggle with the North American colonies saved the Hanoverian dynasty at that time from the outbreak of an English revolution, symptoms of which were alike perceptible in the cry of a Wilkes and the letters of a Junius.[78] Captain Wilkes, born in New York in 1798, forty-three years in the service of the American navy, commands the squadron that from 1838 to 1842 explored the North and South Pacific Ocean by order of the Union government. He has published a report on this expedition in five volumes. He is also the author of a work on *Western America,* which contains some valuable information on California and the Oregon district. It is now certain that Wilkes improvised his *coup de main* * independently and without instructions from Washington.

The two intercepted commissioners of the Southern

* An impetuous and unexpected attack.—*Ed.*

Confederacy—Messrs. Mason and Slidell—form a contrast in every respect. Mason, born in 1798, is descended from one of those aristocratic families of Virginia that fled from England after the Royalists had been defeated at the battle of Worcester. The grandsire of our hero belongs to the circle of men who, along with Washington, Jefferson, etc., are designated by the Americans as "the revolutionary fathers." John Slidell is neither, like Mason, of aristocratic lineage, nor, like his colleague, a slaveholder by birth. His native town is New York, where his grandfather and his father lived as honest tallow-chandlers. Mason, after he had occupied himself for some years with the study of law, stepped on the political stage. He figured repeatedly since 1826 as a member of the House of Representatives of Virginia; made his appearance in 1837 in the House of Representatives of the American Congress for a session; but his importance only dates from 1847. In that year Virginia elected him to the American Senate, in which he held his seat until the spring of 1861. Slidell, who is now sixty-eight years old, was obliged to leave New York hurriedly in consequence of adultery and a duel, in short, of a scandal. He betook himself to New Orleans, where he lived first by gambling, later by practicing law. Having become first a member of the legislature of Louisiana, he soon made his way to the House of Representatives and finally to the Senate of the American Congress. As a director of election rogueries during the presidential election of 1844 and, later, as a participant in a swindle in state lands, he had even somewhat shocked the sort of morals that prevail in Louisiana.

Mason inherited influence; Slidell acquired it. The two men found and supplemented each other in the American Senate, the bulwark of the slave oligarchy. In accordance with the American Constitution, the Senate elects a special Committee of Foreign Relations, which plays about the same rôle as the Privy Council formerly played in England, before the so-called Cabinet, a quantity theoretically unknown to the English constitution, usurped the Privy Council's functions. Mason was for a long time chairman of this committee; Slidell, a prominent member of it.

Mason, firmly convinced that every Virginian is a demi-god and every Yankee a plebeian rascal, never sought to conceal his contempt for his Northern colleagues. Haughty, overbearing, insolent, he knew how to knit his brows in a somber, Zeus-like frown and in fact transported to the Senate the manners native to the plantation. A fanatical eulogist of slavery, a shameless slanderer of the North and particularly of the Northern working class, a blusterer against England, Mason wearied the Senate with the prolix importunity of a persistent flow of speech that vainly sought to hide its complete vacuity under a hollow pomp. As a sort of demonstration, he went around in recent years in Virginian home-made gray linen; but, and this is characteristic of the man, the gray coat was adorned with loud buttons, all of which came from a state of New England, from Connecticut.

Whilst Mason played the *Jupiter Tonans* * of the slave oligarchy on the proscenium, Slidell worked behind the scenes. With a rare talent for intrigue, tireless perseverance and an unscrupulous lack of regard, but at the same time wary, covert, never strutting, but always insinuating himself, Slidell was the soul of the Southern conspiratorial conclave. One may judge the man's repute from the fact that when in 1845, shortly before the outbreak of war with Mexico, he was sent thither as Ambassador, Mexico refused to treat with such an individual.[79] Slidell's intrigues made Polk President. He was one of the most pernicious counselors of President Pierce and the

* Jupiter thundering.—*Ed.*

evil genius of Buchanan's administration.[80] The two, Mason and Slidell, were the chief sponsors of the law on runaway slaves; they brought about the bloodbath in Kansas, and both were wirepullers for the measures whereby Buchanan's administration smuggled all the means to secession into the hands of the South, whilst it left the North defenseless.[81]

As early as 1855 Mason declared on a public occasion in South Carolina that "for the South only one way lies open—immediate, absolute and eternal separation." In March 1861 he declared in the Senate that "he owed the Union government no *allegiance*," but retained his seat in the Senate and continued to draw his senatorial salary as long as the safety of his person allowed—a spy in the supreme council of the nation and a fraudulent parasite on the public exchequer.

Mason's great-grandmother was a daughter of the celebrated Sir William Temple. He is therefore a distant relative of Palmerston. Mason and Slidell appeared to the people of the North not merely as their political opponents, but as their *personal enemies*. Hence the general jubilation over their capture, which in its first days has overwhelmed regard for the danger threatening from England.

Die Presse, December 8, 1861.

10.

THE CONTROVERSIES OVER THE *TRENT* CASE

London, December 7, 1861.

THE Palmerston press—and on another occasion I will show that in foreign affairs Palmerston's control over nine-tenths of the English press is just as *absolute* as

Louis Bonaparte's over nine-tenths of the French press—the Palmerston press feels that it works under "pleasing difficulties." On the one hand, it admits that the Crown lawyers have reduced the charge against the United States to a *mere mistake in procedure,* to a *technical error.* On the other hand, it boasts that on the basis of such a legal quibble a *categorical ultimatum* has been presented to the United States such as can only be justified by a gross violation of law, but not by formal error in the exercise of a recognized right. Accordingly, the Palmerston press now pleads the *material* question of law again. The great importance of the case appears to enjoin a brief examination of the *material* legal question.

By way of introduction, it may be observed that not a single English paper ventures to blame the *San Jacinto* for the visitation and search of the *Trent.* This point, therefore, falls outside the controversy.

Besides, we again call to mind the relevant passage in Victoria's proclamation of neutrality of May 13, 1861. The passage reads:

Victoria R.

Whereas we are happily at peace with the Government of the United States . . . we do hereby strictly charge and command all our loving subjects . . . to abstain from violating or contravening . . . our Royal Proclamation . . . by breaking or endeavoring to break any blockade lawfully and actually established . . . or by *carrying officers . . . dispatches . . .* or any article or articles considered contraband of war. . . . All persons so offending will incur and be liable to the several penalties and penal consequences by the said Statute or by the law of nations in that behalf imposed or denounced. And we do hereby declare, that all our subjects, and persons entitled to our protection, who may misconduct themselves . . . will do so at their peril . . . and . . . will . . . incur our high displeasure by such misconduct.*

* For the original proclamation of Victoria see M. Bernard, *Historical Account of the Neutrality of Great Britain during the American Civil War* [London, 1870], pp. 135-6.—*Ed.*

This proclamation of Queen Victoria, therefore, in the first place declared dispatches to be contraband and subjects the ship that carries such contraband to the "penalties of the law of nations." What are these penalties?

Wheaton, an American writer on international law whose authority is recognized on both sides of the Atlantic Ocean alike, says in his *Elements of International Law*, p. 565:

The fradulent carrying of dispatches of the enemy will also subject the *neutral* vessel, in which they are transported to *capture and confiscation.* The consequences of such a service are indefinite, infinitely beyond the effect of any contraband that can be conveyed. "The carrying of two or three cargoes of military stores," says Sir W. Scott, "is necessarily an assistance of limited nature; but in the transmission of despatches may be conveyed the entire plan of a campaign, that may defeat all the plans of the other belligerent. . . . The confiscation of the noxious article, which constitutes the penalty for contraband . . . would be ridiculous when applied to *despatches.* There would be *no* freight dependent on their transportation and therefore this penalty could not, in the nature of things, be applied. The vehicle, in which they are carried, must, therefore, be *confiscated.*" *

Walker, in his *Introduction to American Law,* says:

. . . neutrals may not be concerned in bearing *hostile dispatches,* under the penalty of confiscation of the vehicle, and of the cargo also. . . .**

Kent, who is accounted a decisive authority in English courts, states in his *Commentaries:*

If, on search of a ship, it is found that she carries *enemy dispatches,* she incurs the penalty of capture and of confiscation by judgment of a prize court.***

* H. Wheaton, *Elements of International Law* (London, 1857), pp. 565-66 (Sixth Edition).—*Ed.*
** T. Walker, *Introduction to American Law* (Boston, 1855), p. 713, Third Edition.—*Ed.*
*** For Kent's discussion of dispatches and the right of search see his *Commentaries on American Law* (New York, 1826), vol. i, pp. 141-47.

Dr. Robert Phillimore, Advocate of Her Majesty in Her Office of Admiralty, says in his latest work on international law, p. 370:

Official communications from an official person on the public affairs of a belligerent Government are such *despatches* as impress an hostile character upon the carriers of them. The mischievous consequences of such a service cannot be estimated, and extended far beyond the effect of any Contraband that can be conveyed, for it is manifest that by the carriage of such despatches the most important operations of a Belligerent may be forwarded or obstructed.... The penalty is confiscation of the ship which conveys the despatches and ... of the cargo, if both belong to the same master.*

Two points are therefore established. Queen Victoria's proclamation of May 13, 1861, subjects *English* ships that forward the dispatches of the Confederacy, to the penalties of international law. International law, according to its English and American commentators, inflicts the *penalty* of capture and confiscation on such ships.

Palmerston's organs consequently *lied* on higher command—and were naïve enough to believe their lie. The captain of the *San Jacinto* had neglected to seek for *dispatches* on the *Trent* and therefore he had likewise found none; the *Trent* had consequently become shotproof through this oversight. The American journals of November 17 to 20, which *could* not yet have been aware of the English lie, *unanimously* state, on the contrary, that the dispatches *have been carried off* and are already in print, for the purpose of submitting them to Congress in Washington. This entirely alters the state of the case. By reason of these dispatches, the *San Jacinto* had the right to take the *Trent* in tow and every American prize court had the duty to confiscate her and her cargo. With

* R. Phillimore, *Commentaries upon International Law* (Philadelphia, 1857), vol. iii, 370 [284].—*Ed.*

the *Trent*, her passengers also came within reach of American jurisdiction.

Messrs. Mason, Slidell and Co., as soon as the *Trent* had touched at Monroe, came under American jurisdiction as rebels. If, therefore, instead of towing the *Trent* herself to an American port, the Captain of the *San Jacinto* contented himself with carrying off the dispatches and their bearers, he in no way worsened the position of Mason, Slidell and Co., whilst, on the other hand, his *error in procedure* benefited the *Trent*, her cargo and her passengers. And it would be indeed unprecedented, if England wished to declare war on the United States because Captain Wilkes committed an error in procedure harmful to the United States, but useful to England.

The question whether Mason, Slidell and Co. were themselves contraband, was only raised and could only be raised because the Palmerston journals had broadcast the *lie* that Captain Wilkes had neither sought for dispatches, nor carried off dispatches. For in this case Mason, Slidell and Co. in fact constituted the sole objects on the ship *Trent* that could possibly fall under the category of contraband. Let us, however, disregard this aspect for the moment. The proclamation of Queen Victoria designates *"officers"* of a belligerent party as contraband. Are *"officers"* merely military officers? Were Mason, Slidell and Co. *"officers"* of the Confederacy? *"Officers,"* says Samuel Johnson in his dictionary of the English language, are *"men employed by the public,"* that is, in German: *öffenliche Beamten.** Walker gives the same definition. (See his dictionary, edition of 1861.)

According to the usage of the English language, therefore, Mason, Slidell and Co., these emissaries, *id est,*** officials of the Confederacy, come under the category of

* Public officials.—*Ed.*
** That is.—*Ed.*

"officers," whom the royal proclamation declares to be contraband. The Captain of the *Trent knew* them in this capacity and therefore rendered himself, his ship and his passengers confiscable. If, according to Phillimore and all other authorities, a ship becomes confiscable as the carrier of an enemy dispatch, because it violates neutrality, in still higher degree is this true of the *person* who carries the dispatches. According to Wheaton, even an enemy *ambassador,* so long as he is in transit, may be intercepted. In general, however, the basis of all international law is that any member of the belligerent party may be regarded and treated as a "belligerent" by the opposing party. "Whilst a man," says Vattel, "continues a citizen of his own country, he is the enemy of all those with whom his nation is at war." * One sees, therefore, that the English Crown lawyers reduced the contentious point to a *mere error in procedure,* not error *in re,*** but error *in forma,**** because, actually, no *material violation of law* is in question. The Palmerston organs chatter about the material question of law again because a mere error in procedure, *in the interest of the Trent* at that, gives no plausible pretext for a high-flown ultimatum.

Meanwhile, important voices have been raised in this sense from diametrically opposite sides: on the one side, Messrs. Bright and Cobden; on the other David Urquhart. These people are enemies in principle and in person: the first two, peace-making cosmopolitans; the other, the *"last Englishman";* the former always ready to sacrifice every international right to international trade; the other hesitating not a moment: *"Fiat Justitia, pereat mundus," ****** and by "justice" he understands "English"

---

* E. Vattel, *The Law of Nations; or Principles of the Law of Nature* (Philadelphia, 1835), p. 321.
** In the matter.—*Ed.*
*** In the form.—*Ed.*
**** Let justice be done though the world perish.—*Ed.*

justice. The voices of Bright and Cobden are important, because they represent a powerful section of the middle-class interests and are represented in the ministry by Gladstone, Milner-Gibson and also, more or less, by Sir Cornwall Lewis. The voice of Urquhart is important because international law is his life-study and every one recognizes him as an *incorruptible* interpreter of this international law.

The usual newspaper sources will communicate Bright's speech on behalf of the United States and Cobden's letter, which is conceived in the same sense. Therefore I will not linger over them.

Urquhart's organ, *The Free Press,* states in its last number, published on December 4:

> We must bombard New York! Such were the frantic cries which met the ears of every one who traversed the streets of London on the evening of this week day, on the arrival of the intelligence of a trifling warlike incident. The act was one which England has committed as a matter of course—namely the seizure on board of a neutral of the persons and property of her enemies.

The Free Press further develops the point that, in 1856 at the Congress of Paris, Palmerston, without authority from Parliament or the Crown, had sacrificed English maritime rights *in the interest of Russia,* and then says that in order to justify this sacrifice, Palmerston's organs stated at that time: "If we maintained the right of search, we should assuredly be *involved in a war with the United States on the occasion of the first war in Europe.* The very 'organs of public opinion' ... now call on us to bombard New York because the United States act on those laws which are theirs no less than our own."

With regard to the utterances of the "organs of public opinion," *The Free Press* remarks:

"The bray of Baron Münchausen's thawing post-horn was nothing to the clangor of the British press on the capture of Messrs. Mason and Slidell." * Then humorously, it places side by side, in "strophe" and "antistrophe," the contradictions by which the English press seeks to convict the United States of a "breach of law."

Die Presse, December 11, 1861.

11.

THE WASHINGTON CABINET AND THE WESTERN POWERS

ONE of the most striking surprises of a war so rich in surprises as the Anglo-French-Russian was incontestably the declaration on maritime law agreed to at Paris in the spring of 1856. When the war against Russia began, England suspended her most formidable weapons against Russia: confiscation of enemy-owned commodities on neutral ships and privateering. At the conclusion of the war, England broke these weapons in pieces and sacrificed the fragments on the altar of peace. Russia, the ostensibly vanquished party, received a concession that, by a series of "armed neutralities," [82] wars and diplomatic intrigues, she had tried in vain to extort since Catherine II. England, the ostensible victor, renounced, on the contrary, the great means of attack and defense that had grown up out of her sea power and that she had maintained for a century and a half against a world in arms.

The humanitarian grounds that served as a pretext for the Declaration of 1856 vanish before the most superficial examination. Privateering is no greater *barbarism* than the action of volunteer corps or guerillas in land warfare. The privateers are the guerillas of the sea. Con-

* *The Free Press*, December 4, 1861.—*Ed.*

fiscation of the private goods of a belligerent nation also occurs in land warfare. Do military requisitions, for example, hit only the cash-box of the enemy government and not the property of private persons also? The nature of land warfare safeguards enemy possessions that are on neutral soil, therefore under the sovereignty of a neutral power. The nature of sea warfare washes away these barriers, since the sea, as the common highway of the nations, cannot fall to the sovereignty of any neutral power.

As a matter of fact, however, the Declaration of 1856 veils under its philanthropic phrases a great inhumanity. In principle it transforms war from a war of peoples into a war of governments. It endows property with an inviolability that it denies to persons. It emancipates trade from the terrors of war and thereby makes the classes carrying on trade and industry callous to the terrors of war. For the rest, it is self-understood that the humanitarian pretexts of the Declaration of 1856 were only addressed to the European gallery, just like the religious pretexts of the Holy Alliance!

It is a well-known fact that Lord Clarendon, who signed away English maritime rights at the Congress of Paris, acted, as he subsequently confessed in the Upper House, without the foreknowledge or instructions of the Crown. His sole authority consisted in a *private letter* from Palmerston. Up to the present Palmerston has not dared to demand the sanction of the English Parliament for the Declaration of Paris and its signature by Clarendon. Apart from the debates on the contents of the Declaration, there was fear of debates on the question whether, independently of Crown and Parliament, an English minister might usurp the right to sweep away the old basis of English sea power with a stroke of the pen. That this ministerial *coup d'état* did not lead to stormy interpellations, but, rather, was silently accepted as a *fait accompli*,* Palmerston owed to the influence of the Manchester school.** It found to be in accordance with the interests represented by it, and therefore with philanthropy, civilization and progress also, an innovation which would allow English commerce to continue to pursue its business with the enemy undisturbed on neutral ships, whilst sailors and soldiers fought for the honor of the nation. The Manchester men were jubilant over the fact that by an unconstitutional *coup de main* the minister had bound England to international concessions whose attainment in the constitutional parliamentary way was wholly improbable. Hence the indignation of the Manchester party in England at the present moment over the disclosures of the blue book submitted by Seward to the Congress in Washington!

As is known, the United States was the only great power that refused to accede to the Declaration of Paris of 1856. If they renounced privateering, then they would have to create a great state navy. Any weakening of their means of war at sea simultaneously threatened them on land with the incubus of a standing army on the European scale. Nevertheless, President Buchanan stated that he was ready to accept the Declaration of Paris, provided that the same inviolability would be assured to all property, enemy or neutral, found on ships, with the exception of contraband of war. His proposal was rejected. From Seward's blue book it now appears that Lincoln, immediately after his assumption of office, offered England and France the adhesion of the United States to the Declaration of Paris, so far as it abolishes privateering, on condition that the prohibition of privateering should be extended to the parts of the United States in revolt,

* Accomplished fact.—*Ed.*
** School of political ecoonmy holding to free trade principles.—*Ed.*

that is, the Southern Confederacy. The answer that he received amounted in practice to recognition of the belligerent rights of the Southern Confederacy.[83]

"Humanity, progress and civilization" whispered to the Cabinets of St. James and the Tuileries that the prohibition of privateering would extraordinarily reduce the chances of secession and therefore of dissolution of the United States. The Confederacy was therefore recognized in all haste as a belligerent party, in order afterwards to reply to the Cabinet at Washington that England and France could naturally not recognize the proposal of one belligerent party as a binding law for the other belligerent party. The same "noble uprightness" inspired all the diplomatic negotiations of England and France with the Union government since the outbreak of the Civil War, and had the *San Jacinto* not held up the *Trent* in the Bahama straits, any other incident would then have sufficed to provide a pretext for the conflict that Lord Palmerston aimed at.

Die Presse, December 25, 1861.

12.

THE OPINION OF THE JOURNALS AND THE OPINION OF THE PEOPLE

London, December 25, 1861.

CONTINENTAL politicians, who imagine that in the London press they possess a thermometer for the temper of the English people, inevitably draw false conclusions at the present moment. With the first news of the *Trent* case the English national pride flared up and the call for war with the United States resounded from almost all sections of society. The London press, on the other hand, affected moderation and even *The Times* doubted whether a *casus belli* existed at all.

Whence this phenomenon? Palmerston was uncertain whether the Crown lawyers were in a position to contrive any legal pretext for war. For, a week and a half before the arrival of the *La Plata* at Southampton, agents of the Southern Confederacy from Liverpool had turned to the English Cabinet, denounced the intention of American cruisers to put out from *English* ports and intercept Messrs. Mason, Slidell, etc., on the high seas, and demanded the intervention of the English government. In accordance with the opinion of its Crown lawyers, the latter refused the request. Hence, in the beginning, the peaceful and moderate tone of the London press in contrast to the warlike impatience of the people. So soon, however, as the Crown lawyers—the Attorney-General and the Solicitor-General, both themselves members of the Cabinet—had worked out a technical pretext for a quarrel with the United States, the relationship between the people and the press turned into its opposite. The war fever increased in the press in the same measure as the war fever abated in the people. At the present moment a war with America is just as unpopular with all sections of the English people, the friends of cotton and the cabbage-junkers * excepted, as the war-howl in the press is overwhelming.

But now, consider the London press! At its head stands *The Times,* whose chief editor, Bob Lowe, was formerly a demagogue in Australia, where he agitated for separation from England. He is a subordinate member of the Cabinet, a kind of minister for education, and a mere creature of Palmerston. *Punch* is the court jester of *The Times* and transforms its *sesquipedalia verba* ** into

---

* *Krautjunker,* a contemptuous term for country squires.—*Ed.*
** Words of a foot and a half.—*Ed.*

snappy jokes and spiritless caricatures. A principal editor of *Punch* was accommodated by Palmerston with a seat on the Board of Health and an annual salary of a thousand pounds sterling.

The *Morning Post* is in part Palmerston's private property. Another part of this singular institution is sold to the French Embassy. The rest belongs to the *haute volée** and supplies the most precise reports for court flunkeys and ladies' tailors. Among the English people the *Morning Post* is accordingly notorious as the *Jenkins* (the stock figure for the lackey) of the press.

The *Morning Advertiser* is the joint property of the "licensed victuallers," that is, of the public houses, which, besides beer, may also sell spirits. It is, further, the organ of the Anglican *bigots* and ditto of the *sporting characters*, that is, of the people who make a business of horse-racing, betting, boxing and the like. The editor of this paper, Mr. Grant, previously employed as a stenographer by the newspapers and quite uneducated in a literary sense, has had the honor to get invited to Palmerston's private *soirées*. Since then he has been enthusiastic for the "truly English minister" whom, on the outbreak of the Russian war, he had denounced as a "Russian agent." It must be added that the pious patrons of this liquor-journal stand under the ruling rod of the Earl of Shaftesbury and that Shaftesbury is Palmerston's son-in-law. Shaftesbury is the pope of the low churchmen, who blend the *spiritus sanctus*** with the profane spirit of the honest *Advertiser*.

The Morning Chronicle! Quantum mutatus ab illo! *** For well-nigh half a century the great organ of the Whig Party and the not unfortunate rival of *The Times*, its star paled after the Whig war. It went through meta-

* High rank.—*Ed.*
** Holy spirit.—*Ed.*
*** How much changed from that!—*Ed.*

morphoses of all sorts, turned itself into a *penny paper* and sought to live by "sensations," thus, for example, by taking the part of the poisoner, Palmer. It subsequently sold itself to the French Embassy, which, however, soon regretted throwing away its money. It then threw itself into anti-Bonapartism, but with no better success. Finally, it found the long missing buyer in Messrs. Yancey and Mann—the agents of the Southern Confederacy in London.

The *Daily Telegraph* is the private property of a certain Lloyd. His paper is stigmatized by the English press itself as *Palmerston's mob paper*. Besides this function it conducts a *chronique scandaleuse*.* It is characteristic of this *Telegraph* that, on the arrival of the news about the *Trent,* by *ordre* from above it declared *war to be impossible.* In the dignity and moderation dictated to it, it seemed so strange to itself that since then it has published half-a-dozen articles about this instance of moderation and dignity displayed by it. As soon, however, as the *ordre* to change its opinion reached it, the *Telegraph* now sought to compensate itself for the constraint put upon it by outbawling all its comrades in howling loudly for war.

The *Globe* is the ministerial evening paper which receives official subsidies from all Whig ministeries.

The Tory papers, *The Morning Herald* and the *Evening Standard* both belonging to the same *boutique,*** are governed by a double motive: on the one hand, hereditary hate for "the *revolted* English colonies"; on the other hand, a chronic ebb in their finances. They know that a war with America must shatter the present coalition Cabinet and pave the way for a Tory Cabinet. With the Tory Cabinet official subsidies for *The Herald* and *The*

* Chronicle of scandal.—Ed.
** Shop.—*Ed.*

Standard would return. Accordingly, hungry wolves cannot howl louder for prey than these Tory papers for an American war with its ensuing shower of gold!

Of the London daily press, *The Daily News* and *The Morning Star* are the only papers left that are worth mentioning; both work counter to the trumpeters of war. *The Daily News* is restricted in its movement by a connection with Lord John Russell; *The Morning Star* (the organ of Bright and Cobden) is diminished in its influence by its character as a "peace-at-any-price paper."

Most of the London weekly papers are mere echoes of the daily press, therefore overwhelmingly warlike. *The Observer* is in the ministry's *pay*. *The Saturday Review* strives for *ésprit* * and believes it has attained it by affecting a cynical elevation above "humanitarian" prejudices. To show *"ésprit,"* the corrupt lawyers, parsons and schoolmasters that write this paper have smirked their approbation of the slaveholders since the outbreak of the American Civil War. Naturally, they subsequently blew the war-trumpet with *The Times*. They are already drawing up plans of campaign against the United States displaying an ignorance which is hair-raising.

The Spectator, The Examiner and, particularly, *MacMillan's Magazine* must be mentioned as more or less respectable exceptions.

One sees: On the whole, the London press—with the exception of the cotton organs, the provincial papers form a commendable contrast—represents nothing but Palmerston and again Palmerston. Palmerston wants war; the English people don't want it. Imminent events will show who will conquer in this duel, Palmerston or the people. In any case, he is playing a more dangerous game than Louis Bonaparte at the beginning of 1859.[84]

Die Presse, December 31, 1861.

* Spirit.—*Ed.*

13.

FRENCH NEWS HUMBUG

ECONOMIC CONSEQUENCES OF WAR

London, December 31, 1861.

THE belief in miracles seems to be withdrawn from one sphere only in order to settle in another. If it is driven out of nature, it now rises up in politics. At least, that is the view of the Paris newspapers and their confederates in the telegraph agencies and the newspaper-correspondence shops. Thus, Paris evening papers of yesterday announce: Lord Lyons has stated to Mr. Seward that he will wait until the evening of December 20, but then depart for London, in the event of the Cabinet at Washington's refusing to surrender the prisoners. Therefore, the Paris papers already knew *yesterday* the steps that Lord Lyons took after receiving the dispatches transmitted to him on the *Europa*. Up to *today,* however, news of the arrival of the *Europa* in New York has not yet reached Europe. The *Patrie* and its associates, *before* they are informed of the arrival of the *Europa* in America, publish in Europe news of the events that ensued in the United States on the heels of the *Europa's* departure. The *Patrie* and its associates manifestly believe that legerdemain requires no magic. One journal over here remarks in its stock exchange article that these Paris inventions, quite like the provocatory articles in some English papers, serve not only the political speculations of certain persons in power, but just as much the *stock exchange speculations* of certain private individuals.

The Economist, hitherto one of the loudest bawlers of the war party, publishes in its last number a *letter from a Liverpool merchant* and a leading article in which the

English public is warned not on any account to under-estimate the effects of a war with the United States. England imported grain worth £15,380,301 during 1861; of the whole amount nearly £6,000,000 fell to the United States. England would suffer more from the inability to buy American grain than the United States would suffer from the inability to sell it. The United States would have the advantage of *prior information*. If they decided for war, then telegrams would fly forthwith from Washington to San Francisco, and the American ships in the Pacific Ocean and the China seas would commence war operations many weeks before England could bring the news of the war to India.

Since the outbreak of the Civil War the American-Chinese trade, and the American-Australian trade quite as much, has diminished to an enormous extent. So far, however, as it is still carried on, it buys its cargoes in most cases with English letters of credit, therefore with English capital. On the contrary, English trade from India, China and Australia, always very considerable, has grown still more since the interruption of the trade with the United States. American privateers would therefore have a great field for privateering; English privateers, a relatively insignificant one. English investments of capital in the United States are greater than the whole of the capital invested in the English cotton industry.[85] American investments of capital in England are nil. The English navy eclipses the American, but not nearly to the same extent as during the war of 1812 to 1814.

If at that time the American privateers already showed themselves far superior to the English, then how about them now? An effective blockade of the North American ports, particularly in winter, is quite out of the question.

In the inland waters between Canada and the United States—and superiority here is decisive for the land warfare in Canada—the United States would, with the opening of the war, hold absolute sway.

In short, the Liverpool merchant comes to the conclusion:

"Nobody in England dares to recommend war for the sake of mere cotton. It would be cheaper for us to feed the whole of the cotton districts for three years at state expense than to wage war with the United States on their behalf for one year."

Cæterum censeo * that the *Trent* case will not lead to war.

Die Presse, January 4, 1862.

14.

A PRO-AMERICA MEETING

London, January 1, 1862.

THE anti-war movement among the English people gains from day to day in energy and extent. Public meetings in the most diverse parts of the country insist on *settlement by arbitration* of the dispute between England and America. Memoranda in this sense rain on the chief of the Cabinet, and the independent *provincial press* is almost unanimous in its opposition to the war-cry of the London press.

Subjoined is a detailed report of the meeting held last Monday in Brighton, since it emanated from the working class, and the two principal speakers, Messrs. Cunningham and White, are influential members of Parliament who both sit on the ministerial side of the House.

* For the rest I think.—*Ed.*

Mr. Wood (a worker) proposed the first motion, to the effect "that the dispute between England and America arose out of a misinterpretation of international law, but not out of an intentional insult to the British flag; that accordingly this meeting is of the opinion that the whole question in dispute should be referred to a neutral power for decision by arbitration; that under the existing circumstances a war with America is not justifiable, but rather merits the condemnation of the English people." In support of his motion Mr. Wood, among other things, remarked:

It is said that this new insult is merely the last link in a chain of insults that America has offered to England. Suppose this to be true, what would it prove in regard to the cry for war at the present moment? It would prove that so long as America was undivided and strong, we submitted quietly to her insults; but now, in the hour of her peril, take advantage of a position favorable to us, to revenge the insult. Would not such a procedure brand us as cowards in the eyes of the civilized world?

Mr. Cunningham: ... At this moment there is developing in the midst of the Union an avowed *policy of emancipation* (*Applause*), and I express the earnest hope that no intervention on the part of the English government will be permitted (*Applause*). ... Will you, freeborn Englishmen, allow yourselves to be embroiled in an anti-republican war? For that is the intention of *The Times* and of the party that stands behind it. ... I appeal to the workers of England, who have the greatest interest in the preservation of peace, to raise their voices and, in case of need, their hands for the prevention of so great a crime (*Loud Applause*). ... *The Times* has exerted every endeavor to excite the warlike spirit of the land and by bitter scorn and slanders to engender a hostile mood among the Americans. ... I do not belong to the so-called peace party. *The Times* favored the policy of Russia and put forth (in 1853) all its powers to mislead our country into looking on calmly at the military encroachments of Russian barbarism in the East. I was amongst those who raised their voices against this false policy. At the time of the introduction of the *Conspiracy Bill*, whose object was to facilitate the extradition of political refugees, no expenditure of effort seemed too great to *The Times*, to force this Bill through the Lower House. I was one of the ninety-nine members of the House who withstood this encroachment on the liberties of the English people and brought about the minister's downfall [86] (*Applause*). This minister is now at the head of the Cabinet. I prophesy to him that should he seek to embroil our country in a war with America without good and sufficient reasons, his plan will fail ignominiously. I promise him a fresh ignominious defeat, a worse defeat than was his lot on the occasion of the Conspiracy Bill (*Loud Applause*).... I do not know the official communication that has gone to Washington; but the opinion prevails that the Crown lawyers have recommended the government to take its stand on the quite narrow legal ground that the Southern commissioners might not be seized without the ship that carried them. Consequently the handing over of Slidell and Mason is to be demanded as the *sine qua non*.*

Suppose the people on the other side of the Atlantic Ocean does not permit its government to hand them over. Will you go to war with it for the bodies of these two envoys of the slavedrivers?... There exists in this country an anti-republican war party. Remember the last Russian war. From the secret dispatches published in Petersburg it was clear beyond all doubt that the articles published by *The Times* in 1855 were written by a person who had access to the secret Russian state papers and documents. At that time Mr. Layard read the striking passages in the Lower House, and *The Times*, in its consternation, immediately changed its tone and blew the war-trumpet next morning.... *The Times* has repeatedly attacked the Emperor Napoleon and supported our government in its demand for unlimited credits for land fortifications and floating batteries. Having done this and raised the alarm cry against France, does *The Times* now wish to leave our coast exposed to the French emperor by embroiling our country in a trans-Atlantic war ... ? It is to be feared that the present great preparations are intended by no means only for the *Trent* case but for the eventuality of a recognition of the government of the

---

* That which is absolutely indispensable.—*Ed.*

slave states. If England does this, then she will cover herself
with everlasting shame.

Mr. White: It is due to the working class to mention that they
are the originators of this meeting and that all the expenses
of organizing it are borne by their committee.... The present
government never had the good judgment to deal honestly and
frankly with the people.... I have never for a moment believed
that there was the remotest possibility of a war developing
out of the *Trent* case. I have said to the face of more than one
member of the government that not a single member of the
government believed in the possibility of a war on account of
the *Trent* case. Why, then, these powerful preparations? I
believe that England and France have reached an understanding to recognize the independence of the Southern states next
spring. By then Great Britain would have a fleet of superior
strength in American waters. Canada would be completely
equipped for defense. If the Northern states are then inclined
to make a *casus belli* out of the recognition of the Southern
states, Great Britain will then be prepared....

The speaker then went on to develop the dangers of a
war with the United States, called to mind the sympathy
that America showed on the death of General Havelock,
the assistance that the American sailors rendered to the
English ships in the unlucky Peiho engagement,[87] etc.
He closed with the remark that the Civil War would end
with the abolition of slavery and England must therefore
stand unconditionally on the side of the North.

The original motion having been unanimously adopted,
a memorandum for Palmerston was submitted to the
meeting, debated and adopted.

Die Presse, January 5, 1862.

15.

THE HISTORY OF SEWARD'S
SUPPRESSED DISPATCH

London, January 14, 1862.

THE defunct *Trent* case is resurrected, this time, however, as a *casus belli* not between England and the United States, but between the English people and the English government. The new *casus belli* will be decided in Parliament, which assembles next month. Without doubt you have already taken notice of the polemic of *The Daily News* and *The Star* against the *Morning Post* for suppressing and denying Seward's peace dispatch of November 30, which on December 19 was read to Lord John Russell by the American Ambassador, Mr. Adams. Permit me, now, to return to this matter. With the assurance of the *Morning Post* that Seward's dispatch had not the remotest bearing on the *Trent* affair, stock exchange securities fell and property worth millions changed hands, was lost on the one side, won on the other. In business and industrial circles, therefore, the wholly unjustifiable semi-official lie of the *Morning Post* disclosed by the publication of Seward's dispatch of November 30 arouses the most tremendous indignation.

On the afternoon of January 9 the peace news reached London. The same evening the *Evening Star* (the evening edition of the *Morning Star*) interpellated the government concerning the suppression of Seward's dispatch of November 30. The following morning, January 10, the *Morning Post* replied as follows:

It will of course be asked why is it that we have not heard of this sooner seeing that Mr. Seward's dispatch must have reached Mr. Adams some time in December? The explanation of this is very simple. It is that the dispatch received by Mr.

Adams was *not communicated to the English government*.*
On the evening of the same day *The Star* gave the lie
to the *Post* completely and declared its "rectification" to
be a miserable subterfuge. The dispatch had in fact not
been "*communicated*" to Lord Palmerston and Lord Russell by Mr. Adams, but had been "*read out*."

Next morning, Saturday, January 11, *The Daily News*
entered the lists and proved from the *Morning Post's*
article of December 21 that the latter and the government
were fully acquainted with Seward's dispatch at that
time and deliberately falsified it. The government now
prepared to retreat. On the evening of January 11 the
semi-official *Globe* declared that Mr. Adams had, to be
sure, communicated Seward's dispatch to the government
on December 19; this, however, "contained no offer of the
kind which Lord Russell supposed the Federal government might have been willing to make any more than
that immediate apology for Captain Wilkes' outrage on
our flag." ** This shamefaced confession of a deliberate
deception of the English people for three weeks only
fanned the flame higher, instead of quenching it. A cry of
anger resounded through all the organs of the industrial
districts of Great Britain, which yesterday finally found
its echo even in the Tory newspapers. The whole question, it was clearly observed, was placed on the order of
the day, not by politicians, but by the commercial public.
Today's *Morning Star* remarks on the subject:

Lord John Russell made himself an accomplice in that suppression of the truth which is the virtual suggestion of false-
hood—he allowed the *Morning Post* to state, uncontradicted,
the very opposite of the truth, but he is incapable of having
dictated that mendacious and incalculably pernicious article
which appeared on the 21st of December. . . . There can be only
one man high enough in office, and low enough in character, to

* *Morning Post*, January 10, 1862.—*Ed.*
** *Globe*, January 11, 1862.—*Ed.*

have inspired the atrocious composition ... The Minister who mutilated the Afghan dispatches is alone capable of having suppressed ... Mr. Seward's message of peace. ... The foolish leniency of the House of Commons condoned the one offense. Will not Parliament and people unite in the infliction of punishment for the other? *

Die Presse, January 18, 1862.

16.

A *COUP D'ÉTAT* OF LORD JOHN RUSSELL

London, January 17, 1862.

LORD JOHN RUSSELL's position during the recent crisis was a thoroughly vexatious one, even for a man whose whole parliamentary life proves that he has seldom hesitated to sacrifice real power for official position. No one forgot that Lord John Russell has lost the Premiership to Palmerston, but no one seemed to remember that he has gained the Foreign Office from Palmerston. All the world considered it a self-evident axiom that Palmerston directed the Cabinet in his own name and foreign policy under the name of Russell. On the arrival of the first peace news from New York, Whigs and Tories vied with one another in trumpet-blasts to the greater glory of Palmerston's statesmanship, whilst the Minister for Foreign Affairs, Lord John Russell, was not even a candidate for praise as his assistant. He was absolutely ignored. Hardly, however, had the scandal caused by the *suppressed* American dispatch of November 30 broken out, when Russell's name was resurrected from the dead.

Attack and defense now made the discovery that the *responsible* Minister for Foreign Affairs was called Lord *John Russell!* But now even Russell's patience gave way.

* *Morning Star,* January 14, 1862.—*Ed.*

Without waiting for the opening of Parliament and contrary to every ministerial convention, he published forthwith in the official *Gazette* of January 12 his own correspondence with Lord Lyons. This correspondence proves
that Seward's dispatch of November 30 was read by Mr.
Adams to Lord John Russell on December 19; that Russell expressly acknowledged this dispatch as an *apology*
for the act of Captain Wilkes, and that Mr. Adams, after
Russell's disclosures, considered a peaceful outcome of
the dispute as certain. After this *official* disclosure, what
becomes of the *Morning Post* of December 21, which
denied the arrival of any dispatch from Seward relating
to the *Trent* case; what becomes of the *Morning Post*
of January 10, which blamed Mr. Adams for the suppression of the dispatch, what becomes of the entire war
racket of the Palmerston press from December 19, 1861,
to January 8, 1862? Even more! Lord John Russell's dispatch to Lord Lyons of December 19, 1861, proves that
the English Cabinet presented *no war ultimatum;* that
Lord Lyons did *not* receive instructions to leave Washington seven days after delivering "this ultimatum"; that
Russell ordered the ambassador to avoid every semblance
of a threat, and, finally, that the English Cabinet had determined to make a *definitive decision* only *after receipt*
of the American answer. The whole of the policy
trumpeted by the Palmerston press, which found so many
servile echoes on the Continent, is therefore a mere
chimera. It has never been carried out in real life. It
only proves, as a London paper states today, that Palmerston "sought to thwart the declared and binding policy
of the *responsible* advisers of the Crown."

That Lord John Russell's *coup de main* struck the
Palmerston press like a bolt from the blue, one fact proves
most forcibly. *The Times* of yesterday *suppressed* the
Russell correspondence and made no mention of it what-

ever. Only today a reprint from the *London Gazette* figures in its columns, introduced and prefaced by a leading article that carefully avoids the real issue, *the issue between the English people and the English Cabinet,* and touches on it merely in the ill-humored phrase that "Lord Russell has exerted all his ingenuity to extract an apology" out of Seward's dispatch of November 30. On the other hand, the wrathful *Jupiter Tonans* of Printing House Square lets off steam in a second leading article, in which Mr. Gilpin, a member of the ministry, the President of the Board of Trade and a partisan of the Manchester school, is declared to be unworthy of his place in the ministry. For last Tuesday, at a public meeting in Northampton, whose parliamentary representative he is, Gilpin, a former bookseller, a demagogue and an apostle of moderation, whom nobody will take for a hero, criminally urged the English people to prevent by public demonstrations an untimely recognition of the Southern Confederacy, which he inconsiderately stigmatized as an offspring of slavery. As if, *The Times* indignantly exclaims, as if Palmerston and Russell—*The Times* now remembers the existence of Lord John Russell once more —had not fought all their lives to put down slavery! It was surely an indiscretion, a *calculated* indiscretion on the part of Mr. Gilpin, to call the English people into the lists against the pro-slavery longings of a ministry to which he himself belongs. But Mr. Gilpin, as already mentioned, is no hero. His whole career evidences little capacity for martyrdom. His indiscretion occurred on the *same day* as Lord Russell carried out his *coup de main.* We may therefore conclude that the Cabinet is not a "happy family" and that its individual members have already familiarized themselves with the idea of "separation."

No less noteworthy than the English ministerial

sequel to the *Trent* drama is its *Russian epilogue.* Russia, which during the entire racket stood silently in the background with folded arms, now springs to the proscenium, claps Mr. Seward on the shoulders—and declares that the moment for the definitive regulation of the maritime rights of neutrals has at last arrived. Russia, as is known, considers herself called on to put the urgent questions of civilization on the agenda of world history at the right time and in the right place. Russia becomes unassailable by the maritime powers the moment the latter give up, with their belligerent rights against neutrals, their power over Russia's export trade. The Paris Convention of April 16, 1856, which is in part a verbatim copy of the Russian "Armed" Neutrality Treaty of 1780 against England, is meanwhile not yet *law* in England. What a trick of destiny if the *Anglo-American* dispute ended with the English Parliament and the English Crown sanctioning a concession that two British ministers made to Russia on their own authority at the end of the *Anglo-Russian* war.

Die Presse, January 21, 1862.

17.

A LONDON WORKERS' MEETING

London, January 28, 1862.

THE working class, so preponderant a component part of a society that within living memory has no longer possessed a *peasantry*, is known to be unrepresented in Parliament. Nevertheless, it is not without political influence. No important innovation, no decisive measure has ever been carried through in this country without *pressure from without*, whether it was the opposition that required such pressure against the government or the government that required the pressure against the opposition. By *pressure from without* the Englishman understands great, extra-parliamentary popular demonstrations, which naturally cannot be staged without the lively coöperation of the working class. Pitt understood how to use the masses against the Whigs in his Anti-Jacobin War. The Catholic emancipation, the Reform Bill, the abolition of the Corn Laws, the Ten Hours Bill, the war against Russia, the rejection of Palmerston's Conspiracy Bill,[88] all were the fruit of stormy extra-parliamentary demonstrations, in which the working class, sometimes artificially incited, sometimes acting spontaneously, now as a *persona dramatis*,* now as the chorus, played the principal part or, according to circumstances, the noisy part. So much the more striking is the attitude of the English working class in regard to the American Civil War.

The misery that the stoppage of the factories and the shortening of the labor time, *motivated* by the blockade of the slave states, has produced among the workers in the northern manufacturing districts is incredible and in daily process of growth.[89] The other component parts of the working class do not suffer to the same extent; but they suffer severely from the reaction of the crisis in the cotton industry on the remaining branches of production, from the curtailment of the export of their own products to the North of America in consequence of the Morrill tariff and from the annihilation of this export to the South in consequence of the blockade. At the present moment, English interference in America has accordingly become a bread-and-butter question for the working class. Moreover, no means of inflaming its wrath against the United States is scorned by its *"natural supe-*

* Person of the drama.—*Ed.*

riors." The sole great and widely circulating workers' organ still existing, *Reynolds's Weekly Newspaper,* has been purchased expressly in order that for six months it might reiterate weekly in raging diatribes the *cæterum censeo* of English intervention. The working class is accordingly fully conscious that the government is only waiting for the intervention cry from below, the *pressure from without,* to put an end to the American blockade and English misery. Under these circumstances, the obstinacy with which the working class keeps silent, or breaks its silence only to raise its voice against intervention and *for* the United States, is admirable. This is a new, brilliant proof of the indestructible excellence of the English popular masses, of that excellence which is the secret of England's greatness and which, to speak in the hyperbolic language of Mazzini, made the common English soldier seem a demi-god during the Crimean War and the Indian insurrection.

The following report on a great *workers' meeting* that took place yesterday in Marylebone, the most populous district of London, may serve to characterize the "policy" of the working class:

Mr. Steadman, the chairman, opened the meeting with the remark that the question was one of a decision on the part of the English people in regard to the *reception of* Messrs. Mason and Slidell. "It has to be considered whether these gentlemen have come on a voyage here to free the slaves from their chains or to forge a new link for these chains."

Mr. Yates: On the present occasion the working class dare not keep silent. The two gentlemen who are sailing across the Atlantic Ocean to our land are the agents of slaveholding and tyrannical states. They are in open rebellion against the lawful Constitution of their country and come here to induce our government to recognize the independence of the slave states. It is the duty of the working class to pronounce its opinion

now, if the English government is not to believe that we
regard its foreign policy with indifference. We must show
that the money expended by this people on the emancipation of
slaves cannot be allowed to be uselessly squandered. Had our
government acted honestly, it would have supported the
Northern states heart and soul in suppressing this fearful
rebellion.

After a detailed defense of the Northern states and the
observation that "Mr. Lovejoy's violent tirade against
England was called forth by the slanders of the English
press," the speaker proposed the following motion:

This meeting resolves that the agents of the rebels, Mason
and Slidell, now on the way from America to England, are
absolutely unworthy of the moral sympathies of the working
class of this country, since they are slaveholders as well as
the confessed agents of the tyrannical faction that is at once
in rebellion against the American republic and the sworn enemy
of the social and political rights of the working class in all
countries.

Mr. Whyune supported the motion. It was, however,
self-understood that every personal insult to Mason and
Slidell must be avoided during their presence in London.

Mr. Nichols, a resident *"of the extreme North* of the
United States," as he announced, who was in fact sent
to the meeting by Messrs. Yancey and Mann as the
*advocatus diaboli,** protested against the motion.

I am here, because here freedom of speech prevails. With
us at home, the government has permitted no man to open his
mouth for three months. Liberty has been crushed not only in
the South, but also in the North. The war has many foes in the
North, but they dare not speak. No less than two hundred
newspapers have been suppressed or destroyed by the mob.
The Southern states have the same right to secede from the
North as the United States had to separate from England.

* Devil's advocate.—*Ed.*

Despite the eloquence of Mr. Nichols, the first motion was carried unanimously. He now sprang up afresh: "If they reproached Messrs. Mason and Slidell with being slaveholders, the same thing would apply to Washington and Jefferson, etc."

Mr. Beale refuted Nichols in a detailed speech and then brought forward a second motion:

In view of the ill-concealed efforts of *The Times* and other misleading journals to represent English public opinion on all American affairs falsely; to embroil it in war with millions of our kinsmen on any pretext whatever, and to take advantage of the momentary perils of the republic to defame democratic institutions, this meeting regards it as the very special duty of the workers, since they are not represented in the Senate of the nation, to declare their sympathy with the United States in their titanic struggle for the maintenance of the Union; to denounce the shameful dishonesty and advocacy of slaveholding on the part of *The Times* and kindred aristocratic journals; to express themselves most emphatically in favor of the strictest policy of non-intervention in affairs of the United States and in favor of the settlement of all matters that may be in dispute by commissioners or arbitration courts nominated by both sides; to denounce the war policy of the organ of the stock exchange swindlers, and to manifest the warmest sympathy with the strivings of the Abolitionists for a final solution of the slave question.

This motion was unanimously adopted, as well as the final motion "to forward to the American government *per medium* of Mr. Adams a copy of the resolutions framed, as an expression of the feelings and opinions of the working class of England."

Die Presse, February 2, 1862.

18.

ANTI-INTERVENTION FEELING

London, January 31, 1862.

LIVERPOOL's commercial greatness derives its origin from the *slave trade*. The sole contributions with which Liverpool has enriched the poetic literature of England are odes to the slave trade. Fifty years ago Wilberforce could set foot on Liverpool soil only at the risk of his life. As in the preceding century the slave trade, so in the present century the trade in the product of slavery—cotton—formed the material basis of Liverpool's greatness. No wonder, therefore, that Liverpool is the center of the English friends of secession. It is in fact the *sole* city in the United Kingdom where during the recent crisis it was possible to organize a quasi-public meeting in favor of a war with the United States. And what does Liverpool say now? Let us hearken to one of its great daily organs, the *Daily Post*.

In a leading article entitled "The Cute Yankees" it is stated among other things:

The Yankees, with their usual adroitness, contrived to convert a loss into a gain. In point of fact they have so managed affairs as to make England subservient to their advantage....
Great Britain has the advantage of displaying her power ...
(but to what end?) The Yankees were always in favor of the unlimited privilege of neutrals, but Great Britain was opposed to it (this privilege was contested to the limit during the Anti-Jacobin War, the Anglo-American War of 1812 to 1814, and again, more recently, in 1842, during the negotiations between Lord Ashburton and the Secretary of State, Daniel Webster).
Now our opposition must cease. *The Yankee principle is virtually recognized.* Mr. Seward establishes the fact ... (declares that England has given way in principle and that through the *Trent* case the United States have obtained a con-

cession to secure which they had hitherto exhausted every means of diplomacy and of war in vain).

More important still is the *Daily Post's* admission of the revulsion in public feeling, even in Liverpool.

The Confederates—it says—have certainly done nothing to forfeit the good opinion entertained of them. Quite the contrary. They have fought manfully and made dreadful sacrifices. If they do not obtain their independence every one must admit that they deserve it.... Public opinion, however, has now run counter to their claims. They are no longer the fine fellows they were six months ago. They are pronounced by implication to be a very sorry set.
...A reaction has in fact set in. The anti-slavery people, who, to use a vulgarism, shrunk in their shoes in the presence of popular excitement, now come forth to thunder big words against man-selling and the slave-owners of the Southern states.... The walls of the town were yesterday posted with a great placard full of denunciation and angry invective, and a London evening paper, the *Sun*, remembered *something to Mr. Mason's disadvantage* ... "the author of the accursed Fugitive Slave Law ..." The Confederates have lost by the *Trent* affair. It was to be their gain; it has turned out to be their ruin. The sympathy of this country will be withdrawn from them and they will have to realize as soon as possible their peculiar situation. They have been very ill-used but they will have no redress.*

After this admission by such a friend of secession as the Liverpool daily paper it is easy to explain the altered language that some important organs of Palmerston now suddenly make use of before the opening of Parliament. Thus *The Economist* of last Saturday has an article entitled, "Shall the Blockade be Respected?"

It proceeds in the first place from the *axiom* that the blockade is a mere *paper blockade* and that its violation is therefore permitted by international law. France demanded the blockade's forcible removal. The practical

* *Liverpool Daily Post,* January 13, 1862.—*Ed.*

decision of the question lay accordingly in the hands of England, who had a great and pressing motive for such a step. In particular she was in need of American cotton. One may remark incidentally that it is not quite clear how a "mere paper blockade" can prevent the shipping of cotton.

"But nevertheless," cries *The Economist, "England must respect* the blockade." Having motivated this judgment with a series of sophisms, it finally comes to the gist of the matter.

It would be undesirable in a case of this kind—it says—for our government to take any steps or to enter any course of action in which they would not carry the whole country cordially and spontaneously with them. ... Now we doubt whether the great body of the British people are yet *prepared* for any interposition which would *even have the semblance* of siding with, or aiding the establishment of, a slave republic. The social system of the Confederate states is based on slavery; the Federalists have done what they could ... to persuade us that slavery lay at the root of the Secession movement, and that they, the Federalists, were hostile to slavery;—and slavery is our especial horror and detestation. ...

But the real error of the popular movement is here:— ... it is the *Restoration* and not the *Dissolution* of the Union that would be the consolidation and perpetuation of Negro servitude, and that it is in the independence of the South and not in her defeat, that we can alone look with confidence for the early amelioration and ultimate extinction of the slavery we abhor. ... We hope soon to make this clear to our readers. But *it is not clear yet. The majority of Englishmen still think otherwise;* and as long as they do, any intervention on the part of our government which should place us in a position of actual opposition to the North, and inferential alliance with the South, would scarcely be supported by the hearty coöperation of the British nation.*

In other words: the attempt at such intervention would cause the downfall of the ministry. And this also ex-

* *The Economist,* January 25, 1862.—*Ed.*

plains why *The Times* pronounces itself so decidedly against any intervention and for England's neutrality.

Die Presse, February 4, 1862.

19.

ON THE COTTON CRISIS

SOME days ago the annual meeting of the Chamber of Commerce of Manchester took place. It represents Lancashire, the greatest industrial district of the United Kingdom and the chief seat of British cotton manufacture. The chairman of the meeting, Mr. C. Potter, and the principal speakers at it, Messrs. Bazley and Turner, represent Manchester and a part of Lancashire in the Lower House. From the proceedings of the meeting, therefore, we learn *officially* what attitude the great center of English cotton industry will adopt in the "Senate of the nation" in face of the American crisis.

At the meeting of the Chamber of Commerce *last year* Mr. Ashworth, one of England's biggest cotton barons, had celebrated with Pindaric extravagance the unexampled expansion of the cotton industry during the last decade. In particular he stressed the point that even the commercial crises of 1847 and 1857 had produced no falling off in the export of English cotton yarns and textile fabrics. He explained the phenomenon by the wonder-working powers of the free trade system introduced in 1846. Even then it sounded strange that this system, though unable to spare England the crises of 1847 and 1857, should be able to withdraw a *particular* branch of English industry from the influence of those crises. But what do we hear today? All the speakers, Mr. Ashworth included, confess that since 1858 an unprecedented glutting of the Atlantic markets has taken place and that in consequence of steadily continuing *overproduction* on a mass scale the present stagnation *was bound* to occur, even without the American Civil War, the Morrill tariff and the blockade. Whether without these aggravating circumstances the falling off in last year's exports would have been as much as £6,000,000, naturally remains an open question, but does not appear improbable when we hear that the principal markets of Asia and Australia are stocked with sufficient English cotton manufactures for twelve months.

Thus, according to the confession of the Manchester Chamber of Commerce, which in *this* matter speaks with authority, the crisis in the English cotton industry has so far been the result not of the American blockade, but of English overproduction. But what would be the consequences of a continuation of the American Civil War? To this question we again receive an unanimous answer: Measureless suffering for the working class and ruin for the smaller manufacturers. "It is said in London," observed Mr. Cheatham, "that they have still plenty of cotton to go on with; but it is not a question of cotton; but it is a question of *price,* and at present prices the capital of the millowners is being destroyed."

The Chamber of Commerce, however, declares itself to be decidedly *against any intervention* in the United States, although most of its members are sufficiently swayed by *The Times* to consider the dissolution of the Union to be unavoidable.

The last thing—says Mr. Potter—that we should do is to recommend, anything like intervention. The last place where such a thing could be entertained, was Manchester. Nothing would tempt them to recommend something which is morally wrong.

Mr. Bazley: The American quarrel must be left to the principle of non-intervention. The people of that vast country
must really settle their own affairs.

Mr. Cheatham: The leading opinion in this district is wholly
opposed to intervention in the American dispute. It is necessary to make a clear pronouncement on this, because strong
pressure would be put upon the Government if there was any
doubt of it.

What, then, does the Chamber of Commerce recommend? The English government ought to remove all the
obstacles of an administrative character that still im-
pede cotton imports into India. In particular, it ought
to lift the import duty of 10 per cent with which English
cotton yarns and textile fabrics are burdened in India.
The régime of the East India Company had hardly been
done away with, India had hardly been incorporated in
the British Empire,[90] when Palmerston introduced this
import duty on English manufactures through Mr. Wil-
son, and that at the same time as he sold Savoy and
Nice for the Anglo-French commercial treaty.[91] Whilst
the French market was opened to English industry to a
certain extent, the East Indian market was closed to it
to a greater extent.

With reference to the above, Mr. Bazley remarked that
since the introduction of this tax great quantities of English machinery had been exported to Calcutta and Bombay and factories had been erected there in the English
style. These were preparing to snatch the best Indian
cotton from them. If 15 per cent for freight were added
to the 10 per cent import duty, the rivals artificially
called into being through the initiative of the English
government enjoyed a protective duty of 25 per cent.

In general, bitter resentment was expressed at the
meeting of magnates of English industry at the protectionist tendency that was developing more and more in

the colonies, in Australia in particular. The gentlemen forget that for a century and a half the colonies protested in vain against the "colonial system" of the motherland. At that time the colonies demanded free trade. England insisted on prohibition. Now England preaches free trade, and the colonies find protection against England better suited to their interests.

Die Presse, February 8, 1862.

20.

THE PARLIAMENTARY DEBATE ON THE ADDRESS

London, February 7, 1862.

THE opening of Parliament was a lusterless ceremony. The absence of the Queen and the reading of the Speech from the Throne by the Lord Chancellor banished every theatrical effect. The Speech from the Throne itself is short without being striking. It recapitulates the *faits accomplis* * of foreign politics and, for an estimation of these facts, refers to the documents submitted to Parliament. Only one phrase created a certain sensation, the phrase in which the Queen "trusts there is no reason to apprehend any disturbance of the peace of Europe." This phrase in fact implies that European peace is relegated to the domain of hope and faith.

In accordance with parliamentary practice, the gentlemen who moved the Reply to the Speech from the Throne in the two Houses had already been commissioned by the ministers with this business three weeks ago. In conformity with the usual procedure, their Reply consists of a broad echo of the Speech from the Throne and of

* Accomplished facts.—*Ed.*

fulsome praises that the ministers bestow upon themselves in the name of Parliament. When Sir Francis Burdett anticipated the official movers of the Address in 1811 and seized the opportunity to subject the Speech from the Throne to a cutting criticism, Magna Charta itself appeared to be imperiled. Since that time no further enormity of the kind has happened.

The interest of the debate on the Speech from the Throne is therefore limited to the "hints" of the official Opposition club and the "counter-hints" of the ministers. This time, however, the interest was more academic than political. It was a question of the best funeral oration on Prince Albert, who during his life found the yoke of the English oligarchy by no means light. According to the *vox populi*,* Derby and Disraeli have borne off the academic palm, the first as a natural speaker, the other as a rhetorician.

The "business" part of the debate turned on the United States, Mexico, and Morocco.

With regard to the United States, the *Outs* (those out of office) eulogized the policy of the *Ins* (the *meati possidentes* **). Derby, the Conservative leader in the House of Lords, and Disraeli, the Conservative leader in the Lower House, opposed not the Cabinet, but each other.

Derby in the first place gave vent to his dissatisfaction over the absence of *"pressure from without."* He "admired," he said, the stoical and dignified bearing of the factory workers. As far as the mill owners were concerned, however he must exclude them from his commendation. For them the American disturbance had come in extraordinarily handy, since overproduction and glutting of all markets had in any case imposed on them a restriction of trade.

* Voice of the people.—*Ed.*
** Blessed possessors.—*Ed.*

Derby went on to make a violent attack on the Union government, "which had exposed itself and its people to the most undignified humiliation" and had not acted like "gentlemen," because it had not taken the initiative and voluntarily surrendered Mason, Slidell and company and made amends. His seconder in the Lower House, Mr. Disraeli, at once grasped how very damaging Derby's onslaught was to the hopes of the Conservatives. He therefore declared to the contrary: "When I consider the great difficulties which the statesmen of North America have to encounter...I would venture to say that they have met these manfully and courageously."

On the other hand—with the consistency customary to him—Derby protested against the "new doctrines" of maritime law. England had at all times upheld belligerent rights against the pretensions of neutrals. Lord Clarendon, it was true, had made a dangerous concession at Paris in 1856. Happily, this had not yet been ratified by the Crown, so that "it did not change the position of international law." Mr. Disraeli, on the contrary, manifestly in collusion with the ministry here, avoided touching on this point at all.

Derby approved of the non-intervention policy of the ministry. The time to recognize the Southern Confederacy has not *yet* come, but he demands authentic documents for the purpose of judging "how far the blockade is bona fide and effective and...whether the blockade has been such a one as ought to be recognized and respected by the law of nations." Lord John Russell, on the other hand, declared that the Union government had employed a sufficient number of ships in the blockade, but had not everywhere carried this out consistently. Mr. Disraeli will permit himself no judgment on the nature of the blockade, but demands ministerial papers for enlightenment. He gives such emphatic warning against any premature recognition of the Confederacy since England is compromising herself at the present moment by threatening an American state (Mexico), the independence of which she herself was the first to recognize.

After the United States, it was Mexico's turn. No member of Parliament condemned a war without declaration of war, but they condemned interference in the internal relations of a country under the shibboleth of a "non-intervention policy," and the coalition of England with France and Spain in order to intimidate a semi-defenseless land. As a matter of fact, the *Outs* merely indicated that they reserve Mexico to themselves for party maneuvers. Derby demands documents on both the Convention between the three powers and the mode of carrying it out. He approves of the Convention *because*—in his view—the right way was for each of the contracting parties to enforce its claims *independently* of the others. Certain public rumors caused him to fear that at least one of the powers—Spain—purposed operations verging on betrayal. As if Derby really believed the great power, Spain, capable of the audacity of acting *counter* to the will of England and France! Lord John Russell answered: The three powers pursued *the same* aim and would anxiously avoid hindering the Mexicans from regulating their own affairs.

In the Lower House, Mr. Disraeli defers any judgment prior to scrutinizing the documents submitted. However, he finds "the announcement of the government *suspicious*." The independence of Mexico was first recognized by England. This recognition recalls a notable policy—the anti-Holy-Alliance policy—and a notable man, Canning. What singular occasion, then, drove England to strike the first blow against this independence? Moreover, the intervention has changed its pretext within a very short time. Originally it was a question of satisfaction for

wrong done to English subjects. Now there are whispers
concerning the introduction of new governmental principles and the setting up of a new dynasty. Lord Palmerston refers members to the papers submitted and to the
Convention that prohibits the "subjugation" of Mexico
by the Allies or the imposition of a form of government
distasteful to the people. At the same time, however, he
discloses a secret diplomatic corner. He has it from hearsay that a party in Mexico desires the transformation of
the republic into a monarchy. The strength of this party
he does not know. He, "for his part, only desires that
some form of government be set up in Mexico with which
foreign governments may treat." He declares the *non-
existence of the present government*. He claims for the
alliance of England, France and Spain the prerogative of
the Holy Alliance to decide over the existence or non-
existence of foreign governments. "That is the utmost,"
he adds modestly, "which the government of Great
Britain is desirous of obtaining." Nothing more!

The last "open question" of foreign policy concerned
Morocco. The English government has concluded a convention with Morocco in order to enable her to pay off
her debt to Spain, a debt with which Spain could never
have saddled Morocco without England's leave. Certain
persons, it appears, have advanced Morocco money with
which to pay her installments to Spain, thus depriving
the latter of a pretext for further occupation of Tetuan
and renewal of war.[92] The English government has in
one way or another guaranteed these persons the interest
on their loan and, in its turn, takes over the administration of Morocco's customs houses as security.

Derby found this manner of ensuring the independence
of Morocco *"rather strange,"* but elicited no answer from
the ministers. In the Lower House Mr. Disraeli went into
the transaction further: it was "to some extent uncon-

stitutional," since the ministry had saddled England with
new financial obligations behind Parliament's back.
Palmerston simply referred him to the "documents" submitted.

Home affairs were hardly mentioned. Derby merely
warned members, out of regard "for the state of mind of
the Queen," not to raise "disturbing" controversial questions like parliamentary reform. He is ready to pay his
tribute of admiration regularly to the English working
class, on condition that it suffers its exclusion from popular representation with the same stoicism as it suffers the
American blockade.

It would be a mistake to infer from the idyllic opening
of Parliament an idyllic future. Quite the contrary! Dissolution of Parliament or dissolution of the ministry is
the motto of this year's session. Opportunity to substan-
tiate these alternatives will be found later.

Die Presse, February 12, 1862.

21.

AMERICAN AFFAIRS

PRESIDENT LINCOLN never ventures a step forward before the tide of circumstances and the call of general public opinion forbids further delay. But once "old Abe" has
convinced himself that such a turning-point has been
reached, he then surprises friend and foe alike by a sudden operation executed as noiselessly as possible. Thus, in
the most unassuming manner, he has quite recently carried out a coup that half a year earlier would possibly
have cost him his presidential office and even a few
months ago would have called forth a storm of debate.
We mean the *removal of McClellan* from his post of

Commander-in-Chief of all the Union armies. Lincoln first of all replaces the Secretary of War, Cameron,[93] by an energetic and ruthless lawyer, Mr. Edwin Stanton. To Generals Buell, Halleck, Butler, Sherman and other commanders of whole departments or leaders of expeditions, Stanton then issued an order of the day in which they were notified that in future they would take all orders, open and secret, from the War Department direct and, on the other hand, would have to report directly to the War Department. Finally, Lincoln issued some orders in which he signed himself "Commander-in-Chief of the Army and Navy," an attribute constitutionally pertaining to him. In this "quiet" manner "the young Napoleon" was deprived of the supreme command he had hitherto held over all the armies and restricted to the command of the army on the Potomac,[94] although the *title* of "Commander-in-Chief" was left to him. The successes in Kentucky, Tennessee and on the Atlantic coast have propitiously inaugurated the assumption of the supreme command by President Lincoln.

The post of Commander-in-Chief hitherto occupied by McClellan has been bequeathed to the United States by England and corresponds approximately to the dignity of a Grand Connetable * in the old French army. During the Crimean War even England discovered the inexpediency of this old-fashioned institution. A compromise was accordingly effected by which part of the attributes hitherto pertaining to the Commander-in-Chief were transferred to the Secretary of War.

The requisite material for an estimate of McClellan's Fabian ** tactics on the Potomac is still lacking. That his influence, however, acted as a brake on the general con-

* Grand Constable.—*Ed.*
** Used to designate a policy like that of Quintus Fabius Maximus Verrucosus (d. 203 B.C.) who avoided direct engagements with Hannibal during the Second Punic War.—*Ed.*

duct of the war, is beyond doubt. One can say of McClellan what Macaulay says of Essex: "The military mistakes of Essex sprang for the most part from political compunction. He was honestly, but by no means warmly attached to the cause of Parliament, and next to a great defeat he feared nothing so much as a great victory." McClellan and most of the officers of the regular army who got their training at West Point are more or less bound to their old comrades in the enemy camp by the ties of *esprit de corps.** They are inspired by like jealousy of the *parvenus*** among the "civilian soldiers." In their view, the war must be waged in a strictly businesslike fashion, with constant regard to the restoration of the Union on its *old* basis, and therefore must above all be kept free from revolutionary tendencies affecting matters of principle. A fine conception of a war that is essentially a war of principles! The first generals of the English Parliament fell into the same error. "But," says Cromwell, "how changed everything was as soon as men took the lead who professed *a principle of godliness and religion!*"

The *Washington Star,* McClellan's special organ, declares in one of its latest issues: "The aim of all General McClellan's military combinations is to restore the Union *completely,* exactly as it existed before the outbreak of the rebellion." No wonder, therefore, if on the Potomac, under the eyes of the supreme general, the army was trained to catch slaves! Only recently, by special *ordre,* McClellan expelled the Hutchinson family of musicians from the camp because they—sang anti-slavery songs.

Apart from such "anti-tendencial" demonstrations, McClellan covered the traitors in the Union Army with his saving shield. Thus, for example, he promoted

* Corps spirit.—*Ed.*
** Upstarts.—*Ed.*

Maynard to a higher post, although Maynard, as the papers made public by the inquiry *comité* * of the House of Representatives prove, worked as the agent of the secessionists. From General Patterson, whose treachery determined the defeat at Manassas, to General Stone, who *effected* the defeat at Ball's Bluff in direct agreement with the enemy, McClellan knew how to keep every military traitor from court martial, and in most cases even from dismissal. The inquiry *comité* of Congress has in this respect revealed the most surprising facts. Lincoln resolved to prove by an energetic step that with his assumption of the supreme command the hour of the traitors in epaulets had struck and a *turning point* in the war policy had been reached. By his order, General Stone was arrested in his bed at two o'clock in the morning of February 10 and transported to Fort Lafayette. A few hours later, the order for his arrest, signed by Stanton, appeared; in this the charge of high treason is formulated, to be judged by a court martial. The arrest and putting of Stone on trial took place without any previous communication to General McClellan.

As long as he himself remained in a state of inaction and wore his laurels merely in advance, McClellan was obviously determined to allow no other general to forestall him. Generals Halleck and Pope had resolved on a combined movement to force General Price, who had already been saved once from Frémont by the intervention of Washington, to a decisive battle. A telegram from McClellan forbade them to deliver the blow. General Halleck was "ordered back" by a similar telegram from the capture of Fort Columbus, at a time when this fort stood half under water. McClellan had expressly forbidden the generals in the West to correspond with one another. Each of these was obliged first to address him-

* Committee.—*Ed.*

AMERICAN AFFAIRS

self to Washington, as soon as a combined movement was intended. President Lincoln has now given them back the necessary freedom of action.

How advantageous to secession McClellan's general military policy was, is best proved by the panegyrics that the *New York Herald* continually lavishes upon him. He is a hero after the *Herald's* own heart. The notorious Bennett, the proprietor and editor-in-chief of the *Herald,* had formerly bossed the administrations of Pierce and Buchanan through his "special representatives," alias correspondents, at Washington. Under Lincoln's administration he sought to win the same power again in a roundabout way, by having his "special representative," Dr. Joes, a man of the South and brother of an officer who had deserted to the Confederacy, worm himself into McClellan's favor. Under McClellan's patronage, great liberties must have been allowed this Joes at the time when Cameron was at the head of the War Department. He evidently expected Stanton to guarantee him the same privileges and accordingly presented himself on February 8 at the War Office, where the Secretary of War, his chief secretary and some members of Congress were just taking counsel concerning war measures. He was shown the door. He got up on his hind legs and finally beat a retreat, threatening that the *Herald* would open fire on the present War Department in the event of its withholding from him his "special privilege" of having, in particular, Cabinet deliberations, telegrams, public communications and war news confided to him in the War Department. Next morning, February 9, Dr. Joes had assembled the whole of McClellan's General Staff at a champagne breakfast with him. Misfortune, however, moves fast. A non-commissioned officer entered with six men, seized the mighty Joes and brought him to Fort

McHenry, where, as the *ordre* of the Secretary of War expressly states, he is to be kept under strict watch *as a spy.*

Die Presse, March 3, 1862.

22.

THE SECESSIONISTS' FRIENDS IN THE LOWER HOUSE

RECOGNITION OF THE AMERICAN BLOCKADE

London, March 8, 1862.

Parturiunt montes! * Since the opening of Parliament the English friends of *Secessia* had threatened a "motion" on the American blockade. The resolution has at length been introduced in the Lower House in the very modest form of a motion in which the government is urged "to submit further documents on the state of the blockade"— and even this insignificant motion was rejected without the formality of a division.

Mr. Gregory, the member for Galway, who moved the resolution, had in the parliamentary session of last year, shortly after the outbreak of the Civil War, already introduced a motion for recognition of the Southern Confederacy. To his speech of this year a certain sophistical adroitness is not to be denied. The speech merely suffers from the unfortunate circumstances that it falls into two parts, of which the one cancels the other. One part describes the disastrous effects of the blockade on the English cotton industry and *therefore* demands removal of the blockade. The other part proves from the papers submitted by the ministry, two memorials by Messrs.

* The mountains are in labor.—*Ed.*

Yancey and Mann and by Mr. Mason among them, that the blockade does not *exist* at all, except on paper, and *therefore* should no longer be recognized.[95] Mr. Gregory spiced his argument with successive citations from *The Times*. *The Times*, for whom a reminder of its oracular pronouncements is at this moment thoroughly inconvenient, thanks Mr. Gregory with a *leader* in which it holds him up to public ridicule. Mr. Gregory's motion was supported by Mr. Bentinck, an ultra-Tory who for two years has labored in vain to bring about a secession from Mr. Disraeli in the Conservative camp.

It was a ludicrous spectacle in and by itself to see the alleged interests of English industry represented by Gregory, the representative of Galway, an unimportant seaport in the West of Ireland, and by Bentinck, the representative of Norfolk, a purely agricultural district.

Mr. Forster, the representative of Bradford, a center of English industry, rose to oppose them both. Forster's speech deserves closer examination, since it strikingly proves the unreality of the phrases concerning the character of the American blockade given currency in Europe by the friends of secession. In the first place, he said, the United States have observed all formalities required by international law. They have declared no port in a state of blockade without previous proclamation, without special notice of the moment of its commencement or without fixing the fifteen days after the expiration of which entrance and departure shall be forbidden to foreign neutral ships.

The talk of the legal "inefficacy" of the blockade rests, therefore, merely on the allegedly frequent cases in which it has been broken through. Before the opening of Parliament it was said that 600 ships had broken through it. Mr. Gregory now reduces the number to 400. His evidence rests on two lists handed the government, the one on November 30 by the Southern commissioners Yancey and Mann, the other, the supplementary list, by Mason. According to Yancey and Mann, more than 400 ships broke through between the proclamation of the blockade and August 20, running the blockade either inwards or outwards. According to customs-house reports, however, the total number of the incoming and outgoing ships amounts to only 322. Of this number, 119 departed *before* the declaration of the blockade, 56 *before* the expiration of the time allowance of fifteen days. There remain 147 ships. Of these 147 ships, 25 were river boats that sailed from inland to New Orleans, where they lay idle; 106 were coastal vessels; with the exception of three ships, all were, in the words of Mr. Mason himself, "quasi-inland" vessels.[96] Of these 106, 66 sailed between Mobile and New Orleans.

Any one who knows this coast knows how absurd it is to call the sailing of a vessel behind lagoons, so that it hardly touches the open sea and merely creeps along the coast, a breach of the blockade. The same holds of the vessels between Savannah and Charleston, where they sneak between islands in narrow tongues of land. According to the testimony of the English consul, Bunch, these flat-bottomed boats only appeared for a few days on the open sea. After deducting 106 coastal vessels, there remain 16 departures for foreign ports; of these, 15 were for American ports, mainly Cuba, and one for Liverpool. The "ship" that berthed in Liverpool was a schooner, and so were all the rest of the "ships," with the exception of a sloop. There has been much talk, exclaimed Mr. Forster, of sham blockades. Is this list of Messrs. Yancey and Mann not a sham list? He subjected the supplementary list of Mr. Mason to a similar analysis, and showed further that the number of cruisers that slipped out only amounted to three or four, whereas in the last Anglo-

American war no less than 516 American cruisers broke through the English blockade and harried the English seaboard. "The blockade, on the contrary, had been wonderfully effective from its commencement."

Further proof is provided by the reports of the English consuls; above all, however, by the Southern price lists. On January 11 the price of cotton in New Orleans offered a premium of 100 per cent for export to England; the profit on import of salt amounted to 1500 per cent and the profit on contraband of war was incomparably higher. Despite this alluring prospect of profit, it was just as impossible to ship cotton to England as salt to New Orleans or Charleston. "In fact, however, Mr. Gregory does not complain that the blockade was inefficacious, but that it was too efficacious. He urges us to put an end to it and with it to the crippling of industry and commerce. One answer suffices: Who urges this House to break the blockade? The representatives of the suffering districts? Does this cry resound from Manchester, where the factories have to close, or from Liverpool, where from lack of freight the ships lie idle in the docks? On the contrary. It resounds from Galway and is supported by Norfolk."

On the side of the friends of secession Mr. Lindsay, a large shipbuilder of North Shields, made himself conspicuous. Lindsay had offered his shipyards to the Union, and, for this purpose, had traveled to Washington, where he experienced the vexation of seeing his business propositions rejected. Since that time he has turned his sympathies to the land of *Secessia*.

The debate was concluded with a circumstantial speech by Sir R. Palmer, the Solicitor-General, who spoke in the name of the government. He furnished well grounded juridical proof of the strength and sufficiency of the blockade in international law. On this occasion he in fact tore to pieces—and was taxed with so doing by Lord Cecil

—the "new principles" proclaimed at the Paris Convention of 1856. Among other things, he expressed his astonishment that in a British Parliament Gregory and his associates ventured to appeal to the authority of Monsieur de Hautefeuille. The latter, to be sure, is a brand-newly discovered "authority" in the Bonapartist camp. Hautefeuille's compositions in the *Revue Contemporaine* on the maritime rights of neutrals prove the completest ignorance or *mauvaise foi* * at higher command.

With the complete fiasco of the parliamentary friends of secession in the blockade question, all prospect of a breach between England and the United Sates is eliminated.

Die Presse, March 12, 1862.

23.

THE AMERICAN CIVIL WAR [I]

FROM whatever standpoint one regards it, the American Civil War presents a spectacle without parallel in the annals of military history. The vast extent of the disputed territory; the far-flung front of the lines of operation; the numerical strength of the hostile armies, the creation of which drew barely any support from a prior organizational basis; the fabulous costs of these armies; the manner of leading them and the general tactical and strategical principles in accordance with which the war is waged, are all new in the eyes of the European onlooker.

The secessionist conspiracy, organized, patronized and supported long before its outbreak by Buchanan's administration, gave the South an advantage, by which alone it

* Bad faith.—*Ed.*

could hope to achieve its aim. Endangered by its slave population [97] and by a strong Unionist element among the whites themselves, with a number of free men two-thirds smaller than the North, but readier to attack, thanks to the multitude of adventurous idlers that it harbors—for the South everything depended on a swift, bold, almost foolhardy offensive. If the Southerners succeeded in taking St. Louis, Cincinnati, Washington, Baltimore and perhaps Philadelphia, they might then count on a panic, during which diplomacy and bribery could secure recognition of the independence of all the slave states. If this first onslaught failed, at least at the decisive points, their position must then become daily worse, simultaneously with the development of the strength of the North. This point was rightly understood by the men who in truly Bonapartist spirit had organized the secessionist conspiracy. They opened the campaign in corresponding manner. Their bands of adventurers overran Missouri and Tennessee, while their more regular troops invaded east Virginia and prepared a *coup de main* against Washington. With the miscarriage of this coup, the Southern campaign was, from the *military standpoint,* lost.

The North came to the theater of war reluctantly, sleepily, as was to be expected with its higher industrial and commercial development. The social machinery was here far more complicated than in the South, and it required far more time to give its motion this unwonted direction. The enlistment of the volunteers for three months was a great, but perhaps unavoidable mistake. It was the policy of the North to remain on the defensive in the beginning at all decisive points, to organize its forces, to train them through operations on a small scale and without the risk of decisive battles, and as soon as the organization was sufficiently strengthened and the traitorous element simultaneously more or less removed from the army, to pass finally to an energetic, unflagging offensive and, above all, to reconquer Kentucky, Tennessee, Virginia and North Carolina. The transformation of the civilians into soldiers was bound to take more time in the North than in the South. Once effected, one could count on the individual superiority of the Northern man.

By and large, and allowing for mistakes which sprang more from political than from military sources, the North acted in accordance with those principles. The guerrilla warfare in Missouri and West Virginia, while it protected the Unionist populations, accustomed the troops to field service and to fire, without exposing them to decisive defeats. The great disgrace of Bull Run was to some extent the result of the earlier error of enlisting volunteers for three months. It was senseless to allow a strong position, on difficult terrain and in possession of a foe little inferior in numbers, to be attacked by raw recruits in the front ranks. The panic which took possession of the Union army at the decisive moment, the cause of which has still not been clarified, could surprise no one who was in some degree familiar with the history of peoples' wars. Such things happened to the French troops very often from 1792 to 1795; they did not, however, prevent these same troops from winning the battles of Jemappes and Fleurus, Moutenotte, Castiglione and Rivoli. The jests of the European press over the Bull Run panic had only one excuse for their silliness—the previous bragging of a section of the North American press.

The six months' respite that followed the defeat of Manassas was utilized by the North better than by the South. Not only were the Northern ranks recruited in greater measure than the Southern. Their officers received better instructions; the discipline and training of the troops did not encounter the same obstacles as in the

South. Traitors and incompetent interlopers were more and more removed, and the period of the Bull Run panic already belongs to the past. The armies on both sides are naturally not to be measured by the standard of great European armies or even of the former regular army of the United States. Napoleon could in fact drill battalions of raw recruits in the depots during the first month, have them on the march during the second and during the third lead them against the foe; but then every battalion received a sufficient stiffening of officers and non-commissioned officers, every company some old soldiers and on the day of the battle the new troops were brigaded together with veterans and, so to speak, framed by the latter. All these conditions were lacking in America. Without the considerable mass of military experience that emigrated to America in consequence of the European revolutionary commotions of 1848-1849, the organization of the Union Army would have required a much longer time still.[98] The very small number of the killed and wounded in proportion to the sum total of the troops engaged (customarily one in twenty) proves that most of the engagements, even the latest in Kentucky and Tennessee, were fought mainly with firearms at fairly long range, and that the incidental bayonet charges either soon halted before the enemy's fire or put the foe to flight before it came to a hand-to-hand encounter. Meanwhile, the new campaign has been opened under more favorable auspices with the advance of Buell and Halleck through Kentucky to Tennessee. After the reconquest of Missouri and West Virginia, the Union opened the campaign with the advance into Kentucky.[99] Here the secessionists held three strong positions, fortified camps: Columbus on the Mississippi to their left, Bowling Green in the center, Mill Spring on the Cumberland River to the right. Their line stretched three hundred miles from west to east. The extension of this line denied the three corps the possibility of affording each other mutual support and offered the Union troops the chance of attacking each individually with superior forces. The great mistake in the disposition of the Secessionists sprang from the attempt to hold all they had occupied. A single, fortified, strong central camp, chosen as the battlefield for a decisive engagement and held by the main body of the army, would have defended Kentucky far more effectively. It must either have attracted the main force of the Unionists or put the latter in a dangerous position should they attempt to march on without regard to so strong a concentration of troops.

Under the given circumstances the Unionists resolved to attack those three camps one after another, to maneuver their enemy out of them and force him to accept battle in open country. This plan, which conformed to all the rules of the art of war, was carried out with energy and dispatch. Towards the middle of January a corps of about 15,000 Unionists marched on Mill Spring, which was held by 20,000 Secessionists.[100] The Unionists maneuvered in a manner that led the enemy to believe he had to deal only with a weak reconnoitering corps. General Zollicoffer fell forthwith into the trap, sallied from his fortified camp and attacked the Unionists. He soon convinced himself that a superior force confronted him. He fell and his troops suffered a complete defeat, like the Unionists at Bull Run. This time, however, the victory was exploited in quite other fashion.

The stricken army was hard pressed until it arrived broken, demoralized, without field artillery or baggage, in its encampment at Mill Spring. This camp was pitched on the northern bank at the Cumberland River, so that in the event of another defeat the troops had no retreat open to them save across the river by way of a few steamers and river boats. We find in general that almost all the Secessionist camps were pitched on the *enemy* side of the stream. To take up such a position is not only according to rule, but also very practical if there is a bridge in the rear. In such case the encampment serves as the bridge head and gives its holders the chance of throwing their fighting forces at pleasure on both banks of the stream and so maintaining complete command of these banks. Without a bridge in the rear, on the contrary, a camp on the enemy side of the stream cuts off the retreat after an unlucky engagement and compels the troops to capitulate, or exposes them to massacre and drowning, a fate that befell the Unionists at Ball's Bluff on the enemy side of the Potomac, whither the treachery of General Stone had sent them.

When the beaten Secessionists had pitched their camp at Mill Spring, they had at once understood that an attack by the enemy on their fortifications must be repulsed or in a very short time capitulation must follow. After the experience of the morning they had lost confidence in their powers of resistance. Accordingly, when next day the Unionists advanced to attack the camp, they found that the foe had taken advantage of the night to put across the stream, leaving the camp, the baggage, the artillery and stores behind him. In this way the extreme right of the Secessionist line was pushed back to Tennessee, and east Kentucky, where the mass of the population is hostile to the slaveholders' party, was reconquered for the Union.

At the same time—towards the middle of January— the preparations for dislodging the Secessionists from Columbus and Bowling Green commenced. A strong flotilla of mortar vessels and ironclad gunboats was held in readiness, and the news was spread in all directions that it was to serve as a convoy to a large army marching along the Mississippi from Cairo to Memphis and New Orleans. All the demonstrations on the Mississippi, however, were merely mock maneuvers. At the decisive moment the gunboats were brought to the Ohio and thence to the Tennessee, up which they traveled as far as Fort Henry. This place, together with Fort Donelson on the Cumberland River, formed the second line of defense of the Secessionists in Tennessee. The position was well chosen, for in case of a retreat behind the Cumberland the latter stream would have covered its front, the Tennessee its left flank, while the narrow strip of land between the two streams was sufficiently covered by the two forts above-mentioned. The swift action of the Unionists, however, broke through the line itself before the left wing and the center of the first line were attacked.

In the first week of February the gunboats of the Unionists appeared before Fort Henry, which surrendered after a short bombardment. The garrison escaped to Fort Donelson, since the land forces of the expedition were not strong enough to encircle the place. The gunboats now traveled down the Tennessee again, upstream to the Ohio and thence up the Cumberland as far as Fort Donelson. A single gunboat sailed boldly up the Tennessee through the very heart of the State of Tennessee, skirting the State of Mississippi and pushing on as far as Florence in North Alabama, where a series of swamps and banks (known by the name of the Muscle Shoals) forbade further navigation. This fact, that a single gunboat made this long voyage of at least 150 miles and then returned, without experiencing any kind of attack, proves that Union sentiment prevails along the river and will be very useful to the Union troops should they push forward so far.

The boat expedition up the Cumberland now combined its movements with those of the land forces under Generals Halleck and Grant. The Secessionists at Bowling Green were deceived over the movements of the Unionists. They accordingly remained quietly in their camp, while a week after the fall of Fort Henry, Fort Donelson was surrounded on the land side by 40,000 Unionists and threatened on the river side by a strong flotilla of gunboats. Like the camp at Mill Spring and Fort Henry, Fort Donelson had the river lying in the rear, without a bridge for retreat. It was the strongest place the Unionists had attacked up to the present. The works were carried out with the greatest care: moreover the place was capacious enough to accommodate the 20,000 men who occupied it. On the first day of the attack the gunboats silenced the fire of the batteries trained towards the river side and bombarded the interior of the defense works, while the land troops drove back the enemy outposts and forced the main body of the Secessionists to seek shelter right under the guns of their own defense works. On the second day the gunboats, which had suffered severely the day before, appear to have accomplished but little. The land troops, on the contrary, had to fight a long and, in places, hot encounter with the columns of the garrison, which sought to break through the right wing of the enemy in order to secure their line of retreat to Nashville. However, an energetic attack of the Unionist right wing on the left wing of the Secessionists and considerable reenforcements that the left wing of the Unionists received, decided the victory in favor of the assailants. Divers outworks had been stormed. The garrison, forced into its inner lines of defense, without the chance of retreat and manifestly not in a position to withstand an assault next morning, surrendered unconditionally on the following day.

Die Presse, March 26, 1862.

24.

THE AMERICAN CIVIL WAR [II] *

WITH Fort Donelson the enemy's artillery, baggage and military stores fell into the hands of the Unionists; 13,000 Secessionists surrendered on the day of its capture; 1,000 more the next day, and as soon as the outposts of the victors appeared before Clarksville, a town that lies further up the Cumberland River, it opened its gates. Here, too, considerable supplies for the Secessionists had been stored.

The capture of Fort Donelson presents only one riddle: the flight of General Floyd with 5,000 men on the second day of the bombardment. These fugitives were too numerous to be smuggled away in steamboats during the night. With some measures of precaution on the part of the assailants, they could not have got away.

Seven days after the surrender of Fort Donelson, Nashville was occupied by the Federals. The distance between the two places amounts to about 100 English miles, and a march of 15 miles a day, on very wretched roads and during the most unfavorable season of the year, redounds to the honor of the Unionist troops. On receipt of the news of the fall of Fort Donelson, the Secessionists evacuated Bowling Green; a week later they abandoned Columbus and withdrew to a Mississippi island, 45 miles south. Thus Kentucky was completely reconquered for the Union. Tennessee, however, can be held by the Secessionists only if they invite and win a big battle. They are said in fact to have concentrated 65,000 men for this purpose. Meanwhile, nothing prevents the Unionists from bringing a superior force against them.

The leadership of the Kentucky campaign from Somer-

* Conclusion of yesterday's feuilleton.—*Ed., Die Presse.*

set to Nashville deserves the highest praise. The reconquest of so extensive a territory, the advance from the
Ohio to the Cumberland during a single month, evidence
an energy, resolution and speed such as have seldom been
attained by regular armies in Europe. One may compare,
for example, the slow advance of the Allies from Magenta
to Solferino in 1859—without pursuit of the retreating
foe, without endeavor to cut off his stragglers or in any
way to envelop and encircle whole bodies of his troops.

Halleck and Grant, in particular, furnish good ex-
amples of resolute military leadership. Without the least
regard either for Columbus or Bowling Green, they concentrate their forces on the decisive points, Fort Henry
and Fort Donelson, launch a swift and energetic attack
on these and precisely thereby render Columbus and
Bowling Green untenable. Then they march at once to
Clarksville and Nashville, without allowing the retreating Secessionists time to take up new positions in north
Tennessee. During this rapid pursuit the corps of Secessionist troops in Columbus remains completely cut off
from the center and right wing of its army. English papers
have criticized this operation unjustly. Even if the attack
on Fort Donelson failed, the Secessionists kept busy by
General Buell at Bowling Green could not dispatch sufficient men to enable the garrison to follow the repulsed
Unionists into the open country or to endanger their
retreat. Columbus, on the other hand, lay so far off that
it could not interfere with Grant's movements at all. In
fact, after the Unionists had cleared Missouri of the
Secessionists, Columbus was for the latter an entirely useless post. The troops that formed its garrison had greatly
to hasten their retreat to Memphis or even to Arkansas
in order to escape the danger of ingloriously laying down
their arms.

In consequence of the clearing of Missouri and the reconquest of Kentucky the theater of war has so far narrowed that the different armies can coöperate to a certain extent along the whole line of operations and work for the achievement of definite results. In other words, the war now takes on for the first time a *strategic* character, and the geographical configuration of the country acquires a new interest. It is now the task of the Northern generals to find the Achilles heel of the cotton states.

Up to the capture of Nashville no concerted strategy between the army of Kentucky and the army on the Potomac was possible. They were too far apart from one another. They stood in the same front line, but their lines of operation were entirely different. Only with the victorious advance into Tennessee did the movements of the army of Kentucky become important for the entire theater of war.

The American papers influenced by McClellan are going great guns with the "anaconda" * envelopment theory. According to this an immense line of armies is to wind round the rebellion, gradually constrict its coils and finally strangle the enemy. This is sheer childishness. It is a rehash of the so-called *"cordon system"* devised in Austria about 1770, which was employed against the French from 1792 to 1797 with such great obstinacy and with such constant failure. At Jemappes, Fleurus and, more especially, at Moutenotte, Millesimo, Dego, Castiglione and Rivoli, the knock-out blow was dealt to this system. The French cut the "anaconda" in two by attacking at a point where they had concentrated superior forces. Then the coils of the "anaconda" were cut to pieces seriatim.

In well populated and more or less centralized states there is always a center, with the occupation of which by

* A large snake, species of boa, found in South America.—*Ed.*

the foe the national resistance would be broken. Paris is a shining example. The slave states, however, possess no such center. They are thinly populated, with few large towns and all these on the seacoast. The question therefore arises: Does a military center of gravity nevertheless exist, with the capture of which the backbone of their resistance breaks, or are they, as Russia still was in 1812, not to be conquered without occupying every village and every plot of land, in a word, the entire periphery? Cast a glance at the geographical formation of *Secessia,* with its long stretch of coast on the Atlantic Ocean and its long stretch of coast on the Gulf of Mexico. So long as the Confederates held Kentucky and Tennessee, the whole formed a great compact mass. The loss of both these states drives an immense wedge into their territory, separating the states on the North Atlantic Ocean from the states on the Gulf of Mexico. The direct route from Virginia and the two Carolinas to Texas, Louisiana, Mississippi and even, in part, to Alabama leads through Tennessee, which is now occupied by the Unionists. The *sole* route that, after the complete conquest of Tennessee by the Union, connects the two sections of the slave states goes through Georgia. This proves that *Georgia* is *the key to Secessia.* With the loss of Georgia the Confederacy would be cut into two sections which would have lost all connection with one another. A reconquest of Georgia by the Secessionists, however, would be almost unthinkable, for the Unionist fighting forces would be concentrated in a center position, while their adversaries, divided into two camps, would have scarcely sufficient forces to summon to a united attack.

Would the conquest of all Georgia, with the seacoast of Florida, be requisite for such an operation? By no means. In a land where communication, particularly between distant points, depends more on railways than on highways, the seizure of the railways is sufficient. The southernmost railway line between the states on the Gulf of Mexico and the Atlantic coast goes through Macon and Gordon near Milledgeville.

The occupation of these two points would accordingly cut *Secessia* in two and enable the Unionists to beat one part after another. At the same time, one gathers from the above that no Southern republic is capable of living without the possession of Tennessee. Without Tennessee, Georgia's vital spot lies only eight or ten days' march from the frontier; the North would constantly have its hand at the throat of the South, and on the slightest pressure the South would have to yield or fight for its life anew, under circumstances in which a single defeat would cut off every prospect of success.

From the foregoing considerations it follows:

The Potomac is *not* the most important position of the war theater. The taking of Richmond and the advance of the Potomac army further South—difficult on account of the many streams that cut across the line of march—could produce a tremendous moral effect. From a purely military standpoint, they would decide *nothing*.

The decision of the campaign belongs to the Kentucky army, now in Tennessee. On the one hand, this army is nearest the decisive points; on the other hand, it occupies a territory without which Secession is incapable of living. This army would accordingly have to be strengthened at the expense of all the rest and the sacrifice of all minor operations. Its next points of attack would be Chattanooga and Dalton on the Upper Tennessee, the most important railway centers of the entire South. After their occupation the connection between the eastern and western states of *Secessia* would be limited to the connecting lines in Georgia. The further question would then arise of cutting off another railway line with Atlanta and

Georgia, and finally of destroying the last connection between the two sections by the capture of Macon and Gordon.

On the contrary, should the "anaconda" plan be followed, then despite all successes in particular cases and even on the Potomac, the war may be prolonged indefinitely, while the financial difficulties together with diplomatic complications acquire fresh scope.

Die Presse, March 27, 1862.

25.

AN INTERNATIONAL *AFFAIRE* MIRÈS *

London, April 28, 1862.

A MAJOR theme of diplomatic circles here is France's appearance on the Mexican scene. It is found puzzling that Louis Bonaparte should have increased the expeditionary troops at the moment when he promised to reduce them, and that he should want to go forward whilst England draws back. It is known here very well that the impulse for the Mexican expedition came from the Cabinet of St. James and not from that of the Tuileries. It is equally well known that Louis Bonaparte likes to carry out all his undertakings, but particularly the overseas adventures, under England's ægis. As is known, the restored Empire has not yet emulated the feat of its original in quartering the French armies in the capital cities of modern Europe. As a *pis aller*,** on the other hand, it has led them to the capital cities of ancient Europe, to Constantinople, Athens and Rome, and, over and above that, even to Peking. Should the

* Refers to a Paris banker, Isaac Jules Mirès (1809-71).—*Ed.*
** Last resource.—*Ed.*

theatrical effect of a trip to the capital city of the Aztecs
be lost, and the opportunity for military archæological
collections à la Montauban? If, however, one considers
the present state of French finance and the future serious
conflicts with the United States and England to which
Louis Bonaparte's advance into Mexico can lead, one is
then obliged to reject without further question the foregoing interpretation of his proceedings, which is popular with various British papers.

At the time of the Convention of July 17, 1861, when
the claims of the English creditors were to be settled,
but the English plenipotentiary demanded at the same
time an examination of the entire register of the Mexican debts or misdeeds, Mexico's Foreign Minister put
down the debt to France at $200,000, therefore a mere
bagatelle of some £40,000. The account *now* drawn up
by France, on the other hand, by no means confines itself to these modest limits.

Under the Catholic administration of Zuloaga and
Miramon, an issue of Mexican state bonds to the amount
of $14,000,000 was contracted per medium of the Swiss
banking house of J. B. Jecker and Co. The whole sum
that was realized by the first issue of these bonds came
to only 5 per cent of the nominal amount or to $700,000.
The sum total of the bonds issued fell very soon into the
hands of prominent Frenchmen, among them relatives
of the Emperor and fellow wire-pullers of *"haute
politique."* * The house of Jecker and Co. let these gentlemen have the aforesaid bonds for far less than their
original nominal price.

Miramon contracted this debt at a time when he was
in possession of the capital city. Later, after he had come
down to the rôle of a mere guerrilla leader, he again
caused state bonds to the nominal value of $38,000,000

* High politics.—*Ed.*

to be issued through his so-called Finance Minister, Señor Peza-y-Peza. Once more it was the house of Jecker and Co. which negotiated the issue, but on this occasion limited its advances to the modest sum of barely $500,-000, or from one to two per cent to the dollar. Once more the Swiss bankers knew how to dispose of their Mexican property as quickly as possible, and once more the bonds fell into the hands of those "prominent" Frenchmen, among whom were some *habitués* * of the imperial court whose names will live on in the annals of the European bourses as long as the *affaire* Mirès.

This debt, then, of $52,000,000, of which not even $1,200,000 have hitherto been advanced, the administration of President Juarez declines to recognize, on the one hand, because it knows nothing about it and, on the other hand, because Messrs. Miramon, Zuloaga and Peza-y-Peza were possessed of no constitutional authority to contract such a state debt. The above mentioned "prominent" Frenchmen, however, had to carry the contrary view at the decisive place. Lord Palmerston was, for his part, opportunely instructed by some members of Parliament that the whole affair would lead to highly objectional interpellations in the Lower House. Among other things to be feared, was the question whether British land and sea power might be employed to support the gambling operations of certain *rouge-et-noir* ** politicians on the other side of the Channel. Accordingly Palmerston caught eagerly at the Conference of Orizaba to withdraw from a business that threatens us with the filth of an international *affaire* Mirès.

Die Presse, May 12, 1862.

---

* Customary frequenters of any place, especially one of amusement. *—Ed.*
** Red and black, a game of chance.—*Ed.*

26.

THE ENGLISH PRESS AND THE FALL
OF NEW ORLEANS

London, May 16, 1862.

ON the arrival of the first reports of the fall of New Orleans *The Times, Herald, Standard, Morning Post, Daily Telegraph* and other English "sympathizers" with the Southern "nigger-drivers" proved strategically, tactically, philologically, exegetically, politically, morally and fortificationally that the report was one of the "canards" which Reuter, Havas, Wolff and their understrappers so often let fly. The natural means of defense of New Orleans, it was said, had been strengthened not only by newly constructed forts, but by submarine infernal machines of every sort and ironclad gunboats. Then there was the Spartan character of the New Orleanists and their deadly hate of Lincoln's hirelings. Finally, was it not before New Orleans that England had suffered the defeat which brought her second war against the United States (1812 to 1814) to an ignominious end? Consequently there was no reason to doubt that New Orleans would immortalize itself as a second Saragossa or a Moscow [101] of the "South." Besides, it harbored 15,000 bales of cotton, with which it was so easy to light an inextinguishable, self-consuming fire, quite apart from the fact that in 1814 the duly damped cotton bales proved more indestructible by cannon fire than the earthworks of Sebastopol. It was therefore as clear as daylight that the fall of New Orleans was a case of the familiar Yankee brag.

When the first reports were confirmed two days later by steamers arriving from New York, the bulk of the English pro-slavery press persisted in its skepticism. The

Evening Standard, especially, was so positive in its un-
belief that in the same number it published a first leader
which proved the half-moon city's impregnability in
black and white, whilst its "latest news" announced
in large type the impregnable city's fall. *The Times,* however, which has always held discretion for the better part
of valor, veered round. It still doubted, but at the same
time it made ready for all eventualities, since New
Orleans was a city of "rowdies" and not of heroes. On
this occasion *The Times* was right. New Orleans is a
settlement of the dregs of the French *Bohème,* in the
true sense of the word a French *convict colony*—and
never, with the changes of time, has it belied its origin.
Only, *The Times* came *post festum* * to this pretty widespread understanding.

Finally, however, the *fait accompli* struck even the
blindest Thomas. What was to be done? The English
pro-slavery press now proves that the fall of New Orleans
is an advantage for the Confederates and a defeat for
the Federals.

The fall of New Orleans allowed General Lovell to re-
enforce Beauregard's army with his troops; Beauregard
was the more in need of reënforcements since 160,000
men (a gross exaggeration!) were said to have been concentrated on his front by Halleck and, on the other hand,
General Mitchell had cut Beauregard's communications
with the East by breaking the railroad connection of
Memphis with Chattanooga, that is, with Richmond,
Charleston and Savannah.[102] After this cutting of his
communications (which we indicated as the necessary
strategical move long *before* the battle of Corinth),
Beauregard had no longer any railway connections from
Corinth save those with Mobile and New Orleans. After
New Orleans had fallen and he had been made dependent

* After the feast.—*Ed.*

on the single railroad to Mobile, he naturally could no longer procure the necessary provisions for his troops, on that account fell back on Memphis and, in the estimation of the English pro-slavery press, his provisioning capacity is of course increased by the entry of Lovell's troops!

On the other hand, remark the same oracles, the yellow fever will mop up the Federals in New Orleans and, finally, if the city itself is no Moscow, is not its mayor a Brutus? Only read (*cf.* New York) his melodramatically valorous epistle to Commodore Farragut.[103] "Brave words, Sir, brave words!" But hard words break no bones.

The press organs of the Southern slaveholders, however, do not construe the fall of New Orleans so optimistically as their English comforters. This will be seen from the following extracts:

The *Richmond Dispatch* says:

What has become of the ironclad gunboats, the *Mississippi* and the *Louisiana*,[104] from which we expected the salvation of the half-moon city? In respect of their effect on the foe, these ships might just as well have been ships of glass. It is useless to deny that the fall of New Orleans is a heavy blow. The Confederate government is thereby cut off from west Louisiana, Texas, Missouri and Arkansas.

The *Norfolk Day Book* observes:

This is the most serious defeat since the beginning of the war. It augurs privations and want for all classes of society and, what is worse, it threatens the supplies for our army.

The *Atlantic Intelligencer* laments:

We expected a different result. The approach of the enemy was no surprise attack; it had been long foreseen, and we had been promised that should he even pass by Fort Jackson, fearful artillery contrivances would force him to withdraw or assure his annihilation. In all this we have deceived ourselves,

as on every occasion when defenses were supposed to guarantee
the safety of a place or town. It appears that modern inventions
have annihilated the defensive capacity of fortifications. Ironclad gunboats destroy them or sail past them unceremoniously.
Memphis, we fear, will share the fate of New Orleans. Would
it not be folly to deceive ourselves with hope?

Finally, the *Petersburg Express:*

The capture of New Orleans by the Federals is the most
extraordinary and most fateful event of the whole war.

Die Presse, May 20, 1862.

27.

A TREATY AGAINST THE SLAVE TRADE

London, May 18, 1862.

THE Treaty for the suppression of the slave trade concluded between the United States and England on April
7 of this year in Washington [105] is now communicated to
us *in extenso* * by the American newspapers. The main
points of this important document are the following:
The right of search is reciprocal, but can be exercised
only by such warships on either side as have for this purpose received special authority from one of the contracting powers. From time to time the contracting powers
supply one another with complete statistics concerning
the sections of their navies that have been appointed to
keep watch on the traffic in Negroes. The right of search
can be exercised only against merchantmen within a distance of 200 miles from the African coast and south of
32 degrees North latitude, and within 30 nautical miles
of the coast of Cuba. Search, whether of English ships by
American cruisers or of American ships by English

* At length.—*Ed.*

cruisers, does not take place in that part of the sea (there-fore within three nautical miles of the coast) which counts as English or American territory; no more does it take place before the ports or settlements of foreign powers.

Mixed courts, composed half of Englishmen, half of Americans, and resident in Sierra Leone, Capetown and New York, will pass judgment on the prize vessels. In the event of a ship's condemnation, her crew will be handed over to the jurisdiction of the nation under whose flag the ship sailed, so far as this can be done without extra cost. Not only the crew (including the captain, mate, etc.), but also the owners of the vessel will then incur the penalties customary to the country. Compen-sation of owners of merchantmen that have been ac-quitted by the mixed courts, is to be paid within a year by the power under whose flag the capturing warship sailed. Not only the presence of captive Negroes is re-garded as affording legal grounds for the seizure of ships, but also specially made arrangements in the construction of the ship for the traffic in Negroes, manacles, chains and other instruments for safeguarding the Negroes and, lastly, stores of provisions that bear no relation to the requirements of the ships' company. A ship on which such suspicious articles are found has to furnish proof of her innocence and even in the event of acquittal can claim no compensation.

Commanders of cruisers, who exceed the authority con-ferred on them by the Treaty, are to be subjected to punishment by their respective governments. Should the commander of a cruiser of one of the contracting powers harbor a suspicion that a merchant vessel under escort by one or more warships of the other contracting power carries Negroes on board, or was engaged in the African slave trade, or is equipped for this trade, he has then to communicate his suspicion to the commander of the escort and, in company with him, search the suspected ship; the latter is to be conducted to the place of residence of one of the mixed courts if, according to the Treaty, it comes under the category of suspicious ships. The Negroes found on board condemned ships are placed at the disposal of the government under whose flag the capture was made. They are to be set at liberty at once and remain free under guarantee of the government in whose territory they find themselves. The Treaty can only be terminated after ten years. It remains in force for a full year from the date of the notice given by one of the contracting parties.

The traffic in Negroes has been dealt a mortal blow by this Anglo-American Treaty—the result of the American Civil War. The effect of the Treaty will be completed by the Bill recently introduced by Senator Sumner, which repeals the law of 1808 dealing with the traffic in Negroes on the coasts of the United States and punishes the transport of slaves from one port of the United States to another as a crime. This Bill in large measure paralyzes the trade that the states raising Negroes (border slave states) carry on with the states consuming Negroes (the slave states proper).

Die Presse, May 22, 1862.

28.

THE SITUATION IN THE AMERICAN THEATER OF WAR

The capture of New Orleans, as the detailed reports now at hand show, is distinguished as a deed of valor almost unparalleled. The fleet of the Unionists consisted merely of wooden ships: about six warships, each having from 14 to 25 guns, supported by a numerous flotilla of gunboats and mortar vessels. This fleet had before it two forts that blocked the passage of the Mississippi. Within range of the 100 guns of these forts the stream was barred by a strong chain, behind which was a mass of torpedoes, fire-floats and other instruments of destruction. These first obstacles had therefore to be overcome in order to pass between the forts. On the further side of the forts, however, was a second formidable line of defense formed by ironclad gunboats, among them the *Manassas,* an iron ram, and the *Louisiana,* a powerful floating battery. After the Unionists had bombarded the two forts, which completely command the stream, for six days without any effect, they resolved to brave their fire, force the iron barrier in three divisions, sail up the river and risk battle with the "ironsides." The hazardous enterprise succeeded. As soon as the flotilla effected a landing before New Orleans, the victory was naturally won.

Beauregard had now nothing more to defend in Corinth. His position there had only any import so long as it covered Mississippi and Louisiana, and especially New Orleans. He now finds himself strategically in the position that a lost battle would leave him no other choice than to disband his army into guerrillas; for without a large town, where railroads and supplies are concentrated, in the rear of his army, he can no longer hold masses of men together.

McClellan has incontrovertibly proved that he is a military incompetent who, having been raised by favorable circumstances to a commanding and responsible position, wages war not in order to defeat the foe, but rather in order not to be defeated by the foe and thus forfeits his own usurped greatness. He bears himself like the old so-called "maneuvering generals" who excused their anxious avoidance of any tactical decision with the plea that by strategic envelopment they obliged the enemy to give up his positions. The Confederates always escape him, because at the decisive moment he never attacks them. Thus, although their plan of retreat had already been announced ten days before, even by the New York papers (for example, the *Tribune*), he let them quietly retire from Manassas to Richmond. He then divided his army and flanked the Confederates strategically, whilst with one corps of troops he established himself before Yorktown. Siege operations always afford a pretext for wasting time and avoiding battle. As soon as he had concentrated a military force superior to the Confederates, he let them retire from Yorktown to Williamsburg and from there further, without forcing them to join battle. A war has never yet been so wretchedly waged. If the rearguard action near Williamsburg ended in defeat for the Confederate rearguard instead of in a second Bull Run for the Union troops, McClellan was wholly innocent of this result.

After a march of about twelve miles (English) in a twenty-four hours' downpour of rain and through veritable seas of mud, 8,000 Union troops under General Heintzelman (of German descent, but born in Pennsylvania) arrived in the vicinity of Williamsburg and met with only weak pickets of the enemy. As soon, however, as the latter had assured himself of their numerically inferior strength, he dispatched from his picked troops at Williamsburg reënforcements that gradually increased the number of his men to 25,000 strong. By nine o'clock in the morning battle had been joined in earnest; by half past twelve General Heintzelman discovered that the engagement was going in favor of the foe. He sent messenger after messenger to General Kearny, who was eight miles to his rear, but could only push slowly forward in consequence of the complete "dissolution" of the roads by the rain. For a whole hour Heintzelman remained without reënforcements and the 7th and 8th Jersey regiment, which had exhausted its stock of powder, began to run for the woods on either side of the road. Heintzelman now caused Colonel Menill and a squadron of Pennsylvania cavalry to take up a position on both fringes of the forest, with the threat of firing on the fugitives. This brought the latter once more to a standstill.

Order was further restored by the example of a Massachusetts regiment, which had likewise exhausted its powder, but now fixed bayonets to its muskets and awaited the foe with calm demeanor. At length Kearny's vanguard under Brigadier [General] Berry (from the State of Maine) came in sight. Heintzelman's army received its rescuers with a wild "Hurrah"; he had the regimental band strike up "Yankee Doodle" and Berry's fresh forces form a line almost half a mile in length in front of his exhausted troops. After preliminary musket fire, Berry's brigade made a bayonet charge at the double and drove the foe off the battlefield to his earthworks, the largest of which after repeated attacks and counterattacks remained in the possession of the Union troops. Thus the equilibrium of the battle was restored. Berry's arrival had saved the Unionists. The arrival of the brigades of Jameson and Birney at four o'clock decided the victory. At nine o'clock in the evening the retreat of the Confederates from Williamsburg began; on the following day they continued it—in the direction of Richmond—hotly pursued by Heintzelman's cavalry. On the morning after the battle, between six and seven o'clock, Heintzelman had already caused Williamsburg to be occupied by General Jameson. The rearguard of the fleeing foe had evacuated the town from the opposite end only half an hour before. Heintzelman's battle was an infantry battle in the true sense of the word. Artillery hardly came into action. Musket fire and bayonet attack were decisive. If the Congress at Washington wanted to pass a vote of thanks, it should have been to General Heintzelman, who saved the Yankees from a second Bull Run, and not to McClellan, who in his wonted fashion avoided "the tactical decision" and let the numerically weaker adversary escape for the third time.

The Confederate army in Virginia has better chances than Beauregard's army, first because it is facing a McClellan instead of a Halleck, and then because the many streams on its line of retreat flow crosswise from the mountains to the sea. However, in order to avoid breaking up into bands *without a battle,* its generals will sooner or later be forced to accept a decisive battle, just as the Russians were obliged to fight at Smolensk and Borodino,[106] though *against* the will of their generals, who judged the situation correctly. Lamentable as McClellan's military leadership has been, the constant retirements, accompanied by abandonment of artillery, munitions and other military stores, and simultaneously the small, unlucky rearguard engagements, have at any rate badly demoralized the Confederates, as will become manifest on the day of a decisive battle. We arrive, therefore, at the following summary of the situation:

Should Beauregard or Jefferson Davis lose a decisive battle, their armies will then break up into bands. Should one of them win a decisive battle, which is altogether unlikely, in the best case the disbanding of their armies will then be deferred. They are not in a position to make the least lasting use even of a victory. They cannot advance 20 English miles without coming to a standstill and again awaiting the renewed offensive of the foe.

There still remains to examine the chances of guerrilla war. But precisely in respect to the present war of the slaveholders it is most amazing how slight, or rather how wholly lacking is the participation of the population in it. In 1813 the communications of the French were continually interrupted and harassed by Colomb, Lützow, Chernyshev and twenty other leaders of insurgents and Cossacks. In 1812 the population in Russia vanished completely from the French line of march; in 1814 the French peasants armed themselves and slew the patrols and stragglers of the Allies. But here nothing happens at all. Men resign themselves to the *fate of the big battles* and console themselves with *"Victrix causa diis placuit, sed victa Catoni."* * [107] The tall talk of war by water passes off in smoke. There can be hardly any doubt, it is true, that the *white trash,* as the planters themselves call the "poor whites," will attempt guerrilla warfare and brigandage. Such an attempt, however, will very quickly transform the possessing planters into *Unionists.* They will themselves call the troops of the Yankees to their aid. The alleged burnings of cotton, etc., on the Mississippi rest exclusively on the testimony of two Kentuckians who are said to have come to Louisville—certainly not *up* the Mississippi. The conflagration in New Orleans was easily organized. The fanaticism of the merchants of New Orleans is explained by the fact that they were obliged to take a quantity of Confederate treasury bonds for hard cash. The conflagration at New Orleans will be repeated in other towns; assuredly, also, much will be otherwise burnt; but theatrical coups like this can only bring the dissension between the planters and the *"white trash"* to a head and therewith—*"finis Secessiæ"! ***

Die Presse, May 30, 1862.

* "The cause of the victor pleased the gods, but that of the vanquished pleased Cato."—*Ed.*
** "The end of Secession."—*Ed.*

ENGLISH HUMANITY AND AMERICA

29.

ENGLISH HUMANITY AND AMERICA

HUMANITY in England, like liberty in France, has now become an export article for the *traders in politics*. We recollect the time when Tsar Nicholas had Polish ladies flogged by soldiers [108] and when Lord Palmerston found the moral indignation of some parliamentarians over the event "unpolitical." We recollect that about a decade ago a revolt took place on the Ionian Islands [109] which gave the English governor there occasion to have a not inconsiderable number of Grecian women flogged. *Probatum est,** said Palmerston and his Whig colleagues who at that time were in office. Only a few years ago proof was furnished to Parliament from official documents that the tax collectors in India employed means of coercion against the wives of the ryots,** the infamy of which forbids giving further details. Palmerston and his colleagues did not, it is true, dare to justify these atrocities, but what an outcry they would have raised, had a *foreign* government dared to proclaim publicly its indignation over these English infamies and to indicate not indistinctly that it would step in if Palmerston and colleagues did not at once disavow the Indian tax officials. But Cato the Censor himself could not watch over the morals of the Roman citizens more anxiously than the English aristocrats and their ministers over the "humanity" of the war-waging Yankees!

The ladies of New Orleans, yellow beauties, tastelessly bedecked with jewels and comparable, perhaps, to the women of the old Mexicans, save that they do not de-

* It is approved.—*Ed.*
** Indian peasant cultivators who hold land under the *ryotwari* system. —*Ed.*

vour their slaves *in natura*,* are this time—previously it was the harbors of Charleston—the occasions for the British aristocrats' display of humanity. The English women who are starving in Lancashire (they are, however, not ladies, nor do they possess any slaves), have inspired no parliamentary utterance hitherto; the cry of distress from the Irish women, who, with the progressive eviction of the small tenant farmers *en masse* in green Erin, are flung half naked on the street and hunted from house and home quite as if the Tartars had descended upon them, has hitherto called forth only one echo from Lords, Commons and Her Majesty's government—homilies on the absolute rights of landed property.

But the ladies of New Orleans! That, to be sure, is another matter. These ladies were far too enlightened to participate in the tumult of war, like the goddesses of Olympus, or to cast themselves into the flames, like the women of Sagunt.[110] They have invented a new and safe mode of heroism, a mode that could have been invented only by female slaveholders and, what is more, only by female slaveholders in a land where the free part of the population consists of shopkeepers by vocation, tradesmen in cotton or sugar or tobacco, and does not keep slaves, like the *cives* ** of the ancient world. After their men had run away from New Orleans or had crept into their back closets, these ladies rushed into the streets in order to spit in the faces of the victorious Union troops or to stick out their tongues at them or, like Mephistopheles, to make in general "an unseemly gesture," accompanied by insulting words. These Magæras imagined they could be ill-mannered "with impunity."

This was their heroism. General Butler issued a procla-

* In a state of nature.—*Ed.*
** Citizens.—*Ed.*

mation in which he notified them that they should be
treated as street-walkers, if they continued to act as
street-walkers. Butler has, indeed, the makings of a
lawyer, but does not seem to have given the requisite
study to English statute law. Otherwise, by analogy with
the laws imposed on Ireland under Castlereagh, he would
have prohibited them from setting foot on the streets at
all. Butler's warning to the "ladies" of New Orleans has
aroused such moral indignation in Earl Carnarvon, Sir
J. Walsh (who played so ridiculous and odious a rôle
in Ireland) and Mr. Gregory, who was already demanding recognition of the Confederacy a year ago, that the
Earl in the Upper House, the knight and the man "without a handle to his name" in the Lower House, interro-
gated the Ministry with a view to learning what steps it
thought of taking in the name of outraged "humanity."
Russell and Palmerston both castigated Butler, both expected that the government at Washington would disavow him; and the so very tender-hearted Palmerston,
who behind the back of the Queen and without the foreknowledge of his colleagues recognized the *coup d'état*
of December 1851 (on which occasion "ladies" were
actually shot dead, whilst others were violated by
Zouaves *) merely out of "human admiration"—the same
tender-hearted Viscount declared Butler's warning to be
an *"infamy."* Ladies, indeed, who actually own slaves—
such ladies were not even to be able to vent their anger
and their malice on common Union troops, peasants,
artisans and other rabble with impunity! It is "in-
famous."

Among the public here, no one is deceived by this
humanity farce. It is meant in a measure to call forth,
in a measure to fortify the feeling in favor of intervention, in the first place on the part of France. After the

* A body of infantry in the French service, originally Algerians.—*Ed.*

first melodramatic outbursts, the knights of humanity in the Upper and Lower House, likewise as at command, threw their emotional mask away. Their declamation served merely as a prologue to the question whether the Emperor of the French had come to an understanding with the English government in the matter of mediating, and whether the latter, as they hoped, had received such an offer favorably. Russell and Palmerston both declared they did not know of the offer. Russell declared the present moment extremely unfavorable for any mediation. Palmerston, more guarded and reserved, contented himself with saying that at the *present* moment the English government had no intention of mediating.

The plan is that during the recess of the English Parliament France should play her rôle of mediator and, in the autumn, if Mexico is secure, should open her intervention. The lull in the American theater of war has resuscitated the intervention speculators in St. James and the Tuileries from their marasmus. This lull is itself due to a strategic error in the Northern conduct of the war. If after its victory in Tennessee the Kentucky army had rapidly advanced on the railroad centers in Georgia, instead of letting itself be drawn South down the Mississippi on a side track, Reuter and Co. would have been cheated of their business in "intervention" and "mediation" reports. However that may be, Europe can wish nothing more fervently than that the *coup d'état* should attempt "to restore order in the United States" and "to save civilization" there likewise.

Die Presse, June 20, 1862.

30.

A SUPPRESSED DEBATE ON MEXICO AND THE ALLIANCE WITH FRANCE

London, July 16, 1862.

ONE of the most curious of English parliamentary devices is the count out. What is the count out? If less than 40 members are present in the Lower House, they do not form a *quorum,* that is, an assembly capable of transacting business. If a motion is introduced by an independent parliamentarian, which is equally irksome to *both* oligarchical factions, the *Ins* and the *Outs* (those in office and those in opposition), they then come to an agreement that on the day of the debate parliamentarians from both sides will gradually be lacking, *alias* otherwise absent themselves. When the emptying of the benches has reached the necessary maximum, the government whip, that is, the parliamentarian entrusted with party discipline by the ministry of the day, then tips the wink to a brother previously chosen for this purpose. Brother parliamentarian gets up and quite nonchalantly requests the chairman to have the house counted. The counting takes place and, behold, it is discovered that there are less than 40 members assembled. Herewith the proceedings come to an end. The obnoxious motion is got rid of without the government party or the opposition party having put itself in the awkward and compromising position of being obliged to vote it down.

At yesterday's sitting the count out was brought up in an interesting manner. Lord R. Montagu had given notice of a motion for that day which dealt with the communication of new diplomatic documents on *intervention in Mexico.* He began his speech with the following words:

I was warned yesterday that both front benches had agreed to count out the House on this motion. I do not suppose the House will be so indifferent to a subject which affects it so nearly. The papers on the affairs of Mexico had a peculiar interest in themselves. The last of them was delivered on Saturday, and it would be unconstitutional not to submit that policy to discussion by the House.

But Lord R. Montagu had reckoned without his host. After he himself had spoken, Layard had replied to him on behalf of the government and Fitzgerald had delivered himself of some official chatter on behalf of the Tories, Kinglake (a Liberal member) rose. The exordium of his speech concluded with the following words:

The whole series of negotiations disclosed by the papers is a good illustration of the way in which the French government uses its relations with this country as a means to prop the Imperial throne. It is of great moment for the French government to divert attention from affairs at home by causing it to be seen that the French government is engaged in some great transactions abroad, in concert with one of the great settled States of Europe.

Hardly had Kinglake uttered these words when an *"honorable"* member of the House moved that the House be *"counted."* And behold! The House had dwindled to only 33 members. Lord Montagu's motion had been killed by the same count out against which he had protested at the beginning of the debate.

Apart from Kinglake's interrupted speech, only that of Lord Montagu possessed any material interest. Lord R. Montagu's speech contains the following important analysis of the facts of the case:

Sir Charles Wyke had concluded a treaty with Mexico. Out of servility to Louis Bonaparte this treaty was not ratified by Lord John Russell. Sir Charles Wyke concluded the said treaty after France, through her connection with Almonte, the leader of the reactionary party, had entered a path which abrogated the joint convention between England, France and Spain. Lord John Russell himself declared in an official dispatch that this treaty satisfied all the legitimate demands of England. In his correspondence with Thouvenel, however, he promised, in compliance with Bonaparte's wish, *not* to ratify the treaty for the time being. He allowed Thouvenel to communicate this decision to the *Corps Législatif*. Indeed, Lord John Russell lowered himself so far as to promise Thouvenel that he would break off all communication with Sir Charles Wyke until July 1, 1862—a date that gave Thouvenel time to answer. Thouvenel answered that Bonaparte did not contest England's right to act in isolation, but disapproved of the Anglo-Mexican treaty concluded by Sir Charles Wyke. Thereupon Russell ordered Wyke to withold the ratification of the treaty.

England, added Lord Montagu, lends her influence to enforce the fraudulent claims on the Mexican Treasury with which Morny "and *perhaps persons of higher standing* in France" have provided themselves per medium of the Swiss bourse-swindler Jecker.

These operations in Mexico—he continued—were not divulged until after Parliament was prorogued and when no question could be asked about them. . . . The first extra-Parliamentary war was waged in 1857. *The Noble Viscount* (*i.e.*, Palmerston) defended that on the ground that the principle of the previous sanction of Parliament did not apply to Asiatic war; now it was made not to apply to wars in America. It would next not be supposed to apply to wars in Europe. Yet if this were permitted Parliament would become a mere farce. For how could that House control the expenditure, if negotiations were to be carried on in secret and wars were to be begun without sanction?

Lord Montagu wound up with the words:

We combined with the murderer of his country's liberties (i.e. Louis Napoleon) and joined him in planting a despotism on free will. Even now we cannot shake off our accomplice, although we see him doomed to the abhorrence of man and the vengeance of Heaven. (We have already given an abstract of Layard's reply in the *Abendblatt*.)

Die Presse, July 20, 1862.

31.

A CRITICISM OF AMERICAN AFFAIRS

THE crisis which at the moment dominates conditions in the United States has been brought about by two-fold causes: military and political.

Had the last campaign been conducted according to a *single* strategic plan, the main army of the West must then, as previously explained in these columns, have availed itself of its successes in Kentucky and Tennessee to penetrate through north Alabama to Georgia and to seize there the railroad centers at Decatur, Milledgeville, etc. The connection between the Eastern and the Western army of the Secessionists would thereby have been broken and their mutual support rendered impossible. Instead of this, the Kentucky army marched south down the Mississippi in the direction of New Orleans and its victory near Memphis had no other result than to dispatch the greater part of Beauregard's troops to Richmond, so that the Confederates here now suddenly confronted McClellan, who had not exploited the defeat of the enemy's troops at Yorktown and Williamsburg and, on the other hand, had from the first split up his own fighting forces, with a superior army in a superior position. McClellan's generalship, already described by us previously, was in itself sufficient to secure the downfall of the strongest and best disciplined army. Finally, War

Secretary Stanton made an unpardonable mistake. To make an impression abroad, he suspended recruiting after the conquest of Tennessee and so condemned the army to constant attenuation, just when it stood most in need of reënforcements for a rapid, decisive offensive. Despite the strategic blunders and despite McClellan's generalship, with a steady influx of recruits the war, if not decided by now, would neverthless have been rapidly nearing a victorious decision. Stanton's step was so much the more unfortunate as the South was then enlisting every man from 18 to 35 years old to a man and was therefore staking everything on a *single* card. It is those people who have been trained in the meantime that almost everywhere give the Confederates the upper hand and secure the initiative to them. They held Halleck fast, dislodged Curtis from Arkansas, beat McClellan and under Stonewall Jackson gave the signal for the guerrilla raids that now reach as far as the Ohio.

In part, the military causes of the crisis are connected with the political. It was the influence of the Democratic Party that elevated an incompetent like McClellan, because he was formerly a supporter of Breckinridge, to the position of Commander-in-Chief of all the military forces of the North. It was anxious regard for the wishes, advantages and interests of the spokesmen of the *border slave states* that hitherto broke off the Civil War's point of principle and, so to speak, deprived it of its soul. The "loyal" slaveholders of these border states saw to it that the fugitive slave laws dictated by the South were maintained and the sympathies of the Negroes for the North forcibly suppressed, that no general could venture to put a company of Negroes in the field and that slavery was finally transformed from the Achilles' heel of the South into its invulnerable hide of horn. Thanks to the slaves, who perform all productive labors, the entire manhood of the South that is fit to fight can be led into the field!

At the present moment, when secession's stocks are rising, the spokesmen of the border states increase their claims. However, Lincoln's appeal to them shows, where it threatens them with inundation by the Abolition party, that things are taking a revolutionary turn. Lincoln knows what Europe does not know, that it is by no means apathy or giving way under pressure of defeat that causes his demand for 300,000 recruits to meet with such a cold response. New England and the Northwest, which have provided the main body of the army, are determined to enforce a revolutionary waging of war on the government and to inscribe the battle-slogan of "Abolition of Slavery!" on the star-spangled banner. Lincoln yields only hesitantly and uneasily to this pressure from without, but knows that he is incapable of offering resistance to it for long. Hence his fervent appeal to the border states to renounce the institution of slavery voluntarily and under the conditions of a favorable contract. He knows that it is only the continuance of slavery in the border states that has so far left slavery untouched in the South and prohibited the North from applying its great radical remedy. He errs only if he imagines that the "loyal" slaveholders are to be moved by benevolent speeches and rational arguments. They will yield only to force.

So far we have only witnessed the first act of the Civil War—the *constitutional* waging of war. The second act, the revolutionary waging of war, is at hand.

Meanwhile, during its first session the Congress, which has now adjourned, has decreed a series of important measures that we will briefly summarize here.

Apart from its financial legislation, it has passed the Homestead Bill that the Northern popular masses had long striven for in vain;[111] by this a part of the state lands is given gratis for cultivation to the colonists, whether American born or immigrants. It has abolished slavery in [the District of] Columbia and the national capital, with monetary compensation for the former slaveholders.[112] Slavery has been declared "forever impossible" in all the *Territories* of the United States.[113] The Act under which the new State of West Virginia is taken into the Union prescribes abolition of slavery by stages and declares all Negro children born after July 4, 1863, to be born free. The conditions of this emancipation by stages are on the whole borrowed from the law that was enacted 70 years ago in Pennsylvania for the same purpose.[114] By a fourth Act all slaves of rebels are to be emancipated as soon as they fall into the hands of the republican army. Another law, which is now being put into effect *for the first time*, provides that these emancipated Negroes may be militarily organized and sent into the field against the South. The independence of the Negro republics of Liberia and Hayti has been recognized [115] and, finally, a treaty for the abolition of the slave trade has been concluded with England.

Thus, however the dice may fall in the fortunes of battle, it can now safely be said that Negro slavery will not long outlive the Civil War.

Die Presse, August 9, 1862.

32.

ABOLITIONIST DEMONSTRATIONS IN AMERICA

IT was previously observed in these columns that President Lincoln, legally cautious, constitutionally conciliatory, by birth a citizen of the border slave state of

202 THE CIVIL WAR IN THE UNITED STATES

Kentucky, escapes only with difficulty from the control of the "loyal" slaveholders, seeks to avoid any open breach with them and precisely thereby calls forth a conflict with the parties of the North which are consistent in point of principle and are pushed more and more into the foreground by events. The speech that Wendell Phillips delivered at Abington, Massachusetts, on the occasion of the anniversary of the slaves' emancipation in the British West Indies, may be regarded as a prologue to this conflict.

Together with Garrison and G. Smith, Wendell Phillips is the leader of the Abolitionists in New England. For 30 years he has without intermission and at the risk of his life proclaimed the emancipation of the slaves as his battle-cry, regardless alike of the persiflage of the press, the enraged howls of paid rowdies and the conciliatory representations of solicitous friends. Even by his opponents he is acknowledged as one of the greatest orators of the North, as combining iron character with forceful energy and purest conviction. The London *Times*—and what could characterize this magnanimous paper more strikingly—today *denounces* Wendell Phillips' speech at Abington to the government at Washington. It is an "abuse" of freedom of speech.

Anything more violent it is scarcely possible to image— says *The Times*—and anything more daring in time of Civil War was never perpetrated in any country by any sane man who valued his life and liberty. In reading the speech ... it is scarcely possible to avoid the conclusion that the speaker's object was to force the government to prosecute him.*

And *The Times,* in spite of or, perhaps, because of its hatred of the Union government, appears not at all disinclined to assume the rôle of public prosecutor!

In the present state of affairs Wendell Phillips' speech

* *The Times,* August 22, 1862.—*Ed.*

is of greater importance than a battle bulletin. We therefore epitomize its most striking passages.*

The government, he says among other things, fights for the maintenance of slavery, and therefore it fights in vain. Lincoln wages a political war. Even at the present time he is more afraid of Kentucky than of the entire North. He believes in the South. The Negroes on the Southern battlefields, when asked whether the rain of cannon-balls and bombs that tore up the earth all round and split the trees asunder, did not terrify them, answered: "No, massa; we know that they are not meant for us!" The rebels could speak of McClellan's bombs in the same way. They know that they are not meant for them, to do them harm. I do not say that McClellan is a traitor; but I say that if he were a traitor, he must have acted exactly as he has done. Have no fear for Richmond; McClellan will not take it. If the war is continued in this fashion, without a rational aim, then it is a useless squandering of blood and gold. It would be better were the South independent today than to hazard one more human life for a war based on the present execrable policy. To continue the war in the fashion prevailing hitherto, requires 125,000 men a year and a million dollars a day.

But you cannot get rid of the South. As Jefferson said of slavery: "The Southern states have the wolf by the ears, but they can neither hold him nor let him go." In the same way we have the South by the ears and can neither hold it nor let it go. Recognize it tomorrow and you will have no peace. For eighty years it has lived with us, in fear of us the whole time, with hatred for us half the time, ever troubling and abusing us. Made presump-

---

* For the complete speech see W. Phillips, *Speeches, Lectures and Letters*, Series 1 (Boston, 1864), pp. 448-463. The address is entitled "The Cabinet."—*Ed*.

tuous by conceding its present claims, it would not keep within an imaginary border line a year—nay, the moment that we speak of conditions of peace, it will cry victory! We shall never have peace until slavery is uprooted. So long as you retain the present tortoise at the head of our government, you make a hole with one hand in order to fill it with the other. Let the entire nation endorse the resolutions of the New York Chamber of Commerce [116] and then the army will have something for which it is worth while fighting. Had Jefferson Davis the power, he would not capture Washington. He knows that the bomb that fell in this Sodom would rouse the whole nation.

The entire North would thunder with one voice: "Down with slavery, down with everything that stands in the way of saving the republic!" Jefferson Davis is quite satisfied with his successes. They are greater than he anticipated, far greater! If he can continue to swim on them till March 4, 1863, England will then, and this is in order, recognize the Southern Confederacy.... The President has not put the Confiscation Act into operation. He may be honest, but what has his honesty to do with the matter? He has neither insight nor foresight. When I was in Washington, I ascertained that three months ago Lincoln had written the proclamation for a general emancipation of the slaves and that McClellan blustered him out of his decision and that the representatives of Kentucky blustered him into the retention of McClellan, in whom he places no confidence. It will take years for Lincoln to learn to combine his legal scruples as an attorney with the demands of the Civil War. This is the appalling condition of a democratic government and its greatest evil.

In France a hundred men, convinced for good reasons, would carry the nation with them; but in order that our government may take a step, nineteen millions must previously put themselves in motion. And to how many of these millions has it been preached for years that slavery is an institution ordained by God! With these prejudices, with paralyzed hands and hearts, you entreat the President to save you from the Negro! If this theory is correct, then only slaveholding despotism can bring a temporary peace.... I know Lincoln. I have taken his measure in Washington. He is a first-rate *second-rate* man. He waits honestly, like another Vesenius, for the nation to take him in hand and sweep away slavery through him.... In past years, not far from the platform from which I now speak, the Whigs fired off small mortars in order to stifle my voice. And what is the result?

The sons of these Whigs now fill their own graves in the marshes of Chickahominy! Dissolve this Union in God's name and put another in its place, on the cornerstone of which is written: "Political equality for all the citizens of the world...." During my stay in Chicago I asked lawyers of Illinois, among whom Lincoln had practiced, what sort of man he was. Whether he could say No. The answer was: "He lacks backbone. If the Americans wanted to elect a man absolutely incapable of leadership, of initiative, then they were bound to elect Abraham Lincoln... Never has a man heard him say No! ..." I asked: "Is McClellan a man who can say No?" The manager of the Chicago Central Railroad, on which McClellan was employed, answered: "He is incapable of making a decision. Put a question to him and it takes an hour for him to think of the answer. During the time that he was connected with the administration of the Central Railroad, he never decided a single important controversial question."

And these are the two men who, above all others, now hold the fate of the Northern republic in their hands!

Those best acquainted with the state of the army assure us that Richmond could have been taken five times, had the do-nothing at the head of the army of the Potomac allowed it; but he preferred to dig up dirt in the Chickahominy swamps, in order ignominiously to abandon the locality and his dirt ramparts. Lincoln, out of cowardly fear of the border slave states, keeps this man in his present position; but the day will come when Lincoln will confess that he has never believed in McClellan.... Let us hope that the war lasts long enough to transform us into men, and then we shall quickly triumph. God has put the thunderbolt of emancipation into our hands in order to crush this rebellion....

Die Presse, August 30, 1862.

33.

THE SITUATION IN NORTH AMERICA

London, November 4.

GENERAL BRAGG, who commands the Southern army in Kentucky—the other fighting forces of the South ravaging it are restricted to guerrilla bands—with his irruption into this border state issued a proclamation that throws considerable light on the latest combined moves of the Confederacy. Bragg's proclamation, addressed to the States of the Northwest, implies that his success in Kentucky is a matter of course, and obviously calculates on the contingency of a victorious advance into Ohio, the central state of the North. In the first place, he declares the readiness of the Confederacy to guarantee free navigation on the Mississippi and the Ohio. This guarantee only acquires import from the time that the slaveholders find themselves in possession of the border states.

At Richmond, therefore, it was implied that the simultaneous incursions of Lee into Maryland and Bragg into Kentucky would secure possession of the border states at a blow. Bragg then goes on to prove the justification of the South, which only fights for its independence, but, for the rest, wants peace. The real, characteristic point of the proclamation, however, is the offer of a separate peace with the Northwestern states, the invitation to them to secede from the Union and join the Confederacy, since the economic interests of the Northwest and the South are just as harmonious as those of the Northwest and the Northeast are inimically opposed. We see: The South barely fancied itself safely in possession of the border states, when it officially blabbed out its ulterior object of a reconstruction of the Union, to the exclusion of the states of New England.

Like the invasion of Maryland, however, that of Kentucky has also come to grief: as the former in the battle of Antietam Creek, so the latter in the battle of Perryville, near Louisville. As there, so here, the Confederates found themselves on the offensive, having attacked the advance guard of Buell's army. The Federals owed their victory to General McCook, the commander of the advance guard, who held his ground against the foe's far superior forces long enough to give Buell time to bring his main body into the field. There is not, the slightest doubt that the defeat at Perryville will entail the evacuation of Kentucky. The most considerable guerrilla band, formed out of the most fanatical partisans of the slave system in Kentucky and led by General Morgan, has been annihilated at Frankfort (between Louisville and Lexington) at almost the same time. Finally, the decisive victory of Rosecrans at Corinth supervenes, which makes imperative the hastiest retreat of the beaten army commanded by General Bragg.

Thus the Confederate campaign for the reconquest of the lost border slave states, which was undertaken on a large scale, with military skill and with the most favorable chances, has come utterly to grief. Apart from the immediate military results, these struggles contribute in another way to the removal of the main difficulty. The hold of the slave states proper on the border states naturally rests on the slave element of the latter, the same element that enforces diplomatic and constitutional considerations on the Union government in its struggle against slavery. In the border states, however, the principal theater of the Civil War, this element is in practice being reduced to nothing by the Civil War itself. A large section of the slaveholders, with its "black chattels" is constantly migrating to the South, in order to bring its property to a place of safety. With each defeat of the Confederates this migration is renewed on a larger scale.

One of my friends, a German officer,[117] who has fought under the star-spangled banner in Missouri, Arkansas, Kentucky and Tennessee in turn, writes to me that this migration is wholly reminiscent of the exodus from Ireland in 1847 and 1848. Furthermore, the energetic sections of the slaveholders, the youth, on the one hand, and the political and military leaders, on the other, separate themselves from the bulk of their class, since they either form guerrilla bands in their own states and, as guerrilla bands, are annihilated, or they leave home and are enlisted in the army or the administration of the Confederacy. Hence the result: on the one hand, an immense reduction of the slave element in the border states, where it had always to contend with the "encroachments" of competing free labor. On the other hand, removal of the energetic section of the slaveholders and its white following. There is left behind only a sediment of "moderate" slaveholders, who will soon grasp greedily at the pile of money offered them by Washington for the redemption of their "black chattels," whose value will in any case be lost as soon as the Southern market is closed to their sale. Thus the war itself brings about a solution by actually revolutionizing the form of society in the border states.

For the South the favorable season for waging war is over; for the North it is beginning, since the inland rivers are now navigable once more and the combination of land and sea warfare already attempted with so much success is again feasible. The North has eagerly availed itself of the interval. "Ironclads," ten in number, for the rivers of the West, are rapidly nearing completion; to which must be added twice as many semi-armored vessels for shallow waters. In the East many new armored vessels have already left the yards, whilst others are still under the hammer. All will be ready by the first of January, 1863. Ericsson, the inventor and builder of the *Monitor*, is directing the building of nine new ships after the same model. Four of them are already "afloat."

On the Potomac, in Tennessee and Virginia, as well as at different points in the South—Norfolk, Newbern, Port Royal, Pensacola and New Orleans—the army daily receives fresh reënforcements. The first levy of 300,000 men, which Lincoln announced in July, has been fully provided and is in part already at the seat of war. The second levy of 300,000 men for nine months is gradually being raised. In some states conscription has been done away with by voluntary enlistment; in none does it encounter serious difficulties. Ignorance and hatred have decried conscription as an unheard-of occurrence in the history of the United States. Nothing can be more mistaken. During the War of Independence and the second war with England (1812-14) great bodies of troops were conscripted, indeed, even in sundry small wars with the

Indians, without this ever having encountered opposition worth mentioning.[118]

It is a noteworthy fact that during the present year Europe furnished the United States with an emigrant contingent of approximately 100,000 souls and that half of these emigrants consist of Irishmen and Britons. At the recent congress of the English "Association for the Advancement of Science" at Cambridge, the economist Merivale was obliged to remind his countrymen of a fact which *The Times, The Saturday Review, Morning Post* and *The Morning Herald,* not to speak of the *dei minorum gentium,** have so completely forgotten, or want to make England forget, namely, the fact that the majority of the English surplus population finds a new home in the United States.

Die Presse, November 10, 1862.

34.

THE DISMISSAL OF McCLELLAN

McCLELLAN's dismissal! That is Lincoln's answer to the election victory of the Democrats.

The Democratic journals had stated with the most positive assurance that the election of Seymour as Governor of New York State would entail the immediate revocation of the proclamation in which Lincoln declared slavery abolished in *Secessia* from January 1, 1863.[119] The paper that took this prophetic imprint had hardly left the press when their favorite general—their favorite because "next to a great defeat he most feared a decisive victory"—was deprived of his command and went back to private life.

* Gods of lesser peoples.—*Ed.*

We recall that to this proclamation of Lincoln, Mc-Clellan replied with a counter-proclamation, an order of the day to his army, in which he indeed forbade any demonstration against the President's measure, but at the same time let slip the fatal words: "... The remedy for political errors, if any are committed, is to be found only in the action of the people at the polls." * McClellan, at the head of the main army of the United States, therefore appealed from the President to the impending elections. He threw the weight of his position into the scales. A *pronunciamento* in the Spanish manner aside, he could not have demonstrated his hostility to the President's policy more strikingly. Accordingly, after the election victory of the Democrats [120] the only choice left Lincoln was either to sink to the level of a tool of the pro-slave compromise party or with McClellan to remove from under it its point of support in the army.

McClellan's dismissal at the present moment is accordingly a political demonstration. In any case, however, it had become unavoidable. Halleck, the Commander-in-Chief,[121] in a report to the Secretary of War, had charged McClellan with direct insubordination. For, shortly after the defeat of the Confederates in Maryland on October 6, Halleck ordered the crossing of the Potomac, particularly as the lower water-level of the Potomac and its tributaries favored military operations at the time. In defiance of this command McClellan remained immovable, under the pretext of his army's inability to march due to lack of provisions. In the report mentioned, Halleck proves that this was a hollow subterfuge, that, compared with the Western Army, the Eastern army enjoyed great privileges in regard to commissariat and that the supplies still lacking could have been received just as well south as north of the Potomac.[122] A second report

* McClellan's General Order 163, October 7, 1862.—*Ed.*

212 THE CIVIL WAR IN THE UNITED STATES

links up with this report of Halleck's; in it the committee appointed to inquire into the surrender of Harper's Ferry to the Confederates accuses McClellan of having concentrated the Union troops stationed near that arsenal in an inconceivably slow fashion—he let them march only six English miles (about one and a half German miles) a day—for the purpose of its relief. Both reports, that of Halleck and that of the Committee, were in the President's hands prior to the election victory of the Democrats.

McClellan's generalship has been described in these columns so repeatedly that it is sufficient to recall how he sought to substitute strategical envelopment for tactical decision and how indefatigable he was in discovering considerations of general-staff discretion which forbade him either to take advantage of victories or to anticipate defeats. The brief Maryland campaign has cast a false halo about his head.[128] Here, however, we have to consider the facts that he received his general marching orders from General Halleck, who also drew up the plan of the first Kentucky campaign, and that victory on the battlefield was due exclusively to the bravery of the subordinate generals, in particular of General Reno, who fell, and of Hooker, who has not yet recovered from his wounds. Napoleon once wrote to his brother Joseph that on the battlefield there was danger at all points alike and one ran into its jaws most surely when one sought to avoid it. McClellan seems to have grasped this axiom, but without giving it the particular application which Napoleon suggested to his brother. During the whole of his military career McClellan has never been on the battlefield, has never been under fire, a peculiarity that General Kearny strongly stresses in a letter which his brother published after Kearny, fighting under Pope's command, had fallen in one of the battles before Washington.

McClellan understood how to conceal his mediocrity under a mask of restrained earnestness, laconic reticence and dignified reserve. His very defects secured him the unshakable confidence of the Democratic Party in the North and "loyal acknowledgement" on the part of the Secessionists. Among the higher officers of his army he gained supporters through the formation of a general staff of dimensions hitherto unheard of in military history. A section of the older officers, who had belonged to the former army of the Union and had received their training in the Academy at West Point, found in him a point of support for their rivalry with the newly sprung up "civil generals" and for their secret sympathies with the "comrades" in the enemy camp. The soldier, finally, knew his military qualities only by hearsay, whilst for the rest he ascribed to him old merits of the commissariat and was able to tell many glorious tales of his reserved condescension. A single gift of the supreme commander McClellan possessed—that of assuring himself of popularity with his army.

McClellan's successor, Burnside, is too little known to pronounce an opinion about. He belongs to the Republican Party. Hooker, on the other hand, who assumes command of the army corps serving specifically under McClellan, is incontestably one of the doughtiest blades in the Union. "Fighting Joe," as the troops call him, played the largest part in the successes in Maryland. He is an *Abolitionist*.

The same American papers which bring us the news of McClellan's dismissal, acquaint us with utterances of Lincoln in which he resolutely declares that he will not deviate a hair's breadth from his proclamation.

He [Lincoln]—observes *The Morning Star* with justice—has by successive exhibitions of firmness, taught the world to know him as a slow, but solid man, who advances with excessive caution, but does not go back. Each step of his administrative career has been in the right direction and has been stoutly maintained. Starting from the resolution to exclude slavery from the territories, he has come within sight of the ulterior result of all anti-slavery movements—its extirpation from the whole soil of the Union—and has already reached the high vantage ground at which the *Union* ceased to be responsible for the enslavement of a single human being.*

Die Presse, November 29, 1862.

35.

ENGLISH NEUTRALITY

THE SITUATION IN THE SOUTHERN STATES

London, November 29, 1862.

THE negotiations between the Cabinet here and the government at Washington on the corsair *Alabama* [124] are still pending, whilst fresh negotiations on the renewed fitting out of Confederate warships in English ports have already begun. Professor Francis W. Newman, one of the theoretical representatives of English radicalism, publishes in today's *Morning Star* a letter in which, among other things, he says:

When the American Consul at Liverpool had got opinion of counsel as to the illegality of the *Alabama* and sent his complaint to Earl Russell, the law officers of the Crown were consulted and they, too, condemned it as illegal. But so much time was lost in this process that the pirate meanwhile escaped. . . . Is our Government a second time going to wink at the successors of the *Alabama* escaping? Mr. Gladstone has made me fear that they are: in that speech of his at Newcastle . . . he said that he had been informed that the rebel President, whom he panegyrized, was "soon to have a navy."

* *Morning Star*, November 22, 1862.—*Ed.*

Did this allude to the navy his Liverpool friends are building?
... Lord Palmerston and Lord Russell as much as the Tory
Party are animated by a hatred of republicanism strong enough
to overbear all ordinary scruples; while Mr. Gladstone, a probable future Prime Minister, has avowed himself an admirer of
perjured men, leagued together against law to extend slavery.*

Of the papers that arrived from America today, the
Richmond Examiner, an organ of the Confederates, is
perhaps the most interesting. It contains a detailed article
on the situation, the most important features of which I
summarize in the following extract:

The extraordinary and sudden increase in the enemy's sea
power threatens to make our prospects gloomy. This weapon
has acquired such a range that in many respects it seems more
dangerous to us than the power of the enemy on land. The
Yankees now command 200 more warships than at the outbreak of the war. Great preparations have been made for naval
operations during the coming winter and, apart from the
vessels already fit for service, some 50 ironclad warships are in
process of construction. We have every reason to believe that
in the armament and construction of its ships the Yankee fleet
which will descend upon our coast this winter far surpasses
its predecessors. The objectives of the forthcoming expeditions
are of the greatest importance. It is intended to capture our
last seaports, complete the blockade and, finally, open up
points of invasion in Southern districts, in order with the beginning of the new year to put the Emancipation Acts into
practical operation. It would be foolish to deny the advantages
which must accrue to our enemy from the capture of our last
seaports, or to dismiss such misfortune lightly with the con-
soling thought that we can still always beat the foe by waging
war in the interior. ... With Charleston, Savannah and Mobile
in the enemy's hands, the blockade would be carried out with
a severity of which even our sufferings hitherto have given no
idea. We would have to give up all thought of building a fleet
on this side of the Atlantic Ocean and submit anew to the
humiliation of surrendering our shipbuilding to the enemy

* *Morning Star,* November 29, 1862.—*Ed.*

or destroying it ourselves. Our great system of railroad connections in the cotton states would be more or less broken
through, and perhaps too late we would make the discovery
that the land warfare, on which such great hopes are built,
would have to be continued under circumstances which forbade
the maintenance, provisioning and concentration of great
armies.... These disastrous results arising from a capture of
our seaports sink into insignificance, however, before a greater
danger, the greatest danger of this war—the occupation of
points in the cotton states from which the enemy can carry out
his emancipation plan. Great efforts are naturally being made
to safeguard this pet measure of the Abolitionists from falling
through and to prevent the spirit of revenge, which Mr. Lincoln
has corked in a bottle till January 1, from fizzling out in the
harmless hissing of soda-water.... The attempt is now made on
our most defenseless side; the heart of the South is to be
poisoned.... Prediction of future misfortune sounds bad to the
ears of the masses, who blindly believe in the government and
consider boasting to be patriotism.... We do not assert that
Charleston, Savannah and Mobile are not in a condition for
defense. In the South there are naturally whole scores of
military authorities, according to whom these ports are more
impregnable than Gibraltar; but military men and their mouth-
pieces have too often lulled our people into false security....
We heard the same story with regard to New Orleans. According to their description, its defensive works surpassed those of
Tyre against Alexander. Nevertheless, the people woke up one
fine morning to see the enemy's flag waving from its harbor.
The defensive condition of our ports is a secret of official circles.
But the indications of the immediate past are not comforting.
A few weeks ago *Galveston* fell into the enemy's hands almost
without a struggle.[125] The local newspapers had been forbidden
to write about the town's means of defense. No cry for help
resounded save that which struck the deaf ear of the government. The people were not roused. Their patriotism was requested to remain in ignorance, to trust the leaders and to
submit to the decrees of providence. In this way another prize
was presented to the enemy. The method of wrapping all
military matters in a mantle of secrecy has borne bad fruit
for the South. It may have reduced criticism to dead silence

and drawn a veil over the mistakes of the government. But it has not blinded the foe. He always seems accurately instructed on the state of our defense works, whilst our people first learn of their weakness when they have fallen into the hands of the Yankees.

Die Presse, December 4, 1862.

PART THREE

CORRESPONDENCE BETWEEN

KARL MARX

AND

FREDERICK ENGELS

(1861-1866)

CORRESPONDENCE BETWEEN KARL MARX
AND FREDERICK ENGELS (1861-1866)

1. MARX TO ENGELS *

January 11, 1860.

In my opinion, the biggest things that are happening in the world today are on the one hand the movement of the slaves in America started by the death of John Brown, and on the other the movement of the serfs in Russia....[126]

I have just seen in the *Tribune* that there has been a fresh rising of slaves in Missouri, naturally suppressed. But the signal has now been given. If things get serious by and by, what will then become of Manchester?

2. ENGELS TO MARX

January 26, 1860.

Your opinion of the significance of the slave movement in America and Russia is now confirmed. The Harper's

* This and the following extracts relating to the American Civil War are taken from the complete German edition of the works of Karl Marx and Frederick Engels: *Gesamtausgabe, Dritte Abteilung* (*"Der Brief-wechsel zwischen Marx und Engels"*), Band 2 (1854-1860) and *Band 3* (1861-1867) [*Collected Works*, Third Division ("The Correspondence Between Marx and Engels"), vols 2 and 3], Berlin, 1930. A number of the letters are contained in K. Marx and F. Engels, *Correspondence, A Selection with Commentary and Notes*, London and New York, 1934. —*Ed.*

Ferry affair [127] with its aftermath in Missouri bears its fruit; the free Negroes in the South are everywhere hunted out of the states, and I have just read in the first New York cotton report (W. P. Wright and Co., January 10, 1860) that the planters have hurried their cotton on to the ports in order to guard against any probable consequences arising out of the Harper's Ferry affair.

3. ENGELS TO MARX

January 7, 1861.

Things in North America are also becoming exciting. Matters must be going very badly for them with the slaves if the Southerners play so risky a game. The least volunteer *putsch* from the North could set everything ablaze. In any case, it seems that one way or another slavery is rapidly going to come to an end, and then it will be the same with cotton production. But how this will react on England will then soon become manifest. And with such mighty movements an ass like Bonaparte believes he can permanently fish in troubled waters.

4. MARX TO ENGELS

June 9, 1861.

Many thanks for the letter about America. Should anything important (militarily) occur, then always write me your opinion about it. According to the picture that I have formed of General Scott—now, moreover, 76 years old—from the Mexican War (see Ripley [128]), I expect the greatest blunders from him unless the old donkey is controlled by others. Slowness and indecision, above all. For the rest, I see by the facts reported in the *Tribune* that the North now speaks openly of a slave war and the destruction of slavery.

5. ENGELS TO MARX

June 12, 1861.

Unfortunately, I have not collected any newspapers on the American War, and many places, likewise, are not to be found on the map. The main thing is this:

The South had prepared in secret for years, but particularly since the excitement of the presidential election; through the treason of Buchanan's ministers it had obtained money and arms *en masse* at the last moment. Till March 4, therefore, the North was completely paralyzed. Even up to the fall of Sumter Linc[oln] did nothing or could do nothing but concentrate somewhat more and put in somewhat better trim the few troops of the line (18,000 men in all, mostly dispersed in the West against the Indians). Now, after the attack on Sumter, the North was at length sufficiently aroused to reduce all opposition outbursts to silence and thereby to make possible a powerful military action. Seventy-five thousand men were raised, who may now be on the move, but ten times this number seem to have offered themselves, and there may now be as many as 100,000 men on the move, though not yet concentrated by a long way. A further levy by Lincoln is daily expected and will require less time, since everything is now better prepared. The 75,000 men, or rather that part of them which is stationed in the neighborhood of Washington, on the Ohio opposite Kentucky and at St. Louis in Missouri (not counting, therefore, the reserves in Ohio and Pennsylvania), has been sufficient to restore for the present the equilibrium between the forces of the North and South on the line of the Potomac and even to permit for the moment the offensive of the North over a short distance.

The first objective of both the South and the North

was Washington. The offensive of the South against it was far too weak; beyond Richmond the main force appears to have been no longer strong enough for a timely blow. The only thing that was achieved was the dispatch of a mobile column to Harper's Ferry on the Potomac, above Washington. This position is eminently suitable for an offensive against the North (Maryland and Pennsylvania); it lies at the confluence of the Shenandoah, an important river, and the Potomac, is tactically of great strength and completely dominates both streams. The Federal arsenal seems to have been placed there not unintentionally by a government that foresaw and favored a future secession. The occupation of Harper's Ferry interrupts the domination of the Potomac line by the Union troops at a sensitive spot and gives the Southern troops, in the event of their advancing in numbers as far as this line, complete command of both banks forthwith.

On the holding of Washington by the North hung the fate of Maryland and Delaware; cut off from the South, occupied by Union troops, they fell at once to the Union. Second success of the Union.

The reconquest of Missouri by the Germans of St. Louis was the third success, and is of enormous importance, since the possession of St. Louis bars the Mississippi. How far the neutrality of Kentucky is favorable to the North or South will presumably depend on circumstances and events. At any rate, it restricts the theater of war for the present to the territory lying to the west.

Result: After all the preparations of the South, then, it has accomplished nothing more than that the North, with only one month's preparation, has already conquered from it the capital of the country and three slave states, and a fourth slave state does not dare to secede; that the Southern offensive has come to a halt at the Potomac, and the North has already moved across this river, so far without meeting resistance. For every additional man that the South can now put in the field, the North will put three to four. The states that have seceded have about 7,500,000 inhabitants, of whom more than 3,000,000 are slaves; 1,000,000 whites, at least, must be deducted for watching over the slaves, so that barely two and a half million remain to form the mass of the population available for war. If ten per cent of these are raised— the strongest force, I should say, that has ever been raised for defense—that gives, at most, 250,000 men. But so many will certainly not be got together. Switzerland, with nearly the same population—rather more than two million—has about 160,000 militiamen *on paper*. The North, on the other hand, counting the free states only, numbers 20,000,000, who are *all* available, with the exception, perhaps, of California, Utah and the remotest Western Territories. Let us say there is an available population of 17,000,000, and let us take not ten per cent of these, but only its third part, 3⅓ per cent, as available for a war of offense, then that gives over 500,000 men, more than sufficient to overwhelm the South, despite its utmost efforts. As far as the relationship, man to man, is concerned, there is no question that physically and morally the people of the North are considerably superior to those of the South. The combativeness of the Southerner is combined to an appreciable extent with the cowardice of the assassin. Every man goes about armed, but only *to be able to down his adversary* in a quarrel *before the latter expects the attack*. That is on the average.... [*The remainder of the letter is missing.*]

6. Marx to Engels

July 1, 1861.

Please write me *at once* what you think of the movements (military) in Virginia. The blunders of the militia officers—Brigadier-General Pierce,[129] by trade a "tailor" from Massachusetts—will naturally be repeated often enough on both sides. Is Washington still threatened? Do you think the Southerners at Manassas Junction hold an offensive position? Or are not the fellows rather on the point of retreat? In Missouri the defeat of the Southerners seems to be decisive, and the terrible "Colonel Bernstein" has now turned up there too. According to a private letter to Weber, "Colonel Willich" is at the head of a corps from Cincinnati.[130] He does not seem to have gone to the front yet. A closer study of this American business has shown me that the conflict between South and North—after the latter has abased itself for the past fifty years by one concession after another—was finally (apart from the new and shameless demands of "chivalry") brought to a head by the weight thrown into the scales by the extraordinary development of the Northwestern states. The population there, richly mixed with fresh German and English elements, and in addition self-working farmers for the most part, was naturally not so easily intimidated as the gentlemen of Wall Street and the Quakers of Boston. According to the last census (1860), the population there increased by 67% between 1850 and 1860, numbering 7,870,869 in 1860, whereas the total free population of the seceded slave states is about 5,000,000, according to the same census. In 1860 these Northwestern states provided the bulk of the government party and the President.[131] And it was just this part of the North which decided against any recognition of the independence of a Southern Confederacy. Naturally, they

cannot allow the lower part and delta of the Mississippi
to fall into the hands of foreign states. Likewise, it was
the population of these Northwestern states, who in the
Kansas affair (from which the present war actually
dates) came to grips with the border ruffians. Closer
examination of the history of the secession movement
reveals that secession, Constitution (Montgomery), Congress (*ibid.*), etc. are all usurpations. In no place did
they allow the people to vote *en masse*. Very characteristic articles appeared at the time in the Southern papers
on these "usurpations," in which it is not merely a question of seceding from the North, but of consolidating
and intensifying the oligarchy of the 300,000 slavelords
in the South against the 5,000,000 whites.

7. ENGELS TO MARX

July 3, 1861.

Your questions about the state of affairs in Virginia
are more easily put than answered. Is Washington still
threatened? Not immediately, otherwise the Southerners
would not have given up so much ground; but one does
not really know the relative strength of the opposing
forces. If the first main attack of the Northerners should
be decisively repulsed, there's no telling what will happen, as one can't say where they will then come to a
standstill. Still, it's three to one, that the Potomac would
then be a sufficient obstacle.

Position at Manassas Junction—determined by its being necessary for the Southerners to maintain their communications with northwest Virginia by means of the
railway to Paris and Strasburg. Should Manassas Junction be lost, their nearest railway communication with
West Virginia (on the other side of the mountains) is the
line from Richmond via Gordonsville to Staunton—80

miles further south; they lose the chance of rapidly moving their first-line reserves, those immediately behind the front, from west to east, etc., as required, and whatever is in West Virginia may be cut off or driven far afield. That is the significance of the position—if it is tactically of any importance is more than I can say, the maps do not allow of any conclusions. Altogether, the war in West Virginia will in the first place be a fight for the railway junctions.

The affair at Big Bethel has no importance whatever; tactically shockingly mismanaged; to make a night attack with such volunteers, and in divided columns into the bargain, could only end in confusion, one column firing on the other, and flight.

On the other hand, two things seem to be badly carried out in the North: 1. The masses of newly-trained and fully mobile troops appear not to be brought forward at all, but to be left idle some four or five hundred miles from the battlefield, whereas they would be invaluable on the Potomac—and 2. Brave old Scott again seems to have vast encirclement plans, which only result in a vast splitting up of his forces; how far this may lead to defeats cannot be foretold in view of the slack organization and the unknown heroes of the South.

What do you mean about not voting on secession? Here it was in all the papers that the Convention decisions had been ratified in every state by a popular vote.

8. MARX TO ENGELS

July 5, 1861.

With regard to the secession business, the affair is quite incorrectly reported in the English papers. With the exception of South Carolina, there was everywhere the strongest opposition to secession.

First: border slave states. In the winter of 1861 a border state Convention was held. Virginia, Kentucky, Arkansas, Maryland, Delaware, Tennessee and North Carolina were invited to it. For this purpose conventions were held in each of these states in order to send delegates to the General Convention.

Delaware refused even to call a convention for this purpose.

Tennessee ditto. Its democratic legislature took it out of the Union by a *coup de main.* Later, however, election held, to ratify this invalid act. This took place under the reign of terrorism. More than a third did not vote at all. Of the remainder one-third against secession, in particular the whole of east Tennessee, which is now arming against secession.[132]

Kentucky. 100,000 for the Union ticket; only a few thousand for secession.

Maryland declared for the Union, and has now elected six Union men as members of Congress.

North Carolina and even *Arkansas* elected Union delegates, the former even by a large majority.[133] Later terrorized.

Virginia. The people elected a Union Convention (according to majority). A part of these fellows let themselves be bought. At the height of the South fever—fall of Sumter—an Ordinance of Secession passed *secretly* by 88 to 55. All other steps—while the Ordinance was kept secret—for the capture of the Federal Navy Yard at Norfolk and the Federal Armory at Harper's Ferry in secret. Were betrayed to the Federal authorities before their execution. Alliance with Jeff Davis' government resolved upon in secret and great masses of Confederate troops suddenly thrown into the state. Under the protection of these troops (in real Bonapartist style) now elections for secession. Nevertheless 50,000 Union votes, in spite of systematic terrorism. Northwestern Virginia has now, as you know, openly separated from the secession movement.[134]

Second: Gulf States. A real popular vote occurred only in a few states. In most cases, the *Conventions,* elected to decide on the attitude of the Southern states to Lincoln's election (they formed later *their* delegates at the Montgomery Congress), usurped the power not only to decide on secession, but also to recognize the constitution, Jeff Davis, etc. You will get an idea of the methods adopted from the following excerpts from Southern papers.

Texas, in which after South Carolina the greatest slave party and terrorism, nevertheless 11,000 votes for the Union.[135]

Alabama. The inhabitants neither voted on secession nor the new constitution, etc. The Convention elected here passed the Ordinance of Secession with 61 against 39 votes. But the 39 of the Northern counties, inhabited almost entirely by whites, represented more free men than the 61; [136] according to the *United States Constitution* every slaveowner votes for ⅗ of his slaves.

Louisiana. At the election for delegates to the Convention more Union votes were cast than secession votes.[137] But the delegates deserted to the other side.

The west of Carolina, the east of Tennessee, the north of Alabama and Georgia, mountain districts with interests very different from those of the Southern swamps.

The December 2nd character [138] of the whole secession maneuver (the fellows are consequently obliged to provoke a war in order to keep the movement alive under the slogan "The North against the South"), which you can see from the following excerpts, is further revealed by the fact that the traitors in Buchanan's Administration,[139] who stood at the head of the movement—Floyd,

Secretary of War; Toucey, Secretary of the Navy; Cobb, Secretary of the Treasury; Thompson, Secretary of the Interior—together with the leading senators of the South, were most deeply involved in the *dilapidations,* running into many millions, which were referred to a Committee of Enquiry in the course of December 1860 by Congress (the House of Representatives). For a part of these fellows (at least) it was a matter of escaping penal servitude. That is why they are the most willing tools of the 300,000 slaveholder oligarchy. That the latter, as a result of their concentration, position and resources, able for the moment to put down any opposition, obvious. In a part of the "poor whites" they found the mob, who acted for them as substitutes of the Zouaves.

Georgia. The Griffin Union: "It is mockery for the same men who made the Constitution in Montgomery to come back to Georgia and ratify it under the name of a state convention." *The Macon Journal:* "The State Conventions... called for another purpose... assume that they are the people, and under such an assumption of power can appoint delegates to a General Convention without consulting the people. *All the acts of the Congress of their Confederacy are passed in secret session with closed doors,* and what is done is kept from the people." *The Augusta Chronicle and Sentinel* (the biggest Georgia paper): *"The whole movement for secession,* and the formation of a new government, so far at least as Georgia is concerned" (and Georgia has the largest population of all the slave states) "proceed on only *a quasi consent* of the people, and was pushed through, under circumstances of great excitement and frenzy—*by a fictitious majority.* With all the appliances brought to bear, etc., the election of January 4 showed a falling-off of nearly 3,000, and an absolute majority of elected deputies of 79. But, upon assembling, by whee-

dling, coaxing, *buying,* and all the arts of deception, the convention showed a majority of 31 (against Union)....
The Georgia Convention and the *Confederate Congress* have gone forward in their work, as none can deny, without authority from the people."

Alabama. The Mobile Advertiser: "The Convention has adopted the permanent Constitution in behalf of the State of Alabama....[140] The great fact stands forth that the delegates were not chosen for any such purpose." *The North Alabamian:* "The Convention made haste to usurp the prerogative, and ratify the Constitution.... It is a remarkable fact, that the substantial, physical force of the country, the hard-fisted, hard-working men, expected to do all the fighting when the country calls, *were from the beginning opposed to the Ordinance of Secession.*"

Mississippi. Similar complaints about usurpation in *Jackson Mississippian* and the *Vicksburg Whig.*

Louisiana. New Orleans True Delta: "Here secession succeeded only by suppressing the election returns ... the government has been changed into *despotism.*" In the *State Convention* of Louisiana (New Orleans) of March 22, 1861, old *Roselius* (one of the leading politicians in the United States) says: "The Montgomery instrument ... did not inaugurate a government of the people, but *an odious and unmitigated oligarchy.* The people had not been permitted to act in the matter."

In Louisville, Kentucky, on March 16, 1861, Senator Guthrie (pro-slavery man, Secretary of the Treasury under Pierce) said the whole movement was a plot and usurpation. Amongst other things that: "In Alabama a majority of the popular vote was cast against going out, but a small majority of the delegates were for secession, they took Alabama out, and refused the people to have any voice in the matter. The vote of Louisiana, too, was against secession, but the delegates suppressed it."

9. ENGELS TO MARX

November 27, 1861.

Have these Yankees then gone completely crazy to carry out the mad coup with the Confederate Commissioners?[141] The fact that here in the Channel too, a warship was waiting for the mail steamer, proves that general instructions must have been issued from Washington. To take political prisoners by force on a foreign ship, is the clearest *casus belli* there can be. The fellows must be sheer fools to land themselves in for a war with England. If war should actually break out, you can send your letters to New York via Germany or the Havre addressed to an intermediary, but you will have to take care that you don't give any assistance to the enemies of the Queen.

10. MARX TO ENGELS

December 9, 1861.

War, as I have declared in the *Presse* from the first day, will not break out with America, and I only regret that I had not the means to exploit the asininity of the Reuter and *Times*-swayed Stock Exchange during this fool period.

11. MARX TO ENGELS

December 19, 1861.

As for *war with America*, Pam * may *possibly* succeed in bringing it about, but not easily. He must have a *pretext*, and I do *not* think *that Lincoln will furnish it*. A part of the Cabinet, Milner-Gibson, Gladstone, *plus ou moins* ** Lewis, cannot be fooled like John Russell.

Considered in itself, the Americans have not erred, either *materially* or *formally*, according to the *British*

* Palmerston.—*Ed.*
** More or less.—*Ed.*

maritime law prevailing over there. Hence they have resorted to an *error in form,* a technicality, a legal quibble, since Pam wanted a pretext. But this is false too. According to British maritime law two things must be distinguished. Whether a neutral ship carries *belligerent* goods and persons or *contraband of war,* no matter if the latter consists of goods or persons. In the latter case the ship is to be seized with cargo and persons and brought into a port for adjudication. In the former case—if there is *no doubt* that the goods have not *gone over* into the possession of neutrals (which is of itself impossible in the case of persons), the belligerent goods or persons are confiscable on the high sea, while the ship, etc., goes free. England has continually asserted this jurisprudence—apart from the authorities—as I have convinced myself by looking up all the squabbles with neutrals since 1793 in Cobbett's Register.

On the other hand, since the English crown lawyers have restricted the question to an error in form, and thus conceded the Yankees the *right* of confiscating any British ship that carries belligerents and towing it into a port for adjudication, the Yankees can very easily declare—and they will do so, in my opinion—that they are satisfied with this concession, will not violate the *form* in confiscation, etc., in the future, and yield up Mason and Slidell for the nonce.

If Pam wants war absolutely, he can bring it about of course. In my opinion *that is not his purpose.* If the Americans act in the manner I have supposed, Pam will have furnished stupid John Bull another proof that he is "the truly English minister." The fellow will then be allowed to do anything. He will utilize the opportunity to

(1) Force the Yankees to recognize the Paris declaration on the rights of neutrals;

(2) under this pretext call upon and make Parliament

sanction the resignation of the old English maritime law, signed by Clarendon at his (Pam's) instructions behind the back of the crown and without Parliament knowing it in advance, *which he hasn't dared to do as yet.*

Pam is old, and the Russians have endeavored to force through the declaration issued in Paris ever since the time of Catherine II. They still lack two things: *the sanction of the British Parliament, and the adherence of the United States.* Both of these will be accomplished upon this occasion. The show of war seems to me to be merely theatrical accessories in order to exhibit the definitive resignation of his own maritime law to stupid John Bull as a victory won over the Yankees by the pluck of the "truly English minister."

Subsidiary reasons for the war show would be: diversion from Poland (since even fellows like Cunningham of Brighton demand in public meetings the stoppage of further payment of the Dutch-Russian loan) and diversion from Denmark, where Russia is at this instant engaged in pushing aside Glücksburg, the heir presumptive it appointed itself.

It is possible, of course, that the Yankees will not yield, and then Pam is compelled to go to war by his preparations and rodomontades up to now. Yet I should like to bet 100 to 1 against it.

12. MARX TO ENGELS

March 3, 1862.

I should be glad if you supplied me *this week* (by Friday morning) with an *English* article on the American War. You can write *entirely without constraint.* The *Tribune* will print it as the letter of a foreign officer. *Nota bene:* * The *Tribune* hates McClellan, who is in

* Note well.—*Ed.*

league with the Democratic Party and who, *so long as* he was Commander-in-Chief of all the armies, prevented any action not only on the Potomac (where this was perhaps justified), but in *all* theaters of war, particularly in the West, by *direct intervention*. (He was also the soul of the extremely disgraceful intrigue against Frémont.) This Mc, moreover, out of *esprit de corps* and hatred of the civilians, protected all the traitors in the army, *e.g.*, Colonel Maynard and General Stone. The arrest of the latter ensued a day or two after [Mc]Clellan had been deposed as Commander-in-Chief of the whole army. In the same way the shameless Washington "representative" of the *New York Herald* was arrested as a spy contrary to M'Clellan's wishes and after he had entertained the entire staff of M'C[lellan] the day before at a champagne breakfast.

13. ENGELS TO MARX

March 5, 1862.

You shall have the article. The braggarts in the South are now getting a glorious beating. The reception that the gunboats on the Tennessee River have had everywhere as far as Florence, Alabama (here the muscle shoals begin, which interrupt navigation) is most gratifying. Accordingly even in west Tennessee, on the plains, a decisive majority for the Union. Fifteen thousand prisoners, among them the Confederates' best general, Johnston, who decided Bull Run by his rapid concentration in the center, is no joke.[142]

14. MARX TO ENGELS

March 6, 1862.

Of [England's] total exports, amounting to 125,115,133 pounds (1861), 42,260,970 pounds' worth go to English "possessions" and "colonies." If one adds to these England's further exports to Asia, Africa, and America, 23 to 24 per cent at most then remain for export to the European states. If Russia goes forward in Asia at the double quick march of the last ten years, until she concentrates all her efforts on India, then it is all up with John Bull's world market, and this end is further hastened by the protectionist policy of the United States, which now, if only to revenge themselves on John Bull, will assuredly not give it up so soon. Moreover, John Bull discovers with horror that his principal colonies in North America and Australia become protectionists in precisely the same measure as John Bull becomes a free-trader. The self-complacent, brutal stupidity with which John admires Pam's "spirited policy" in Asia and America, will cost him damned dear.

That the Southerners will have concluded peace by July 1862 does not appear to me very probable. When the Northerners have secured (1) the border states—and it is these that were at stake from the beginning—and (2) the Mississippi to New Orleans and Texas, a second period of the war will presumably begin in which the Northerners will not put forth great military efforts, but by quarantining the Gulf states will finally drive these to voluntary re-annexation.

Bull's behavior during the present war is possibly the most barefaced that has ever been witnessed.

In the matter of brutality on the English side, the *Mexican Blue Book* surpasses anything that history has known. Menshikov seems a gentleman, compared with *Sir C. Lennox Wyke*. This canaille not only develops the most unbounded *zèle* in carrying out Pam's secret instructions, but seeks to revenge himself by boorishness for the fact that Señor Zamacona, the Mexican Minister for Foreign Affairs (now out of office) and a former journalist, is invariably his superior in the exchange of diplomatic notes. As regards the fellow's style, here are a few samples from his notes to Zamacona. "The arbitrary act of stopping all payments for the space of two years is depriving the parties interested of their money *for that space of time, which is a dead loss of so much value* to them." "A starving man may justify, in his own eyes, the fact of stealing a loaf on the ground that imperious necessity impelled him thereto; but such an argument cannot, in a moral point of view, justify his violation of the law, which remains as positive, *apart from all sentimentality,* as if the crime had not had an excuse. *If he was actually starving,* he should have first asked the baker to assuage his hunger, but *doing so* (starving?) *of his own free will,* without permission, *is* acting exactly as the Mexican government *has* done towards *its creditors on the present occasion.*" "With regard to the *light* in which you view the question, as *expressed* in your above named note, you will excuse me for stating that it *cannot be treated of partially,* WITHOUT *also* taking into consideration the opinions of those who directly suffer *from the practical operation of such ideas as emanating from yourself.*" "I had a full right to complain of having first of all *heard* of this extraordinary measure by *seeing* it in printed bills *placarded through* the public streets." "I have a duty to perform both to my own God and to that to *which* I am accredited *which* impels me, etc." "I suspend all official relations with the government of this Republic until *that* of Her Majesty shall adopt such measures as *they* shall deem necessary." Zamacona writes to him that the intrigues of the foreign diplomatists for twenty-five years are chiefly to blame for the troubles in Mexico. Wyke replies to him that "the population of Mexico is so degraded as to make them dangerous, not only to themselves, but to everybody coming into contact with them!"

Zamacona writes to him that the proposals which he makes put an end to the autonomy of the republic and run counter to the dignity of any independent state. Wyke answers: "Excuse me for adding that such a proposition as I have made to you does not necessarily become undignified and impracticable simply because *you, an interested person* (*i.e.,* as Mexico's Foreign Minister), are pleased to say so." However, *satis superque.**

15. MARX TO ENGELS

April 28, 1862.

What is of particular interest to the fellows ** at the moment is America, and I wish you would send me an article on the progress of the war (I mean the battle of Corinth), if possible, this week still, and generally that you would now write me every time there's any turn in the military situation. If only to spread correct views on this important matter in Germany. (I have already worked up your former articles for them; they've already been printed.)

16. ENGELS TO MARX

May 5, 1862.

About America:

1. Battle of Corinth. Ranks with all the big, well-fought modern battles where the contending forces are fairly equal, Eylau, Wagram, Lützen, Bautzen (here the French were indeed much stronger, but were without cavalry and therefore powerless to pursue), Borodino, Magenta and Solferino.[143] The battle burns slowly, as

---

* Enough and more than enough.—*Ed.*
** Refers to *Die Presse.—Ed.*

Clausewitz says, like damp powder, exhausts both parties and at the finish the *positive* advantages gained by the victorious side are more of a moral than a material nature. At any rate, the momentary advantage which Beaur[egard] obtained on the Sunday was far more intensive and greater than that which Gr[ant] and Buell obtained on the Monday. The bulk of the trophies remained with the Confederates, despite the fact that they were finally beaten, that is, forced to abandon their attack and to withdraw. So much for the tactical aspect. The strategical aspect, however, is this:

Beauregard had concentrated all the troops that he could obtain, in order, where possible, to fall on the advancing Federal divisions individually. This miscarried; the troops of Grant, Buell and Wallace were sufficient to repel him. If they had lost the battle, the Federals would have lost Tennessee; now they have held it. Beauregard has only his entrenchments at Corinth to thank for not having been obliged to go further south forthwith. Whether these entrenchments are capable of safeguarding him against an attack by Halleck (who has now assumed command), we are not in a position to know. Just as little is the report to be trusted that he has received colossal reënforcements from Mississippi, Louisiana and Alabama. If this is partly the case, then they are merely recruits, who are more in his way than of use to him. On the other hand, at Pittsburg Landing the forces were so nearly in equilibrium that *without reënforcements* Halleck, likewise, will not lightly undertake the storming of an entrenched camp or any other big offensive enterprise. Apart from those in the engagement at Pittsburg Landing, we do not know what other troops the Federals have in Tennessee or Kentucky; it is therefore hard to say how the chances stand. Meanwhile the Unionists have cut the railroad line from Memphis to Chattanooga (*id est,* to Richmond, Charleston and Savannah) both west and east of Corinth. Beaur[egard] is hereby restricted to one railroad (to Mobile and New Orleans) and it is questionable whether he will be able to provision his troops for long in Corinth.

2. Virginia. The hero McClellan is in a dead fix. I think he will bury his false glory here. He has had another division transferred from McDowell to himself, but it will avail little. Only the *armored ships* can save him, another of which (the *Galena*) has left for Monroe. On this subject see today's *Morning Star,* American correspondence, very interesting for Austria. From this you will also see why recently the *Monitor* remained lying idle when the *Merrimac, Yorktown,* etc., captured the three transports. By sweeping the rivers right and left, and by flank and rear fire, these ships could save the ass or traitor once more, just as the gunboats at Pittsburg Landing saved Sherman (who only had young troops that had never been under fire).

3. Mountain Department. Frémont is still in Wheeling, and in consequence thereof the mountainous part of south Virginia, as of east Tennessee, is still in the hands of the enemy. Accordingly, *the best Union districts of all!* Why that is so is not explicable. In any case, the Confederate regiment recruited at the beginning of April in Knoxville, Tennessee, will doubtless desert at the first shot.

Bonaparte is up to his tricks again in America. He will take care not to stir up this wasps' nest. Before the end of the year (*vide* The Morning Star*) his ironclads, as well as all French merchantmen, would be off the ocean, and then adieu to pleasure!

Apropos! In today's *Standard* (or *Morning Herald*) you will have seen that *General Hecker* has become

* See.—*Ed.*

"nigger-catcher-in-chief" (Manhattan). *Be sure and put the paper by.*

17. MARX TO ENGELS

May 6, 1862.

I shall write to Dana once more. I miss the sending of the *Tribune* sadly. This is a mean trick of Greeley and McElrath. From the last numbers of the *Tribune* for March I have learnt two things. Firstly, that McClellan had been *accurately* informed eight days beforehand of the Confederates' retreat. Secondly, that *The Times'* Russell availed himself of his nosing in Washington during the *Trent* affair to gamble on the Stock Exchange in New York....

Bonaparte's present maneuvers in Mexico (the affair originally emanated from Pam) are explained by the fact that Jaurez only recognizes the official debt to France of £46,000. But Miramon and his gang, per medium of the Swiss banker Jecker *et* Co., had issued state bonds to the amount of $52,000,000 (on which about $4,000,000 have been paid). These state bonds—Jecker *et* Co. being only the *hommes de pailles* *—have fallen almost for *zéro* into the hands of Morny *et* Co. They demand recognition of them by Jaurez. *Hinc illae lacrimae.***

Schurz is—a brigadier-general with Frémont! ! !

18. ENGELS TO MARX

May 12, 1862.

What puts me off the Yankees in regard to any success is not the military position, taken by itself. This, solely as a result of the slackness and obtuseness that manifest

---

* Men of straw.—*Ed.*
** Hence these tears.—*Ed.*

themselves throughout the North. Where is there revolutionary energy anywhere among the people? They let themselves get a beating and are quite proud of the lickings they receive. Where throughout the North is there even a single symptom that the people are in earnest about anything? I have never come across such a state of affairs; not in Germany in the worst times. The Yankees, on the contrary, already seem to find most joy in the thought that they will cheat their state creditors.

19. ENGELS TO MARX *

May 23, 1862.

McClellan continues in his well-known manner. The Confederates always escape him because he never has a go at them, his excuse for which is that they are stronger, a good deal, than he. For that reason, indeed, they always run away. Never yet has a war been waged in such a fashion, and for this he then obtains his vote of thanks. Meanwhile these small, unlucky rearguard engagements and the continual desertions are still sufficient to demoralize the Confederates badly,[144] and when it comes to the decisive battle, they will find it out.

The capture of New Orleans is a deed of valor on the part of the fleet. The passing of the forts, that is, was altogether excellent. After this, everything was simple. The moral effect on the Confederates was evidently enormous, and the material effect will have already made itself felt. Beauregard has now nothing more to defend in Corinth; the position had only any meaning so long as it covered Mississippi and Louisiana, and especially New Orleans. B[eauregard] has now been put in such a strategic position that the loss of a single battle leaves

* This letter was almost entirely included by Marx in his article on "The Situation in the American Theatre of War" (*Die Presse*, May 30, 1862). See pp. 185-190.—*Ed.*

him no other choice than to disband his army into guerrillas; for without a large town, where railroads and resources are concentrated, in the rear of his army, he *cannot* hold masses of men together.

If the Confederate army in Virginia is beaten, it must
then, after the previous demoralizing affairs, soon dissolve into guerrillas automatically. It has admittedly
better chances, because the many streams on its line of
retreat flow crosswise from the mountains to the sea, and
because it has this donkey McCl[ellan] opposed to it;
nevertheless, in the nature of things it will be driven
either to accept a decisive battle or to break up into bands
without a battle. Just as the Russians were obliged to
fight at Smolensk and Borodino, though *against* the will
of their generals, who judged the situation correctly.

Should Beaur[egard] or the Virginia army win a battle,
and be it ever so big, this can still avail little. The Confederates are not in a position to make the least use of
it. They cannot advance twenty English miles without
coming to a standstill and must consequently await a renewed attack. They lack everything. For the rest, I consider this case to be quite impossible without direct
treachery.

On a single battle, then, now hangs the fate of the
Confederate armies; it still remains to examine the
chances of guerrilla warfare. Now in respect of precisely
the present war it is most amazing how slight or, much
rather, how wholly lacking is the participation of the
population in it. In 1813, indeed, the communications
of the French were continually interrupted and cut up
by Colomb, Lützow, Chernyshev and twenty other insurgents and Cossack leaders; in 1812 the population in
Russia disappeared completely from the French line of
march; in 1814 the French peasants armed themselves
and slew the patrols and stragglers of the Allies. But

here nothing happens at all. Men resign themselves to *the fate of the big battles* and console themselves with *victrix causa deis*, etc. The tall talk of war to the knife dissolves into mere muck. And shall guerrillas come forth on the terrain? I certainly expect that after the definite dissolution of the armies the white trash of the South will attempt something of the sort, but I am too firmly convinced of the bourgeois nature of the planters to doubt for a moment that this will make them rabid Union men forthwith. The former are bound to attempt this with brigandage, and the planters will everywhere receive the Yankees with open arms. The bonfires on the Mississippi are based exclusively on the two Kentuckians who are said to have come to Louisville—certainly not *up* the Mississippi. The conflagration in New Orleans was easily organized and will be repeated in other towns; assuredly, much will otherwise be burnt also; but this business must necessarily bring the split between the planters and merchants, on one side, and the white trash, on the other, to a head and therewith secession is undone.

The fanaticism of the New Orleans merchants for the Confederacy is simply explained by the fact that the fellows have had to take a quantity of Confederate scrip for hard cash. I know several instances of this here. This must not be forgotten. A good forced loan is a famous means of fettering the bourgeois to the revolution and diverting them from their class interests through their personal interests.

20. MARX TO ENGELS

May 27, 1862.

The blowing up of the *Merrimac* seems to me an evident act of cowardice on the part of the dirty dogs of

Confederacy.[145] The hounds could still risk something. It is wonderfully fine how *The Times* (which supported all the Coercion Bills against Ireland with so much fiery zeal) wails that "liberty" must be lost in the event of the North tyrannizing the South. *The Economist* is also good. In its last number it declares that the Yankees' financial prosperity—the non-depreciation of their paper money—is *incomprehensible* to it (although the matter is perfectly simple). It had hitherto consoled its readers from week to week with this depreciation. Although it now admits that it does not understand what is its business and has misled its readers concerning this, it is at present solacing them with dark doubts about the "military operations," of which it officially knows nothing.

What extraordinarily facilitated the paper operations of the Yankees [146] (the main point being the confidence placed in their cause and therewith in their government) was without question the circumstance that in consequence of secession the West was almost denuded of paper money and therefore of a circulating medium generally. All the banks whose principal securities consisted of the bonds of slave states, were bankrupted. Moreover, currency for millions, which circulated in the West in the form of direct banknotes of the Southern banks, was swept away. Then, partly in consequence of the Morrill tariff, partly in consequence of the war itself, which largely put an end to the import of luxuries, the Yankees had a balance of trade and therefore a rate of exchange favorable to themselves and against Europe the whole time. An unfavorable rate of exchange might have badly affected the patriotic confidence in their paper on the part of the philistines.

For the rest—this comical concern of John Bull for the interest on the national debt that Uncle Sam will have to pay! As if it were not a mere bagatelle in comparison with Bull's national debt; moreover the United States are unquestionably richer today than were the Bulls with their debt of a billion in 1815.

Has Pam not got Bonaparte into a pretty pickle in Mexico?

21. ENGELS TO MARX

May 29, 1862.

Anneke is with Buell's army and from today is writing in the *Augsburger*. I am rather anxious about Halleck's troops; the affair drags on so long, and yet he does not appear to receive any reënforcements, though Spence's lies in *The Times* have surely no significance. Willich is a colonel (the eternal colonel!) and commands the 32nd Indiana regiment....

A certain amount of guerrilla warfare does now seem after all to be beginning; but it is certainly not of great importance, and if only a victory ensues, the reserve forces following in its wake, together with some cavalry, will soon put an end to the business. In case of a defeat, it would of course be vexatious.

22. ENGELS TO MARX

June 4, 1862.

At last, then, we learn from Anneke's letter that, counting Pope and Mitchell's forces, Halleck had rather more than 100,000 men and 300 guns on April 26, and that he was waiting for the arrival of Curtis and Sigel with further reënforcements. Up to April 29 the condition of the army seems to have been passable on the whole; A[nneke] says nothing about sickness. Accordingly, I consider the talk of sickness to be sheer invention. For the rest, it must be said that Stanton and Halleck understand how to make the press and the public mistrustful; in order that the public may get news of some sort, it is surely easy enough to have a correspondent with each army, who is told what he is to write by the general. Presumably, then, the big battle will be fought as soon as Sigel and Curtis are on the spot. The calculations of Spence to the effect that 120,000 men are necessary to keep the border states in order, are ludicrous; hardly a single man seems to be stationed in Kentucky (outside possible training camps for recruits at Louisville, out of whom, however, Sigel's corps will presumably be formed) and, according to Anneke, there were merely convalescents, etc., in Nashville; otherwise, outside the armies of Halleck and McClellan, only Frémont (who, it seems, still has no army at all), Banks (who must be very weak) and McDowell, all of whom, however, count as part of the *active* army, are stationed in the border states. On the other hand, Spence errs in the other direction: 1. At the present moment the armies of the Federals certainly do not number 500,000 men in all; 2. They have assuredly more than 90,000 men distributed along the coast. My calculation is something like this:

On the coast	100,000	men
Sigel and Curtis	30,000	"
Banks and Frémont	30,000	"
McClellan	80,000	"
At Washington	30,000	"
McDowell	30,000	"
Halleck	100,000	"

altogether, therefore, 400,000 men in the field, to whom I add about 60,000 recruits, convalescents and small detachments that may be distributed in Missouri, along both banks of the lower Ohio and Tennessee, and partly in the towns of the Northeast. *Summa summarum,**

* In sum.—*Ed.*

460,000 men. I am supported in this calculation by the new levy of 50,000 men, which will presumably be followed very soon by a second of equal strength; it seems to be desired to maintain the army at a normal strength of 500,000 men.

It was Stanton's biggest blunder and sheer vainglory to suspend recruiting. Materially, that has done much harm and is to blame for all the loss of time at Corinth and Richmond; and morally, this present countermand does much more harm still—apart from the fact that it will be much harder to obtain recruits now. Otherwise, there are people enough available; in consequence of immigration the Northern states must have at least three to four per cent more people of from 20 to 35 years of age than any other country.

For the rest, Monsieur Anneke appears in his letters as the same old grumbling fault-finder and wiseacre who judges the army not according to the circumstances and not according to the adversary either, but by old, schooled European armies, and not even by these as they are, but as they *should* be. The blockhead ought, however, to think of the confusion that he himself must have experienced often enough in Prussian maneuvers.

23. ENGELS TO MARX *

July 30, 1862.

Things go wrong in America, and it is after all Mr. Stanton who is chiefly to blame, for the reason that after the conquest of Tennessee he suspended recruiting out of sheer vainglory and so condemned the army to constant weakening just when it stood most in need of reënforcements for a rapid, decisive offensive. With a steady influx of recruits, even if the war were not de-

* Part of this letter is included by Marx in his article on "A Criticism of American Affairs" (*Die Presse,* August 9, 1862), pp. 198-201.—*Ed.*

cided by now, its success would nevertheless have been beyond doubt. With continual victories recruits would also have come freely. This step was all the sillier as the South was then enlisting all men from 18 to 35 years of age, and was therefore staking everything on a *single* card. It is those people who have joined up in the meantime who now give the Confederates the upper hand everywhere and secure the initiative to them. They held Halleck fast, dislodged Curtis from Arkansas, smote McClellan and under Jackson in the Shenandoah valley gave the signal for the guerrilla raids that now reach as far as the Ohio. No one could have acted more stupidly than Stanton.

Further. When Stanton saw that he could not dislodge McClellan from the command of the Potomac army, he perpetrated the stupidity of weakening him by conferring special commands on Frémont, Banks and McDowell *and of splitting up the forces to the end of removing McClellan.* The consequence of this is, not only that McC[lellan] has been beaten, but also that public opinion now maintains that it is not McC[lellan], but Stanton who is to blame for the defeat. Serves Mr. Stant[on] right.

All that would be of no consequence, it might even be of service, in that the war would at last be waged in a revolutionary way. But there's the trouble. The defeats do not stir these Yankees up; they make them slack. If, merely to obtain recruits, they have already come to the point of declaring themselves prepared to take them *for nine months only,* what is meant is nothing other than this: we are in a bad way, and all we want is the semblance of an army as a means of making a demonstration during the peace negotiations. Those 300,000 volunteers were the criterion, and by refusing to provide them the North declares that to it its whole cause is *au fond* *

* At bottom.—*Ed.*

muck. Furthermore, what cowardice in government and Congress. They are afraid of conscription, of resolute financial steps, of attacks on slavery, of everything that is urgently necessary; they let everything loaf along as it will, and if the semblance of some measure finally gets through Congress, the honorable Lincoln so qualifies it that nothing at all is left of it any longer. This slackness, this collapse like a punctured pig's bladder, under the pressure of defeats that have annihilated one army, the strongest and best, and actually left Washington exposed, this total absence of any elasticity in the whole mass of the people—this proves to me that it is all up. The few mass meetings, etc., do not mean anything; they don't attain even the stir of a presidential election.

In addition, the total lack of talent. One general more stupid than the other. Not one that would be capable of the least initiative or of independent decision. For three months the initiative once more wholly with the adversary. Then, one financial measure more lunatic than the other. Helplessness and cowardice everywhere, save among the common soldiers. The politicians in like case—just as absurd and devoid of counsel. And the populus is more helpless than if it had lingered three thousand years under the Austrian scepter.

For the South, on the contrary—it's no use shutting one's eyes to the fact—it's a matter of bloody earnest. That we get no cotton is already one proof. The guerrillas in the border states are a second. But that after being thus shut off from the world, an agricultural people can sustain such a war and after severe defeats and losses in resources, men and territory, can nevertheless now stand forth as the victor and threaten to carry its offensive right into the North, this is in my opinion decisive. Besides, they fight quite famously, and with the second occupation of Kentucky and Tennessee, what Union feeling still existed there outside the highlands is now surely lost.

If they get Missouri, they get the Territories, too, and then the North can pack up.

As said, if the North does not proceed forthwith in revolutionary fashion, it will get an ungodly hiding and deserve it—and it looks like it.

24. MARX TO ENGELS

July 30, 1862.

As to America, that, says he [Lassalle],[147] is quite interesting. The Yankees have no "ideas." "Individual liberty" is merely a "negative idea," etc., and more of this old, decayed, speculative rubbish.

25. MARX TO ENGELS

August 7, 1862.

I do not altogether share your views on the American Civil War. I do not think that all is up. The Northerners have been dominated from the first by the representatives of the border slave states, who also pushed McClellan, that old partisan of Breckinridge, to the top. The Southerners, on the other hand, acted as one man from the beginning. The North itself has turned the slaves into a military force on the side of the Southerners, instead of turning it against them. The South leaves productive labor to the slaves and could therefore put its whole fighting strength in the field without disturbance. The South had unified military leadership, the North had not. That no strategic plan existed was already obvious from all the maneuvers of the Kentucky army after the conquest of Tennessee. In my opinion all this will take another turn. In the end the North will make war seriously, adopt revolutionary methods and throw over the domination of the border slave statesmen. A single Negro regiment would have a remarkable effect on Southern nerves.[148]

The difficulty of getting the 300,000 men seems to me purely political. The Northwest and New England wish to and will force the government to give up the diplomatic method of conducting war which it has used hitherto, and they are now making terms on which the 300,000 men shall come forth. If Lincoln does not give way (which he will do, however), there will be a revolution.

As to the lack of military talent, the method which has prevailed up till now of selecting generals purely from considerations of diplomacy and party intrigue is scarcely designed to bring talent to the front. General Pope seems to me to be a man of energy, however.[149]

With regard to the financial measures, they are clumsy, as they are bound to be in a country where up to now no taxes (for the whole state) have in fact existed; but they are not nearly so idiotic as the measures taken by Pitt and Co. The present depreciation of money is due, I think, not to economic but to purely political reasons—distrust. It will therefore change with a different policy.

The long and short of the business seems to me to be that a war of this kind must be conducted on revolutionary lines, while the Yankees have so far been trying to conduct it constitutionally.

26. ENGELS TO MARX

September 9, 1862.

The Bull Run affair, No. II,* was a capital bit of work by Stonewall Jackson, who is by far the best chap in

---

* The second Battle of Bull Run took place toward the end of August, 1862.—*Ed.*

America. Had he been supported by a frontal attack of the main Confederate army and had everything gone well (even only tolerably well), then it would probably have been all up with Monsieur Pope. As it is, however, the affair has led to nothing save that the Confederates have gained a great moral advantage—respect for their enterprising spirit and for Jackson—and a few square miles of territory, but have, on the other hand, hastened the unification and concentration of the *whole Federal army* before Washington. We shall now, presumably, get further news by the next steamer of fresh encounters, in which the Federals might well be victorious if their generals were not so bloody stupid. But what is to be done with such a pack of hounds! Pope is the lousiest of the lot; he can only brag, revoke, lie and conceal reverses. Truly, the wiseacre of the general staff. McClellan now appears to one to be again altogether a sensible man. Furthermore, the *ordre* that all future major-generals are to pass the Prussian ensign's examination. It is too pitiable, and the lads in the South, who at least know what they want, strike me as heroes in comparison with the flabby management of the North. Or do you still believe that the gentlemen in the North will crush the "rebellion"?

27. Marx to Engels

September 10, 1862.

As regards the Yankees, I am assuredly still of my previous opinion that the North will finally prevail; certainly the Civil War may go through all sorts of episodes, even armistices, perhaps, and be long drawn out. The South would and could only conclude peace on condition that it received the border slave states. In this event California would also fall to it; the Northwest would follow, and the entire Federation, with perhaps the exception of the New England states, would form a single country once more, this time under the acknowledged supremacy of the slaveholders. It would be the reconstruction of the United States on the basis demanded by the South. This, however, is impossible and will not happen.

The North can, for its part, only conclude peace if the Confederacy limits itself to the old slave states and those confined between the Mississippi River and the Atlantic. In this case the Confederacy would soon come to its blessed end. Intervening armistices, etc., on the basis of a *status quo*, could at most entail pauses in the prosecution of the war.

The manner in which the North wages war is only to be expected from a *bourgeois* republic, where fraud has so long reigned supreme. The South, an oligarchy, is better adapted thereto, particularly as it is an oligarchy where the whole of the productive labor falls on the Negroes and the four millions of "white trash" are filibusters by profession. All the same, I would wager my head that these boys come off second best, despite "Stonewall Jackson." To be sure, it is possible that it will come to a sort of revolution in the North itself first.

Willich is a brigadier-general and, as Kapp has related in Cologne, Steffen is now to take the field also.

It seems to me that you let yourself be swayed a little too much by the military aspect of things.

28. ENGELS TO MARX

October 16, 1862.

What do you think of America? The financial crash, which with these stupid paper-money measures cannot fail to come, seems near. Militarily, the North will now, presumably, get on its feet again somewhat.

29. MARX TO ENGELS

October 29, 1862.

As for America, I believe that the Maryland campaign was decisive in so far is it showed that even in this section of the border states most sympathetic to the South support for the Confederates is weak. But the whole struggle turns on the border states. Whoever gets them dominates the Union. At the same time the fact that Lincoln issued the forthcoming Emancipation Act [150] at a moment when the Confederates were pushing forward in Kentucky, shows that all consideration for the loyal slaveholders in the border states has ceased. The emigration of the slaveowners from Missouri, Kentucky and Tennessee to the South, with their black chattels, is already enormous, and if the war is prolonged for a while, as it is certain to be, the Southerners will have lost all hold there. The South began the war for these territories. The war itself was the means of destroying its power in the border states, where, apart from this, the ties with the South were becoming weaker every day because a market can no longer be found for the breeding of slaves and the internal slave trade. In my opinion, therefore, for the South it will only be a matter now of the defensive. But their sole possibility of success lay in an offensive. If the report is confirmed that Hooker is getting the active command of the Potomac army, that McClellan is being "retired" to the "theoretical" post of Commander-in-Chief and that Halleck is taking over the chief command in the West, then the conduct of the war in Virginia may also take on a more energetic character. Moreover the most favorable time of year for the Confederates is now past.

There is no doubt at all that morally the collapse of

the Maryland campaign was of the most tremendous importance.

As to finance, the United States know from the time of the War of Independence and we know from the Austrian experience, how far one can go with depreciated paper money. It is a fact that the Yankees never exported more corn to England than they have this year, that the present harvest is again far above the average and that the trade balance was never more favorable for them than it has been for the last two years. As soon as the new system of taxation (a very hackneyed one, it is true, exactly in Pitt's style) comes into operation, the paper money which up to now has only been continually *emitted* will also at last begin to *flow back again*. An extension of the paper issue on the present scale will therefore became superfluous and further depreciation will thus be checked. What had made even the present depreciation less dangerous than it was in France, and even in England, in similar circumstances, has been the fact that the Yankees never prohibited *two prices,* a gold price and a paper price. The actual damage done resolves itself into a state debt for which the proper equivalent has never been received and a premium on jobbing and speculation.

When the English boast that their depreciation was never more than 11½ per cent (other people believe that it amounted to more than double this during some time), they conveniently forget that they not only continued to pay their old taxes but every year paid new ones as well, so that the return flow of the banknotes was assured from the beginning, while the Yankees have actually carried on the war for a year and a half *without taxes* (except the greatly diminished import duties), simply by repeating the issue of paper. For a process of this kind, which has now reached the turning point, the actual depreciation is still comparatively small.

The fury with which the Southerners have received Lincoln's Acts proves their importance. All Lincoln's Acts appear like the mean pettifogging conditions which one lawyer puts to his opposing lawyer. But this does not alter their historic content, and indeed it amuses me when I compare them with the drapery in which the Frenchman envelops even the most unimportant point.

Of course, like other people, I see the repulsive side of the form the movement takes among the Yankees; but I find the explanation of it in the nature of "bourgeois" democracy. The events over there are a world upheaval, nevertheless, and there is nothing more disgusting in the whole business than the English attitude towards them.

30. ENGELS TO MARX

November 5, 1862.

As regards America I also think, of course, that the Confederates in Maryland have received an unexpected moral blow of great significance. I am also convinced that the *definite* possession of the border states will decide the result of the war. But I am by no means certain that the affair is going to proceed along such classic lines as you appear to believe. Despite all the screams of the Yankees, there is still no sign whatever available that the people regard this business as a real question of national existence. On the contrary, these election victories of the Democrats go to prove rather that the party which has had enough of the war is growing. If there were only some proof or some indication that the masses in the North were beginning to rise as they did in France in 1792 and 1793, then it would all be very fine. But the only revolution to be expected seems rather to be a Democratic counter-revolution and a rotten peace, including the partition of the border states. That this would not be the end of the affair by a long way—granted. But for the present moment I must say I cannot work up any enthusiasm for a people which on such a colossal issue allows itself to be continually beaten by a fourth of its own population and which after eighteen months of war has achieved nothing more than the discovery that all its generals are idiots and all its officials rascals and traitors. After all the thing must happen differently, even in a bourgeois republic, if it is not to end in utter failure. I entirely agree with what you say about the meanness of the English way of looking at the business.

31. ENGELS TO MARX

November 15, 1862.

I impatiently await the steamer that is bringing news of the New York elections. If the Democrats triumph in the State of New York,[151] then I no longer know what I am to think of the Yankees. That a people placed in a great historical dilemma, which is at the same time a matter of its own existence, can after eighteen months' struggle become reactionary in its mass and vote for climbing down, is a bit beyond my understanding. Good as it is from one aspect that even in America the bourgeois republic exposes itself in thoroughgoing fashion, so that in future it can never again be preached on its own merits, but solely as a means and a form of transition to the social revolution, still it is mortifying that a lousy oligarchy with only half the number of inhabitants proves itself just as strong as the unwieldy, great, helpless democracy. For the rest, if the Democrats triumph, the worthy McClellan and the West Pointers have the better of it most beautifully, and its glory will soon be at an end. The fellows are capable of concluding peace, if the South returns to the Union on condition that the President shall always be a Southerner and the Congress shall always consist of Southerners and Northerners in equal numbers. They are even capable of proclaiming Jeff Davis President of the United States forthwith and to surrender even the whole of the border states, if there is no other way to peace. Then, good-by America.

Of Lincoln's emancipation, likewise, one still sees no effect up to the present, save that from fear of a Negro inundation the Northwest has voted Democratic.

32. MARX TO ENGELS

November 17, 1862.

It seems to me that you are looking too much at only one side of the American quarrel. I have looked at a mass of Southern papers in the American coffee-house and have seen from these that the Confederacy is in a tight corner. The English newspapers have suppressed the battle of "Corinth." The Southern papers describe it as the most extraordinarily bad luck that has befallen them since the armed rising. The State of *Georgia* has declared the Confederate "Conscription Acts" to be null and void.[152] In the person of Floyd the thief, *Virginia* has disputed the right of the *"creatures* (literally) of Jefferson Davis" further to levy troops in his state. Oldham, representative of *Texas* in the Congress of Richmond, has lodged a protest against the transportation of the "picked troops" of the Southwest to the East, that is, Virginia. From all these disputes two things emerge quite incontestably:

That the Confederate government has overreached itself in its violent efforts to fill the ranks of the army;

That the states are asserting their "state rights" against

the separatist Confederacy, just as the latter made them its pretext against the Union.

I regard the victories of the Democrats in the North as a reaction, which was made easy for this conservative and blackleg element by the Federal government's bad direction of the war and financial blunders. It is for the rest a species of reaction met with in every revolutionary movement and at the time of the Convention, for instance, was so strong that it was considered counter-revolutionary to want to submit the death of the King to *suffrage universel* * and under the Directory so strong that Mr. Bonaparte I. had to bombard Paris.

On the other hand, the elections have no bearing on the composition of the Congress prior to December 4, 1863; they serve, therefore, merely as a spur to the Republican government, over whose head the sword hangs. And in any case the Republican House of Representatives will put the term of life allotted to it to better use, if only from hatred of the opposing party.

As to McClellan, he has in his own army Hooker and other Republicans, who will any day arrest him on the order of the government.

In addition, there is the French attempt at intervention, which will call forth a reaction against the reaction.

I do not therefore regard things as so bad. What might be much more injurious in my view is the sheep's attitude of the workers in Lancashire. Such a thing has never been heard of in the world. All the more is this the case as the manufacturing rabble do not even pretend "to make sacrifices" themselves, but leave to the rest of England the honor of keeping their army going for them; that is, impose on the rest of England the costs of maintenance of their variable capital.

During this recent period England has disgraced her-

* Universal suffrage.—*Ed.*

self more than any other country, the workers by their
christian slave nature, the bourgeois and aristocrats by
their enthusiasm for slavery in its most direct form. But
the two manifestations supplement one another.

33. MARX TO ENGELS

November 20, 1862.

If the Mexicans (*les derniers des hommes* *) would but
lick *les crapauds* ** once, but the latter dogs themselves
—the allegedly radical bourgeois—are now talking in
Paris of *"l'honneur du drapeau"*! ***

If Spence does not down the Northerners, nothing will
help; not even McClellan's bad generalship.

34. ENGELS TO MARX

December 30, 1862.

Burnside's defeat is being exaggerated frightfully.[153]
It is clear that it must affect the morale of the army,
but not as seriously by a long way as if it had been beaten
in the open field. The tactical arrangements seem to have
been very bad. Manifestly the flank attack of the left
wing ought first to have been developed before the frontal
attack under Sumner took place. This, however, was let
slip altogether. Sumner seems to have been in a thorough
mess before Franklin had even come to serious fighting.
Then Burnside does not seem to have been able to come
to any decision on the use of his reserves. The successes
of the left wing should have led him to send at least part
of them thither, since it was there that the decisive action had to take place; instead of this he employed them
in front, and here also too late, namely, 1. as a *relief* and

* The lowest of men.—*Ed.*
** The toads.—*Ed.*
*** The honor of the flag.—*Ed.*

not as a support for Sumner's beaten troops, and 2. so shortly before dark that it was night before half came into action. These observations are naturally made on the basis of the poor materials the American papers provide and without knowledge of the terrain. For the rest, it seems to me that Burnside might well have dislodged the *canaille* * wholly by envelopment, especially as he seems to have had certainly 150,000 men against 100,000; but the belief that Washington can only remain covered as long as one disposes one's forces transversely before the foe has evidently kept him from this. The folly of giving the Confederates a month's time in which to establish themselves in the position and then attacking them in front is, however, only to be criticized by a flogging.

35. MARX TO ENGELS

January 2, 1863.

Burnside seems to have committed great tactical blunders in the battle of Fredericksburg. He was obviously nervous in the employment of such great military forces. As far, however, as the fundamental asininity is concerned: 1. In connection with the wait of 26 days, there is unquestionably direct treason at work in the war administration at Washington. Even the New York correspondent of *The Times* admitted that only after weeks did Burnside obtain resources which had been promised him immediately; 2. That nevertheless he then made this attack, shows the moral weakness of the man. The worthy *Tribune* began to cast suspicion on him and threatened him with dismissal. This paper, with its enthusiasm and its ignorance, does great harm.

The Democrats and M'Clellanists naturally cried out in unison, in order to exaggerate the unfortunate position.

* Scum or mob.—*Ed.*

For the "rumor" that M'Clellan, "the Monk" of *The Times,* had been summoned to Washington, we are indebted to Mr. Reuter.

"Politically" the defeat was good. They ought not to have had good luck before January 1, 1863. Anything of the sort could have caused the "Proclamation" to be revoked.

The Times and Co. are utterly furious over the workers' meetings in Manchester, Sheffield and *London.*[154] It is very good that the eyes of the Yankees are opened in this way. For the rest, Opdyke (Mayor of New York and political economist) has already said at a meeting in New York: "We know that the English working class are with us, and that the governing classes of England are against us."

I greatly regret that Germany does not hold similar demonstrations. They cost nothing and "internationally" bring in large returns. Germany would have all the more warrant for these, as in this war she has done more for the Yankees than France in the eighteenth century. It is the old German stupidity of not making herself felt in the world theater and stressing what she actually accomplishes.

36. MARX TO ENGELS

February 13, 1863.

Things go damned slowly in the United States. I hope that J. Hooker bites his way out.[155]

37. ENGELS TO MARX

February 17, 1863.

Things look rotten in Yankeeland. It is true that with the customary irony of world history the Democrats, as against the philistine, have now become the war party, and the bankrupt poetaster Ch. Mackay has again made himself thoroughly ridiculous. I also hear from private sources in New York that the preparations of the North are being continued on a hitherto unheard of scale. But, on the other hand, the signs of moral slackening are increasing daily and the inability to conquer is daily becoming greater. Where is the party whose victory and *avènement* * would be synonymous with prosecution of the war *à outrance* ** and by every means? The *people* has been bamboozled, that is the trouble, and it is lucky that a peace is a physical impossibility, otherwise they would have made one long ago, merely to be able to live for the almighty dollar again.

A Confederate major, who participated in the engagements near Richmond on Lee's staff, told me during the last few days that according to papers which Lee himself had shown him, the rebels had no less than 40,000 stragglers at the end of these actions! He referred specifically to the Western regiments of the Federals with great respect; for the rest, however, he is an ass. [*The conclusion of the letter is missing.*]

38. MARX TO ENGELS

March 24, 1863.

What I consider very important in America's most recent history is that they will again give out *letters of marque.**** Quoad **** England, this will put quite a different complexion on matters and under favorable circumstances may lead to war with England, so that the self-satisfied Bull would see besides his cotton also corn with-

---

* Advent.—*Ed.*
** To a finish.—*Ed.*
*** A commission issued by a government authorizing a private person to take the property of a foreign state or of a foreign citizen as redress for an injury done by such a state or by one of its citizens.—*Ed.*
**** As regards.—*Ed.*

drawn from under his nose. On his own hook, Seward had at the beginning of the Civil War taken the liberty of *accepting* the decisions of the Congress of Paris of 1856 as applicable to America *for the time being.* (This came out on the printing of the dispatches on the *Trent* affair.) The Washington Congress and Lincoln, furious at the outfitting of Southern pirates in Liverpool, etc., have now put an end to this joke. This has given rise to great dismay on the Stock Exchange here but the faithful hounds of the press naturally obey *ordres* and do not mention the matter in the newspapers.

39. ENGELS TO MARX

June 11, 1863.

There are nice goings on in America. Fighting Joe has made an awful fool of himself with his boasts,[156] Rosecrans is asleep, and only Grant operates well. His movement against Vicksburg from southwest to northeast, cutting off the relief army, repulsing it, then rapid advance against Vicksburg and even the impetuous, unavailing assaults, are all very good. I do not believe in the possibility of assembling sufficient relief troops in time. On the other hand, we have so often seen the American generals suddenly operate well for a fortnight and then perpetrate the greatest asininities once more, that one can say nothing whatever about their future movements.

40. MARX TO ENGELS

July 6, 1863.

In my opinion, the expedition of the Southerners against the North has been forced on Lee by the clamor of the Richmond papers and their supporters. I regard it as a complete *coup de désespoir.** For the rest, this war

* Stroke of despair.—*Ed.*

will drag on for a long time, and in the interest of *Europe* that is greatly to be desired.

41. MARX TO ENGELS

August 15, 1863.

The philistines here are raving mad with *The Times,* because *The Times* has taken them in so nicely with the Confederate loan. These honorable men might surely have known that *The Times,* as Cobbett had already revealed to them, is nothing but a "commercial concern," which does not care a damn how the balance falls, if only the balance comes out in its own favor. The fellows from *The Times,* like *J. Spence*—"that man," says the *Richmond Enquirer,* "whom we have paid in solid gold"— obtained the loan scrip in part *for nothing,* in part at a 50 per cent discount on the nominal amount. It was therefore good business to boost it up to 105.

It seems to me very important for the United States that they should, above all, take possession of the remaining ports, Charleston, Mobile, etc., by reason of the collision into which they may any day come with Boustrapa.[157] This imperial Lazarillo de Tormes [158] now caricatures not only his uncle, but even himself. For the "suffrage" in Mexico is surely a fine caricature of the suffrage by which he made not merely himself, but Nice and Savoy French. To my mind, there is no doubt that he will break his neck in Mexico, if he is not already hanged beforehand.

42. MARX TO ENGELS

May 26, 1864.

What do you say of Grant's operations? *The Times,* of course, has admiration only for Lee's strategy, concealed behind retreats. "It," said Tussy [159] this morning, "considers this very canny, I dare say." I wish for nothing more fervently than that Butler may have success. It would be priceless, if he marched into Richmond first. It would be bad if Grant had to retreat, but I think that fellow knows what he is about. At any rate, the first Kentucky campaign, Vicksburg and the beating that Bragg got in Tennessee, are due to him.

43. ENGELS TO MARX

May 30, 1864.

Once more, the Virginian campaign bears the character of indecisiveness or, more strictly speaking, of the difficulty of bringing matters to a decision at all on this terrain. I do not attach any importance to the news per the *Scotia;* it merely signifies that the eight days' rain has saved Lee from the necessity of continually fighting battles *à la* Solferino. And that is a great deal for him. Two more such battles and his army, which had been obliged to take up a new position to the rear every evening, would undoubtedly have been in a very sorry state, hardly able to make a further stand anywhere *before* Richmond. Grant has certainly also gained by the lull, but not in the same measure. The reënforcements that he now obtains will not be worth much. Still, I should not be surprised if Lee soon withdrew to Richmond. There the decisive struggle will then take place.

44. MARX TO ENGELS

June 7, 1864.

The American news seems to me to be very good, and I was particularly delighted with today's leader in the *Times,* in which it proves that Grant is being beaten continuously and will possibly be punished for his defeats— by the capture of Richmond.

45. ENGELS TO MARX

June 9, 1864.

I am very eager to know how things will go in Virginia. The forces still seem very closely balanced, and a trifling contingency, the possibility of smiting a single corps of Grant's separately, can again give Lee the upper hand. The struggle before Richmond may be fought under quite other conditions; for Butler is certainly weaker than Beauregard, otherwise he would not have let himself be forced on the defensive, and even if both are equally strong, Lee still becomes stronger by effecting a junction with Beaur[egard] in Richmond than Grant by one with Butler; for from his entrenched encampment Lee can appear on either side of the James River in full strength, whereas Grant must detach troops (to the south side of the stream). I hope, however, that Grant will carry the thing through all the same; at any rate it is certain that after the first Battle of the Wilderness[160] Lee has evinced little inclination to fight decisive actions in the open field, but has, on the contrary, kept his main force constantly in entrenched positions and only ventured brief offensive skirmishes. I also like the methodical course of Grant's operations. For this terrain and this adversary, that is the only correct method.

46. ENGELS TO MARX

September 4, 1864.

What do you think of things in America? Lee avails himself of his entrenched encampment at Richmond in quite masterly fashion; no wonder it is already the third campaign centering on this place. He holds Grant's hosts fast with relatively few troops and employs the larger part of his men in offensive operations in West Virginia and in threatening Washington and Pennsylvania. Excellent example for the Prussians to study; they can learn from it in detail how a campaign for the entrenched encampment of Coblenz must be conducted, but are naturally far too haughty to learn anything from these improvised generals. Grant—six years ago a lieutenant discharged from the army for intoxication, subsequently a drunken engineer in St. Louis—has much unity of purpose and great contempt for the life of his cannon-fodder; he also seems to be very resourceful as a *small* strategist (that is, in day-to-day movements); but I seek in vain for signs of his having a broad enough outlook to survey the campaign as a whole. The campaign against Richmond seems to me to be miscarrying; the impatience with which G[rant] attacks now at one point, now at another, but nowhere perseveringly with sap and mine, is a bad sign. In general, engineering matters seem to be in a bad state among the Yankees; besides theoretical knowledge, such matters also require a traditional practice, which is not so easily improvised.—Whether Sherman will settle with Atlanta is questionable;[161] still, he has, I believe, better chances. The guerrilla and cavalry raids in his rear will scarcely do him much harm. The fall of Atlanta would be a very hard blow for the South; Rome would straightway fall with it and the South's gun foundries, etc., are situated there; in addition, the railroad connection between Atlanta and South Carolina would be lost.—Farragut is a constant quantity. The fellow knows what he is doing. But whether Mobile itself will fall is very problematical. The town is very strongly fortified and, as far as I know, can only be taken from the landward side, since deep-draught ships cannot approach near enough. But what an imbecility is this dispersal of the attacking forces on the coast, where Charleston and Mobile are attacked simultaneously, instead of one after the other, but each time in full strength.

I do not pay much attention to the peace talk that is becoming so widespread. Not even to the alleged direct negotiations of Lincoln.[162] I regard all this as an election maneuver. As things stand thus far, Lincoln's reëlection appears to me to be pretty certain.

47. MARX TO ENGELS

September 7, 1864.

As regards America, I consider the present moment, *entre nous,** to be very critical. If it brings Grant a great defeat or Sherman a great victory, then it's all right. A chronic series of small checks, precisely at the present election time, would be dangerous. I am entirely of your opinion that thus far Lincoln's reëlection is pretty certain, *still a hundred to one.* But in the model country of the democratic swindle this election time is full of contingencies that may give the logic of events (an expression that Magnus Urquhartus** considers to be just as senseless as "the justice of a locomotive") a quite unexpected smack in the face. An armistice seems to be very necessary for the South, to save it from complete exhaustion. It has been the first to bring up this cry not only in its Northern organs, but directly in the Richmond organs, though now, when it has found an echo in New York, the *Richmond Examiner* throws it back to the Yankees with scorn. That Mr. Davis has decided to treat the Negro soldiers as "prisoners of war" —latest official instruction of his War Secretary—is very characteristic.

---

* Between us.—*Ed.*
** Great Urquhart. See biographical notes, Urquhart, David.—*Ed.*

Lincoln has in his hands great resources with which to carry this election. (Peace proposals on his part are naturally mere humbug!) The election of an opposition candidate would probably lead to a real *revolution*. But all the same one cannot fail to recognize that for the coming eight weeks, in which the issue will in the first instance be decided, much depends on military accident. This is absolutely the most critical point since the beginning of the war. If this is shifted, old Lincoln can then blunder on to his heart's content. For the rest, the old man cannot possibly "make" generals. He could already choose his ministers better. The Confederate papers, however, attack their ministers quite as much as the Yankees do those at Washington. If Lincoln gets through this time—as is very probable—it will be on a much more radical platform and under wholly changed circumstances. In conformity with his legal manner, the old man will then find more radical methods compatible with his conscience.

48. ENGELS TO MARX

November 9, 1864.

The affair at Richmond seems to be nearing the end. But as long as Lee is not compelled to confine himself to the pure defensive, especially to draw all the troops out of the Shenandoah valley to his army, and as long as Richmond is not *completely encircled,* all of Grant's advancing against the works of R[ichmond] or Petersburg means little. It is like Sebastopol, where no encirclement also occurred.—I should like to see what Monsieur de Beauregard will do; probably no more than Hood before him, if as much. I haven't the slightest confidence in this puffed-up hero.

49. MARX TO ENGELS

December 2, 1864.

The worst of such an agitation is that one is much bothered as soon as one participates in it. For example, it was again a matter of an Address, this time to Lincoln,* and again I had to compose the stuff (which was much harder than a substantial work)—in order that the phraseology to which this sort of scribbling is restricted should at least be distinguished from the democratic, vulgar phraseology. . . .

As the Address to Lincoln was to be handed to Adams, *part* of the Englishmen on the Committee wanted to have the deputation introduced by a member of Parliament since it was customary. This hankering was defeated by the majority of the English and the unanimity of the Continentals, and it was declared, on the contrary, that such old English customs ought to be abolished. On the other hand: M. Le Lubez,[163] like a real *crapaud,* wanted to have the Address made out, not to Lincoln, but to the American people. I have made him duly ridiculous and explained to the Englishmen that the French democratic etiquette is not worth a farthing more than the monarchical etiquette.

50. MARX TO ENGELS

February 6, 1865.

. . . Lincoln's answer ** to us is in today's *Times.*

* For the Address of the First International to Lincoln see pp. 281-283.—*Ed.*
** For Lincoln's answer to the Address of the First International, as transmitted by Adams, the American ambassador, see pp. 284-285.—*Ed.*

51. ENGELS TO MARX

February 7, 1865.

In America the opening of the campaign before Richmond in March-April will probably be decisive for the whole year. Should Grant succeed in dislodging Lee from there, then the Confederacy is played out, its armies disperse and the bandit war, as it is already being carried on at present in west Tennessee and in general almost everywhere, is the sole enemy left. At the present time Lee's army is in reality already the only one that the Southerners have; everything depends on its disruption. We can already assume that the territory from which Lee draws his resources is restricted to south Virginia, the Carolinas and, at most, a part of Georgia.

52. MARX TO ENGELS

February 10, 1865.

The fact that Lincoln has replied to us so courteously and to the "Bourgeois Emancipation Society" so rudely and purely formally has made *The Daily News* so angry that it did *not* print the reply to us. When, however, it saw to its sorrow that *The Times* did so, it had to publish it *belatedly* in the *stop press. Levy,* too, has had to swallow the bitter pill. The difference between L[incoln]'s reply to us and to the bourgeois has made such a stir here that the "Clubs" in the West End are shaking their heads over it. You can understand how much good this does our people.

53. MARX TO ENGELS

March 4, 1865.

The Confederacy seems to be at an end.

54. Engels to Marx

April 16, 1865.

What do you say to Richmond? I had expected that instead of running away, Lee would act like a *soldier* and capitulate, in order to secure at least better conditions for the army. But it is better so. He ends now as a shabby fellow; the tragedy ends comically.

55. Marx to Engels

May 1, 1865.

The *chivalry of the South* ends worthily. In this connection the assassination of Lincoln was the greatest piece of folly that they could commit.[164] *Johnson* is stern, inflexible, revengeful and as a former poor white has a deadly hatred of the oligarchy. He will stand less on ceremony with the fellows, and through the assassination he finds the temper of the North adequate to his intentions.

56. Engels to Marx

May 3, 1865.

At Richmond Grant has repeated exactly the battle of Jena—so far as the strategic design is concerned—and with the same result: capture of the whole hostile army. Save that he did not need to march so far to gather the fruits.

Now Johnston has also capitulated[165] and thereby I have won my wager made two months ago: that on May 1 the Southerners would no longer have any army. Such as still offer resistance will be taken as brigands and rightly so. In any case, Johnson will insist on confiscation of the large landed property[166] and thereby make the pacification and reorganization of the South a somewhat more acute matter. Lincoln would hardly have insisted on this.

The Southern sympathizers here solaced themselves for the hypocritical howl that they had to set up because of the murder by prophesying that in four weeks there would be a Grant I., Emperor of America. The donkeys have deceived themselves nicely!

For the rest, the " 'Ighnesses" must surely feel frightfully angry that the murder of Lincoln has produced such a colossal effect throughout the world. None of them has yet had the honor.

57. MARX TO ENGELS

May 9, 1865.

Today I have to submit an "Address to President Johnson." *

58. MARX TO ENGELS

May 20, 1865.

Cutting enclosed, in which is my Address to Johnson.

59. MARX TO ENGELS

June 24, 1865.

Johnson's policy disquiets me.[167] Ridiculous affectation of severity against single persons; up to the present extremely vacillating and weak in substance. The reaction has already begun in America and will soon be greatly strengthened, if the hitherto prevailing slackness does not quickly cease.

60. ENGELS TO MARX

July 15, 1865.

I, too, like Mr. Johnson's policy less and less. His hatred of Negroes comes out more and more violently,

* For the Address of the First International to Johnson, see pp. 285-287.—*Ed.*

while as against the old lords of the South he lets all power go out of his hands. If things go on like this, in six months all the old villains of secession will be sitting in Congress at Washington. Without colored suffrage nothing whatever can be done there, and J[ohnson] leaves it to the vanquished, the ex-slaveholders, to decide upon this matter. It is too absurd. However, one must certainly reckon with things developing differently from what Messrs. the Barons imagine. The majority of them are surely totally ruined and will be glad to sell land to migrants and speculators from the North. These will come soon enough and change many things. The mean whites, I think, will gradually die out. With this stock there is nothing more to be done; what is left after two generations will merge with the migrants into a stock entirely different. The Negroes will probably become small squatters as in Jamaica. So that finally, indeed, the oligarchy goes down, but the process could now be brought to a speedy conclusion on the spot at one time, whilst, as it is, it becomes long drawn out.

61. MARX TO ENGELS

April 23, 1866.

After the Civil War phase the United States are really only now entering the revolutionary phase, and the European wiseacres, who believe in the omnipotence of Mr. Johnson, will soon be disillusioned.

APPENDIX

1.

ADDRESS
OF THE INTERNATIONAL WORKINGMEN'S
ASSOCIATION TO ABRAHAM LINCOLN

To the Editor of the Bee-Hive.

Sir,

You will oblige the Central Council of the International Workingmen's Association by publishing the following, which has been forwarded through Mr. Adams, United States Minister.

Respectfully yours,

W. R. CREMER, Hon. Gen. Secretary.

To Abraham Lincoln,
President of the United States of America.

Sir,

We congratulate the American people upon your re-election by a large majority. If resistance to the Slave Power was the reserved watchword of your first election, the triumphant war cry of your re-election is Death to Slavery.

From the commencement of the titanic American strife the workingmen of Europe felt instinctively that the star-spangled banner carried the destiny of their class.

The contest of the territories which opened the dire epopée, was it not to decide whether the virgin soil of immense tracts should be wedded to the labor of the emigrant or prostituted by the tramp of the slave driver?

When an oligarchy of 300,000 slaveholders dared to inscribe for the first time in the annals of the world "slavery" on the banner of armed revolt, when on the very spots where hardly a century ago the idea of one great democratic republic had first sprung up, whence the first Declaration of the Rights of Man was issued, and the first impulse given to the European revolution of the eighteenth century; when on those very spots counter-revolution, with systematic thoroughness, gloried in rescinding "the ideas entertained at the time of the formation of the old constitution," and maintained "slavery to be a beneficent institution," indeed, the only solution of the great problem of the "relation of capital to labor," and cynically proclaimed property in man "the cornerstone of the new edifice"—then the working classes of Europe understood at once, even before the fanatic partisanship of the upper classes for the Confederate gentry had given its dismal warning, that the slaveholders' rebellion was to sound the tocsin for a general holy crusade of property against labor, and that for the men of labor, with their hopes for the future, even their past conquests were at stake in that tremendous conflict on the other side of the Atlantic. Everywhere, therefore, they bore patiently the hardships imposed upon them by the cotton crisis, opposed enthusiastically the pro-slavery intervention—importunities of their betters—and, from most parts of Europe, contributed their quota of blood to the good cause.

While the workingmen, the true political power of the North, allowed slavery to defile their own republic, while before the Negro, mastered and sold without his concurrence, they boasted it the highest prerogative of the white-skinned laborer to sell himself and choose his own master, they were unable to attain the true freedom of labor, or to support their European brethren in their struggle for emancipation; but this barrier to progress has been swept off by the red sea of civil war.

The workingmen of Europe feel sure that, as the American War of Independence initiated a new era of ascendancy for the middle class, so the American anti-slavery war will do for the working classes. They consider it an earnest of the epoch to come that it fell to the lot of Abraham Lincoln, the single-minded son of the working class, to lead the country through the matchless struggle for the rescue of an enchained race and the reconstruction of a social world.

Signed, on behalf of the International Workingmen's Association, the Central Council—

Longmaid, Worley, Whitlock, Fox, Blackmore, Hartweil, Pidgeon, Lucraft, Weston, Dell, Nieass, Shaw, Lake, Buckley, Osborne, Howell, Carter, Wheeler, Stanisby, Morgan, Grossmith, Dick, Denoual, Jourdain, Morrissot, Leroux, Bordage, Bosquet, Talandier, Dupont, L. Wolff, Aldrovandi, Lama, Solustri, Nusperli, Eccarius, Wolff, Lessner, Pfänder, Lochner, Thaub, Bolliter, Rypczinski, Hansen, Schantzenback, Smales, Cornaline, Petersen, Otto, Bagnagatti, Setacci; Georges Odgers, President of Council; P. V. Lubez, Corresponding Secretary for France; Karl Marx, Corresponding Secretary for Germany; G. P. Fontana, Corresponding Secretary for Italy; J. E. Holtorp, Corresponding Secretary for Poland; H. F. Jung, Corresponding Secretary for Switzerland, William R. Cremer, Hon. Gen. Secretary, 18, Greek Street, Soho.

Bee-Hive (London), January 7, 1865.

2.

THE AMERICAN AMBASSADOR'S REPLY TO ADDRESS OF THE INTERNATIONAL WORKINGMEN'S ASSOCIATION

To the Editor of the Times.
Sir,

Some few weeks since a congratulatory address was sent from the Central Council of the above Association to Mr. Lincoln. The address was transmitted through the United States' Legation and the following reply has been received. Its publication will oblige,

Respectfully yours,

W. R. CREMER.

Legation of the United States,
London, Jan. 31.

Sir,

I am directed to inform you that the address of the Central Council of your association, which was duly transmitted through this legation to the President of the United States has been received by him. So far as the sentiments expressed by it are personal, they are accepted by him with a sincere and anxious desire that he may be able to prove himself not unworthy of the confidence which has been recently extended to him by his fellow-citizens, and by so many of the friends of humanity and progress throughout the world. The government of the United States has a clear consciousness that its policy neither is nor could be reactionary, but at the same time it adheres to the course which it adopted at the beginning, of abstaining everywhere from propagandism and unlawful intervention. It strives to do equal and exact justice to all states and to all men, and it relies upon the beneficial results of that effort for support at home and for respect and good-will throughout the world. Nations do not exist for themselves alone, but to promote the welfare and happiness of mankind by benevolent intercourse and example. It is in this relation that the United States regard their cause in the present conflict with slavery-maintaining insurgents as the cause of human nature, and they derive new encouragement to persevere from the testimony of the workingmen of Europe that the national attitude is favored with their enlightened approval and earnest sympathies.

I have the honor to be, Sir, your obedient servant,

CHARLES FRANCIS ADAMS.

Mr. A. W. Cremer, Hon. Gen. Secretary of the International Workingmen's Association, 18, Greek St., W.

The Times, February 6, 1865.

3.

ADDRESS
OF THE INTERNATIONAL WORKINGMEN'S ASSOCIATION TO PRESIDENT JOHNSON

To Andrew Johnson,
President of the United States.
Sir,

The demon of the "peculiar institution," for the supremacy of which the South rose in arms, would not allow his worshipers to honorably succumb on the open field. What he had begun in treason, he must needs end in infamy. As Philip II's war for the Inquisition bred a Gerard, thus Jefferson Davis's pro-slavery war a Booth.

It is not our part to call words of sorrow and horror, while the heart of two worlds heaves with emotion. Even the sycophants who, year after year, and day by day, stuck to their Sisyphus work of morally assassinating Abraham Lincoln, and the great republic he headed stand now aghast at this universal outburst of popular feeling, and rival with each other to strew rhetorical flowers on his open grave. They have now at last found out that he was a man, neither to be browbeaten by adversity, nor intoxicated by success, inflexibly pressing on to his great goal, never compromising it by blind haste, slowly maturing his steps, never retracing them, carried away by no surge of popular favor, disheartened by no slackening of the popular pulse; tempering stern acts by the gleams of a kind heart, illuminating scenes dark with passion by the smile of humor, doing his titanic work as humbly and homely as heaven-born rulers do little things with the grandiloquence of pomp and state; in one word, one of the rare men who succeed in becoming great, without ceasing to be good. Such, indeed, was the modesty of this great and good man, that the world only discovered him a hero after he had fallen a martyr.

To be singled out by the side of such a chief, the second victim to the infernal gods of slavery, was an honor due to Mr. Seward. Had he not, at a time of general hesitation, the sagacity to foresee and the manliness to foretell "the irrepressible conflict"? Did he not, in the darkest hours of that conflict, prove true to the Roman duty to never despair of the republic and its stars? We earnestly hope that he and his son will be restored to health, public activity, and well-deserved honors within much less than "90 days."

After a tremendous war, but which, if we consider its vast dimensions, and its broad scope, and compare it to the Old World's 100 years' wars,[168] and 30 years' wars,[169] and 23 years' wars,[170] can hardly be said to have lasted 90 days, yours, Sir, has become the task to uproot by the law what has been felled by the sword, to preside over the arduous work of political reconstruction and social regeneration. A profound sense of your great mission will save you from any compromise with stern duties. You will never forget that to initiate the new era of the emancipation of labor, the American people devolved the responsibilities of leadership upon two men of labor—the one Abraham Lincoln, the other Andrew Johnson.

Signed on behalf of the International Workingmen's Association, London, May 13, 1865, by the Central Council—

Charles Kaub, Edward Coulson, F. Lessner, Carl Pfänder, N. P. Stanen, Karl Schapper, William Dell, George Lochner, George Eccarius, John Osborne, P. Peterson, A. Janks, H. Klimosch, John Weston, H. Bolliter, B. Lucraft, J. Buckley, Peter Fox, M. Salvatells, George Howell, Bordage, A. Valtier, Robert Shaw, J. H. Longmaid, M. Morgan, G. W. Wheeler, J. D. Nieass, W. C. Worley, D. Stanisby, F. de Lassasire, F. Carter; Emile Holtorp, Secretary for Poland; Karl Marx, Secretary for Germany; H. Jung, Secretary for Switzerland; E. Dupont, Secretary for France; E. Whitlock, Financial Secretary; G. Odgers, President; W. R. Cremer, Hon. Gen. Secretary.

Bee-Hive, May 20, 1865.

REFERENCE NOTES

1. On the eve of the Civil War, a number of congressmen attempted to settle the coming struggle through a series of parliamentary maneuvers. In December, 1860, Crittenden of Kentucky proposed (1) the passage of a constitutional amendment to restore the Missouri Compromise Line and (2) the enactment of a law to guarantee the protection of slavery in the District of Columbia. By throwing open the great Southwest to slave penetration and by safeguarding slavery in the Federal capital, the plan was partly, though not entirely, satisfactory to the slavocracy. Opposition to the Crittenden proposal came chiefly from Lincoln's free-soil followers. Without adequate support from this decisive Northern element, the plan was finally dropped. A similar fate was accorded the compromise proposals of Corwin, Weed and McKean.

2. The Missouri Compromise was the beginning of a series of political struggles which finally culminated in civil war. In 1820, the slave South found itself in a peculiar situation. Control of the House of Representatives had definitely passed into the hands of the free North. Under these circumstances, the South could stop the enactment of pro-Northern legislation or hostile Southern measures only if it dominated the Senate. Its hegemony in that body depended upon the entrance of Missouri as a slave state. To prevent the South from having a majority of one state in the upper house the North demanded the admission of Maine. After prolonged and bitter debate, both states were admitted, an "equilibrium of forces" in the Senate being thus maintained. In addition, the Missouri Compromise provided for the prohibition of slavery in the Louisiana Territory north of the 36° and 36′ line.

The seriousness of the parliamentary struggle of 1820 was fully appreciated at the time. On February 7, 1820, Jefferson wrote to Hugh Nelson: "It [the Missouri question] is the most portentous one which ever yet threatened our Union. In the gloomiest moment of the revolutionary war I never had any apprehensions equal to what I feel from this source." (T. Jefferson, *Writings,* ed. P. L. Ford, New York, 1899, vol. x, p. 156.)

3. In 1854, the Kansas-Nebraska bill was passed. In the first place, the measure provided for the formation of two territories on the assumption that Nebraska would enter the Union as a free and Kansas as a slave state. Under these circumstances, Northern and

Southern strength in the Senate would be equalized. Secondly, the act provided for the repeal of the Missouri Compromise line of 1820. By so doing, the measure gave the slave power what it most desired: the recognition that the area of slavery in the United States was unlimited. To attract the support of the Western democracy, the bill allowed for the doctrine of popular sovereignty, that is, the people of the territory were to decide for themselves whether they wanted slavery or not. The enactment of the Kansas-Nebraska Bill was significant in that it directly led to the Kansas Civil War, a struggle which served as a prologue to the dramatic events of 1861-65.

4. The statement refers to James Buchanan who was nominated by the Democratic Party in 1856.

5. The slave power's control of the Supreme Court was clearly indicated in the notorious Dred Scott decision of 1857. Dred Scott, a slave, was brought by his master, Dr. Emerson, into the Louisiana Territory above the 36° 30' line where slavery was legally prohibited. Here Dred lived for a number of years, married and raised a family. Eventually the Scotts were brought back to the slave state of Missouri. After their master's death, they were sold to a New Yorker, Sanford, whom they eventually sued for their freedom.

The case came before the Supreme Court which consisted not only of a majority of Southerners but was at the time presided over by a Southerner, Chief Justice Taney. The latter, writing the majority decision, held that the Missouri Circuit Court had no jurisdiction over the case since the Scotts were not and could never be citizens within the meaning of the Constitution. Instead of resting the matter here, the Chief Justice seized the opportunity to express an opinion not vital to the case. In this opinion Taney gave the slave power what it wanted the most: the right of taking its chattels to any territory of the United States and of holding them there in bondage no matter what Congress or the territorial legislature said to the contrary. Though the powerful dissenting opinion of Justice Curtis of Massachusetts theoretically demolished the majority decision of the Court, it nevertheless remained for the Civil War to destroy it completely.

6. Despite the illegality of the African slave trade, Southern planters continued to import chattels after 1808. Although accurate statistics are lacking, contemporary sources indicate that more Negroes were carried across the Atlantic after that year than ever before. In 1840, it was estimated that as many as 150,000 were annually sent to the New World, as compared with 45,000 toward the end of the

eighteenth century. Although all of these slaves were not shipped directly to the United States, most of them probably arrived here. During the 'fifties, slave vessels were openly fitted out in New York and Maine; according to Du Bois, 85 vessels were engaged in the illicit traffic. On the eve of the Civil War, Senator Douglas went so far as to assert that the number of Negroes imported was greater than ever before. In the meantime, Great Britain and the United States made hypocritical attempts to stop the slave trade by stationing a few ships off the African coast.

7. With the passage of the Kansas-Nebraska Act, a Northern anti-slavery group, headed by Thayer of Massachusetts, formed an Emigrant Aid Society. This organization proposed to send free-soil sympathizers to Kansas in order to see that that territory entered the Union as a free state. In the meantime, the slave power organized bands of ruffians recruited from the riff-raff element of western Missouri.

In October, 1854, the Missouri rabble invaded Kansas, but were driven back. However, they soon returned and by means of terrorism forced the "election" of a pro-slavery delegate to Congress. Similarly, in March, 1855, they "elected" a legislature friendly to the slave power, a body which the free-soil element refused to recognize. Under these circumstances, the latter established their own assembly, drew up a constitution and asked for admission into the Union. In the meantime, Shannon, a lackey of the slave interests, was appointed governor of the territory. Civil War broke out in 1856; the free-soil element, led by John Brown, the militant abolitionist, organized military units and proceeded to disband the pro-slavery forces. Governor Shannon was then replaced by a more brazen follower of the slave power, Woodson, who called upon all "good citizens" to crush the "insurrection." This call was obviously an appeal to the Missouri riff-raff who, taking the cue, again invaded Kansas and this time laid waste to Ossawattomie. The free-soil element then moved on Lecompton and were prevented from taking the town only by the arrival of Federal troops. Meanwhile, a new governor, Geary of Pennsylvania, was appointed; by prompt action, he was able to compel the border ruffians to leave the territory.

8. The Republican Party was founded during the 'fifties to check the encroachments of the reactionary slave oligarchy. With the gradual disappearance of the Whig Party after the election of 1852, the field was practically left to the pro-slavery Democratic Party. The repeal of the Missouri Compromise in 1854 brought this fact closer home. Mass meetings protesting the action of Congress were held throughout the North. Out of these emerged the Republican

Party, the first state convention of which was held at Jackson, Michigan, July 6, 1854. The formation of a national organization was stimulated by events in Kansas (1854-56) heightened by Northern indignation over the Ostend Manifesto (1854). In 1856, the new party entered its first presidential campaign with Frémont heading the ticket. Four years later it secured the election of Lincoln under the slogan of "Free speech, free soil, free labor and free men."

9. In 1856, Frémont, the Republican candidate, received 1,341,264 votes; Buchanan, the Democratic nominee, secured 1,838,169.

10. In 1850, Illinois, Indiana, Iowa, Ohio, Michigan, Wisconsin and the Minnesota Territory had a population of 4,721,551; ten years later there were 7,773,820 people in this region. (*All population figures used in reference notes are taken from the official census returns.*)

11. Buchanan was American ambassador to England during the Pierce administration.

12. For the Republican Party's condemnation of the slave trade, see the Republican platform of 1860, ninth resolution (E. Stanwood, *A History of Presidential Elections*, Boston, 1888, p. 230).

13. In October, 1859, John Brown, heading a band of eighteen, five of whom were Negroes, tried to capture the Federal arsenal and armory at Harper's Ferry, Virginia. Part of a more ambitious undertaking whose ultimate end was the emancipation of slaves throughout the South, the raid proved unsuccessful. Colonel Robert E. Lee, the future military commander of the Southern forces, led a detachment of United States marines, and captured Brown and a number of his followers. Amid popular excitement, they were tried for treason and found guilty. In December, 1859, Brown was hanged at Charles Town. His execution was vigorously condemned in the North where the militant abolitionist was hailed as a martyr and a hero.

14. See J. C. Calhoun, *Works*, ed. R. K. Crallé (New York, 1854), vol. iv, pp. 340-341, 343.

15. In July, 1832, Jackson signed a "systematically protective tariff," which aroused widespread dissatisfaction in South Carolina. John C. Calhoun took the lead in crystallizing sentiment within his state in favor of nullification and secession. A special session of the South Carolina legislature was held and the calling of a convention ordered. The latter adopted an ordinance nullifying the tariff acts of 1828 and 1832 and openly proclaimed the right of a state to secede if

an attempt was made to coerce it. The ordinance was to go into effect in February, 1833.

In the meantime, President Jackson acted swiftly. After announcing his intention to enforce all Federal laws in South Carolina, he dispatched troops and ships to Charleston. With none of the other Southern states showing any disposition to follow her, South Carolina soon acquiesced. (For Jackson's statement on the tariff as a pretext for secession see his letter to the Rev. Andrew J. Crawford, dated May 1, 1833, in A. Jackson, *Correspondence*, ed. J. S. Bassett and J. F. Jameson, Washington, 1931, vol. v, p. 72.)

16. The Morrill Tariff passed the Senate on February 20, 1861, and was signed by the President on March 2. As early as February 4, 1861, delegates from six seceded states had met at Montgomery to form the Southern Confederacy.

17. The reference is to the potato famine of 1845-47. Conditions were particularly bad in Ireland where tenant-farmers, unable to pay their rent, were evicted in wholesale fashion by their landlords. The resentment of the peasantry fired up in revolt in 1848. The suppression of the uprising resulted in a mass emigration to the United States; from 1848 to 1854 inclusive, over one million Irish immigrants came to America.

18. On October 6, 1861, King William of Prussia visited Napoleon III at Compiègne. The two rulers discussed the possibilities of a Franco-Prussian alliance for the purpose of isolating England. They also took up the old question of rectifying the French frontier as settled in 1815.

19. The Duc d'Aumale was the son of King Louis Philippe, while "Plon-Plon" or the "Red Prince" was a relative of Napoleon III. "Plon-Plon," whose real name was Joseph Charles Paul Napoleon, was regarded as the leader of the "left" Bonapartists. He issued a series of pamphlets in defiance of the existing regime and attempted to organize the Paris workers in Bonapartist police unions.

20. In September, 1861, two princes of the House of Orléans, the Comte de Paris and the Duc de Chartres, accompanied by the Prince de Joinville, arrived in Washington and received permission to enter the Union army as aides-de-camps. The two princes were made captains and were assigned to the Army of the Potomac. They saw active service during the Peninsular Campaign of 1862. It is interesting to note that their companion, the Prince de Joinville, wrote an account of the campaign, part of which was published in *Appleton's Annual Cyclopaedia 1862* (pp. 85-86). Later, one of the Orléanist princes, the Comte de Paris, wrote a book on the American Civil War, the first volume of the American edition appearing in 1875.

21. Louis Napoleon Bonaparte (later Napoleon III) was living in London at the time the Chartist movement reached its height. In 1848, he, together with other "aristocratic foreigners," enrolled in a voluntary police force to help crush Chartist demonstrations.

22. In 1856, Napoleon III, acting in concert with Great Britain, demanded from China reparations and concessions for the "murder" of a French missionary. Canton was seized, the Taku forts taken and China forced to accept the Treaties of Tientsin (1858). The latter gave France and England further commercial concessions in the Far East as well as indemnities. In the meantime, Napoleon, with Spanish aid, took the desirable port of Saigon in Cochin-China and in 1862 acquired three additional provinces in that region.

23. The reference is to the disastrous defeats suffered by the Union forces in the summer of 1861. The Northern army was routed at Bull Run (Manassas) and was forced to evacuate Springfield.

24. Refers to the victories won by the armies of Napoleon III during the Crimean and Italian Wars.

25. In October, 1859, Spain went to war with Morocco on the pretext that Arab tribesmen had invaded the neighborhood of Melilla and Ceuta. Morocco put up a stout resistance, but was eventually defeated. Peace was concluded on April 26, 1860. In 1861, the reactionary ruler of Santo Domingo, Sanatana, proclaimed the Dominican Republic a part of the Spanish dominions.

26. The Holy Alliance was created in 1815 at the Congress of Vienna on the initiative of the Russian tsar, Alexander I, and the Austrian minister, Metternich, to fight revolution in Europe. The Holy Alliance undertook a number of repressive measures against the revolutionary movements in Spain and Italy; it completely lost its significance with the downfall of Metternich in 1848.

27. In 1857, a liberal constitution was adopted in Mexico which curtailed the privileges of the clergy and provided for a popular election. Under the new constitution, General Comonfort was elected president. A coup d'état, engineered by the church party, soon secured his removal and placed General Zuloaga in control. The progressive forces then proclaimed Juarez the constitutional president of Mexico. Under these circumstances, civil war broke out in 1858. After three years of bitter fighting, Juarez emerged victorious, the reactionary generals Zuloaga and Miramon having been defeated. In 1861, he entered Mexico City and was reëlected president. During the course of the war, church property was confiscated

and everything done to reduce the power of the reactionary Catholic establishment.

28. While in a West Indian port, Captain Wilkes, commander of the American warship *San Jacinto*, read in a newspaper that two Confederate commissioners, Mason and Slidell, accompanied by their secretaries, Eustis and McFarland, were about to pass through the Bahama Channel on the British mail steamer *Trent*. After consulting works on international law, Wilkes convinced himself that he could legally board the English vessel and remove the Southern agents. Consequently, on November 8, 1861, he stopped the *Trent*, arrested the four men and sailed for Boston.

Throughout the entire affair, Wilkes acted on his own initiative, a point made clear by the American Secretary of State, Seward, in a letter to Adams dated November 30. On the same day, Earl Russell communicated with Lord Lyons, the British Ambassador at Washington, instructing the latter to give Seward at least seven days to comply with Britain's request for the release of the Confederate commissioners. However, almost three weeks elapsed before the British minister acquainted Seward with the tenor of Russell's letter and another four days passed before it was officially read. On December 26, the American Secretary of State replied to the British government: although justifying the action of Wilkes on the grounds of international law, Seward expressed his willingness to release the Confederate agents since that procedure was more in accord with the traditional American policy to promote neutral rights on the high seas. With this dispatch the incident was closed and on January 1, 1862, the Southern emissaries were placed on board the British warship *Rinaldo* and taken to England.

29. Refers to a famous English commercial corporation engaged in shipbrokerage and marine insurance. The name is derived from Edward Lloyd (d. 1726) at whose coffeehouse the merchants and underwriters of London were accustomed to meet.

30. Refers to the *American Union* written by James Spence and published in London during the year 1861.

31. At this time, the British fleet in North American waters numbered 65 first class frigates, well-armed corvettes and sloops mounting 850 guns.

32. On June 1, 1812, Madison, in a message to Congress, pointed out that "British cruisers had been in the continued practice of violating the American flag . . . and of seizing and carrying off persons

under it. ..." He assured Great Britain that if the United States had done what she was doing, England would be prompt "to avenge" this "crying enormity." (*American State Papers, Class I, Foreign Relations*, Washington, 1832, vol. iii, p. 405.)

33. At the Ghent peace conference of 1814, England was in an excellent position to carry on treaty negotiations. With Napoleon in exile, she found herself free from European strife and consequently could, if she wanted, strengthen her army in America and wage a more vigorous struggle. On the other hand, the American position was desperate; with New England threatening secession, the Federal government was on the verge of civil war. Under these circumstances, the British delegation refused to make any concessions. In the Treaty of Ghent, signed on December 24, 1814, no mention was made of the impressment of seamen or the rights of neutrals on the high seas. Even the question of boundary disputes was postponed for future negotiations.

34. In 1841, Lord Ashburton, who owned large tracts of lands in Maine, was sent to America to settle a number of vexing questions. After some negotiations with Webster, American Secretary of State, a treaty was signed (1842). By its terms, the United States secured seven-twelfths of the territory in dispute between Maine and Canada. Arrangements were likewise made for the mutual extradition of criminals and the "suppression" of the slave trade.

35. A few days after the seizure of the Southern commissioners, Davis sent a message to the Confederate Congress which was designed for British rather than Southern consumption. Hoping to appeal to the patriotic "instincts" of the English people, Davis asserted that the North was claiming "a general jurisdiction over the high seas ..." and that the arrest of the Confederate agents "in the streets of London would have been as well founded as that [of apprehending] them where they were taken. ..."

36. General Winfield Scott, who was in Paris when news of the *Trent* incident reached Europe, expressed the opinion that the seizure of the Southern commissioners could not have been authorized by the Federal government. "I am sure," wrote Scott, "that the president and people of the United States would be but too happy to let these men go ... if by it they could emancipate the commerce of the world."

37. For example, at Dublin, Ireland, 5,000 gathered to cheer a speaker who openly asserted that if England were to declare war upon the United States, Ireland would fight on the American side.

38. No class in England suffered more as a result of the cotton crisis than did the proletariat. For British workers, especially those engaged in the textile industry, the scarcity of cotton meant unemployment or at best part-time work. For example, in the town of Blackburn, 8,424 workers were unemployed, 7,438 were on part-time, and only 10,113 had full-time jobs. By November 1862, 31.8% of the city's population was on relief. Similar conditions existed in Stockport where 6,000 wage-earners were out of work, 6,000 were partially employed and 5,000 were working the entire day. In November 1862, 35.9% of the population of Glossop was living on charity, while in May of the same year, 28.9% of the people of Ashton-under-Lyne was receiving relief.

39. In 1793, Republican France found herself faced by a counter-revolutionary coalition of European powers led by England. In the war which followed, France, under the revolutionary Jacobins, carried the struggle to her enemies. By 1795, she practically broke up the coalition.

40. In the autumn of 1861, the Confederate privateer *Nashville*, which had seized a $3,000,000 booty of war and which was attempting to elude a Federal fleet, arrived off the English coast. The British authorities, though well aware of the state of affairs, allowed the *Nashville* to enter Southampton and to carry out disembarkation. This represented a clear violation of neutrality.

41. The Orders in Council, issued by England during the year 1807, declared that all ships trading with France or her allies were liable to capture and directed neutral vessels in certain instances to touch at British ports. Especially injurious to American trade, these decrees were bitterly condemned by the United States as an infringement upon neutral rights. The obnoxious orders were finally suspended on June 23, 1812, five days after the United States declared war on Britain.

42. Jackson's statement as to the tariff being a pretext for secession refers to the action of South Carolina in 1832 (see reference note 15). South Carolina suffered her first attack of nullification in 1828 when her legislature appointed a committee of seven to protest the constitutionality of the protective tariff of that year. The committee drew up a report which was actually written by John C. Calhoun, then Vice-President of the United States. This paper, which came to be known as the *South Carolina Exposition*, declared the Tariff Act of 1828 unconstitutional and requested Congress to repeal it. The protest was accepted by the state legislature and was then sent to the Senate of the United States which received it for publication in

its journal (February, 1829). The reason South Carolina did not openly call for more decisive action (that is, publicly proclaim the right of secession) in her *Exposition* of 1828 was due to her belief that a lower tariff would be adopted as soon as President-elect Jackson was inauguarated.

43. Faneuil Hall, called the "Cradle of Liberty," served as a meeting place for Boston revolutionaries during the American War of Independence. It was donated to the city by Peter Faneuil, a wealthy merchant.

44. In his inaugural speech, Lincoln made it clear that he was in favor of allowing the people to amend the constitution, if they so desired. "While I make no recommendation of amendment," he said, "I fully recognize the full authority of the people over the whole subject.... I will venture to add, that to me the Convention mode seems preferable, in that it allows amendments to originate with the people themselves...." (A. Lincoln, *Inaugural Address, March 4, 1861*, reprinted in H. Greeley, *The American Conflict*, Hartford, 1864, vol. i, p. 425.)

45. The votes cast in the election of 1860 were distributed as follows:

	Popular Vote	Electoral College Vote
Lincoln	1,866,452	180
Douglas	1,375,157	12
Breckinridge	847,953	72
Bell	590,631	39

Thus, the combined popular vote of Douglas and Breckinridge was 356,658 more than that of Lincoln.

46. See reference note 2.

47. See reference note 3.

48. See reference note 5.

49. The Fugitive Slave Act of 1850 provided that the Federal government use all the means at its disposal to assist masters in regaining possession of runaway slaves. It likewise denied the alleged slave the right of trial by jury or of testifying in his own behalf.

50. In 1854, a homestead or free-soil bill came before the Senate; the measure was immediately opposed by a number of Southern Democrats who held that it was "tinctured" with abolitionism. They

argued that under its provisions, the West would be settled by small farmers hostile to the slave interests. Although the measure was defeated, similar proposals were later introduced and finally in 1860 a homestead bill providing for a cash payment of $.25 per acre was passed. However, the Democratic president, Buchanan, reflecting the interests of the slave power, vetoed the measure. In the same year, the Republican Party in its national platform endorsed a free-soil bill; however, it was not until 1862, after the slave states had withdrawn, that a homestead act with no provision for an acreage charge was passed.

51. By securing new slave territory, the Southern oligarchy hoped to create a sufficient number of states to give it control of the Senate; in this way it expected to have enough votes to block any popular measure proposed by the more representative House. Having already despoiled Mexico of territory in the late 'forties, the land-hungry slavocracy turned to Spain in the 'fifties. In 1854, the ministerial lackeys of the slave power, Soule, Mason and Buchanan, American ambassadors to Spain, France and England respectively, met at Ostend and issued a manifesto offering to purchase Cuba from Spain and threatening to seize the island, if she refused.

The publication of this bellicose announcement was well-timed; England and France were occupied by the Crimean War, Spain was in dire financial straits and British bondholders were growing more fearful concerning the security of their Cuban investments. Although conditions seemed outwardly favorable, the slave power did not achieve its purpose. Faced by opposition within the United States and fearful of European hostility, the Washington government was forced to repudiate the adventurist scheme. Yet, despite this set-back, the slaveholding interests did not give up hope; four years later, during Buchanan's administration, efforts were made to revive the manifesto.

52. From 1857 to 1859, American capitalists, headed by Charles P. Stone, displayed great interest in the mines and fertile fields of Sonora. In fact, emigrant aid societies were established with a view of ultimately absorbing the country. The Mexican policy of Buchanan was in perfect harmony with these economic tendencies. Soon after his inauguration, Buchanan authorized the American minister to Mexico to pay that nation twelve to fifteen millions for Lower California and a large portion of Sonora and Chihuahua. In 1858, the President recommended to Congress that the American government should assume a temporary protectorate over Sonora and Chihuahua and that it should establish military posts there.

53. During the 'fifties, the slave power coveted not only Cuba and northern Mexico but also Central America. Filibustering expeditions

were particularly directed against Nicaragua which was to serve as a base for the establishment of a great slave empire. In these undertakings, William Walker played a leading part; however, it was not until after his first expedition that he was actually supported by the slavocracy which awoke to the opportunities offered. In 1855, Walker made himself master of Granada; his proclamation to re-establish and legalize slavery secured for him the backing of Southerners. The aid of the latter, however, was not strong enough to protect him from a coalition of Central American states. In 1857, Walker was overthrown and although he made various attempts to regain his position, his efforts were unsuccessful.

54. The movement to reopen the African slave trade was launched during the late 'fifties; on the whole, however, it never attracted a large number of adherents. Although the Southern Commercial Convention of 1859 went on record as favoring legislation providing for the revival of the slave traffic, all efforts to pass such bills in Georgia, Alabama, Louisiana and Texas failed. The failure of the movement was due largely to opposition within the slaveholding class, especially on the part of slave breeders in the "border" and eastern states who feared depressed prices resulting from an oversupply of chattels.

55. On December 9, 1857, Douglas, under the pressure of his constituents, declared in the Senate, "...if this constitution [Lecompton] is to be forced down our throats, in violation of the fundamental principle of free government, under a mode of submission that is a mockery and insult, I will resist it to the last.... I should regret any social or political estrangement even temporarily; but if it must be ...I will stand on the great principle of popular sovereignty... and I will endeavor to defend it against assault from any and all quarters." (S. A. Douglas, *Speech on the President's Message delivered in the Senate of the United States, December 9, 1857*, Washington, 1857, p. 15.)

56. In 1856, six Northwestern states, Ohio, Michigan, Indiana, Illinois, Wisconsin and Iowa, gave Frémont 559,864 votes out of 1,341,-264 cast for him. In other words, 41.7% of the total vote given to Frémont came from the Northwest.

57. On this point, the Republican platform of 1860 stated, "That the normal condition of all the territory of the United States is that of freedom; that as our Republican fathers, when they had abolished slavery in all of our national territory, ordained that no person should be deprived of life, liberty, or property without due process of law, it becomes our duty... to maintain this provision of the Constitution against all attempts to violate it; and we deny the authority of Congress, of a territorial legislature, or of any individual, to give legal existence to slavery in any Territory of the United

States." (As quoted in E. Stanwood, *History of Presidential Elections*, Boston, 1888, pp. 229-30.)

58. In 1860, the seven Northwestern states of Indiana, Illinois, Iowa, Michigan, Minnesota, Ohio and Wisconsin had a population of 7,773,820, while the white population of the fifteen slave states of the South was 8,036,940.

59. Leporello, the servant of Don Juan, represents the typical rogue.

60. For official figures in respect to the population of Delaware and other Southern states, with specific reference to Negro population, see *Population of the United States in 1860; compiled from the Original Returns of the Eighth Census*, Washington, 1864, pp. 598-599.

61. In the early part of 1861, the people of Tennessee opposed the calling of a convention by a vote of 69,673 to 57,798. The Union stronghold of East Tennessee voted against a convention by a 25,611 majority, while Middle Tennessee followed suit but with a substantially smaller margin. On the other hand, West Tennessee supported the move by 15,118 votes.

62. On June 8, 1861, the people of Tennessee voted as follows on the question of secession:

	For	Against
East Tennessee	14,780	32,923
Middle Tennessee	58,265	8,198
West Tennessee	29,127	6,117
Military Camps	2,741	—
	104,913	47,238

63. As early as March, 1861, a convention, held in Missouri, declared itself opposed to secession by a vote of 89 to 1. Yet, the slave power dominated the state machinery to such an extent that Missouri was slowly but surely drawn into the orbit of Confederate influence. In order to avert this, a convention, reflecting the real sentiments of the people, gathered in Jefferson City during the latter part of July. At this meeting Governor Jackson, leader of the slave party, was deposed and Gamble, a Union man, elected in his place. Thus, by August, 1861, the state government of Missouri was definitely brought over to the support of the Union cause.

64. Prior to 1848, a considerable number of Germans, hoping to establish an independent state, made their way to Texas where they were eagerly welcomed by the authorities. They were followed in

1848 and 1849 by thousands of German revolutionaries; by 1850, the German element, according to one estimate, formed one-fifth of the white population of the state. The majority of those coming over after the revolution of 1848 were anti-slavery men. In 1853, the latter organized an abolition society, the *Frier Verein*. One year later, a convention was held in San Antonio demanding the end of slavery. When the Civil War broke out, most Germans in the state opposed secession and throughout the struggle, they remained loyal to the Union government.

65. The slave power in Georgia, rather than risk the possibility of a popular rejection of the Montgomery Constitution, submitted it for ratification to a state convention. The latter, under the control of the slavocracy, accepted the Constitution on March 16, 1861, without a dissenting vote. The same procedure was adopted in other Southern states where hand-picked conventions, rather than the people, proceeded to ratify the new instrument of government.

66. In August, 1861, General Frémont issued a proclamation confiscating the property of all persons in Missouri taking up arms against the Washington government or abetting the enemy in any way. The manifesto further declared that the slaves of such traitors were to be regarded as freemen. To carry out his proclamation the Union general established bureaus of abolition and issued decrees of freedom. Lincoln officially directed Frémont to revoke the order.

67. In 1833, Parliament passed a law abolishing slavery throughout the Empire. In the British West Indies, the government paid the slaveholders at the rate of £2 for each chattel set free. The purchase price had to be covered by further taxes on the population, *i.e.*, in the first place on the Negroes themselves.

68. See Brownson's review of A. Cochin's *L'Abolition de l'Esclavage* in *Brownson's Quarterly Review, Third New York Series* (New York, 1861), vol. ii, pp. 510-46.

69. Crédit Mobilier was a French bank founded in 1852 by the brothers Péreire. The object of the bank was the organization of credit for industry, the final result of which would be, in the view of its founders, the establishment of a banking monopoly over the whole of industry. In point of fact, the new bank was only an instrument of Bonapartism and a means for the subordination of industry to stock exchange speculation. Marx exposed the connection of Bonapartism with the Crédit Mobilier and analyzed the class character of the whole arrangement. (See Marx's articles in the *New York Daily Tribune*, June 21, 24 and July 11, 1856. The series is entitled "The French Crédit Mobilier.")

70. For the text of the convention, consult *Appleton's Annual Cyclopaedia, 1861* (New York, 1862), pp. 466-67.

71. About 1861, English, French and Spanish claims upon the Mexican government were estimated as follows:

British bondholders' debt......................	$60,621,843.00
Spanish convention............................	7,270,600.75
English-Spanish convention....................	5,000,000.00
French convention.............................	263,490.00
	$73,155,933.75

72. Refers to the King of Naples who reigned from 1859-61. In 1861, the Neapolitan kingdom became part of united Italy.

73. Frémont turned over his command to Hunter on November 2, 1861.

74. Battle fought in McClellan's department resulting in a Northern defeat. Although the casualties were relatively small, the outcome of the battle was distinctly depressing to Union sympathizers.

75. See reference note 28.

76. See reference note 40.

77. Captain Wilkes apparently intended to do just that. In reporting the transaction to the Secretary of the Navy, he wrote, "It was my determination to have taken possession of the *Trent*, and send her to Key West as a prize, for resisting the search, and carrying these passengers ... but the reduced number of my officers and crew, and the large number of passengers on board, bound for Europe, who would be put to great inconvenience, decided me to allow them to proceed." (As quoted in M. Bernard, *Historical Account of the Neutrality of Great Britain during the American Civil War*, London, 1870, p. 191.)

78. The pseudonym of an English radical publicist, Sir Phillip Francis (1740-1818), author of a series of pamphlets which contained sharp attacks on the oligarchical government of George III.

79. In November, 1845, Slidell was sent by President Polk to Mexico in order to adjust the Texan boundary claims and to purchase New Mexico and possibly California. The Mexican government having refused to deal with him, he soon returned to the United States.

80. Slidell played an important rôle in the canvass of 1852 and helped elect Pierce president. The latter offered him a diplomatic post in Central America, but the Louisianan refused. In 1853, he became a member of the Senate and three years later aided in the election of his friend Buchanan. The latter proposed to include Slidell in his Cabinet but the Louisianan preferred to continue to serve the slave interests of his state in the Senate. As the confidential adviser of Buchanan, Slidell exerted considerable influence and helped shape the policies of the administration.

81. On the eve of the Civil War, the Buchanan cabinet utilized its executive powers to strengthen the South and disarm the North. Floyd, the Secretary of War, played a notorious and decisive rôle in this connection. In the first place, he disposed of the armed forces in such a manner as to render them useless in case of a Southern uprising. In 1860, out of 16,000 men in the regular army, 15,000 were garrisoned west of the Mississippi and only 1,000 east. Of the latter, very few were placed in the key forts of the South and consequently these posts were easy marks for surprise attacks. This state of affairs was fully realized by General Scott, who in October and December, 1860, advised that more men be stationed in these forts. His recommendation, however, was flatly refused by the treacherous Floyd who a little later declared before a Southern audience that if he had given in to Scott, the Confederacy would never have come into being.

In the second place, the Secretary of War aided the slave power by furnishing it with arms and munitions, transferring cannons from Northern arsenals to Southern and using Congressional appropriations to equip the militia of the South. In his efforts to weaken the North, Floyd was assisted by another pro-slavery cabinet minister, Toucey. As Secretary of the Navy, Toucey did nothing to strengthen the American fleet; on the contrary, it reached its lowest point of efficiency since the War of 1812. In the meantime, the Secretary of Treasury, Cobb, a Georgian slaveholder, was leaving his department without a dollar and thus was, in the words of Toombs, another traitor, depriving the North of the "sinews of war."

82. During the American War of Independence, British captains and admirals claimed the right to search and seize neutral vessels trading with America or bearing contraband of war. Against this practice, Catherine II of Russia objected and in 1780 a league was formed with Sweden and Denmark to uphold the protest with force, if necessary. Prussia, Portugal, the Two Sicilies and Holy Roman Empire later joined. In 1800, Bonaparte succeeded in making Russia revive the league against England; this time the "Armed Neutrality of the North" included Russia, Prussia, Sweden and Denmark.

83. For pertinent extracts from the diplomatic correspondence between the British and American governments on the subject of the adhesion of the United States to the Declaration of Paris, see *Appleton's Annual Cyclopaedia, 1861* (New York, 1862), pp. 266-68.

84. In 1859, Napoleon III found himself in an extremely difficult position. A war between Sardinia and Austria was imminent; the French liberals demanded that Bonaparte support the former against the latter. The French emperor hesitated because he felt that a united Italy under Sardinian leadership would threaten his ambition to dominate Italian policies and at the same time alienate the sympathies of his clerical supporters. After much wavering, he decided to ally himself with Sardinia when the latter promised him Nice and Savoy.

85. At the outbreak of the Civil War, a considerable amount of British capital was invested in American enterprises. English capitalists were interested in such railroads as the New York and Erie, the Baltimore and Ohio, the Philadelphia and Reading and the Illinois Central; in such New York and Philadelphia banks as the Manhattan Company and the Girard Bank; in such insurance firms as the New York Life and American Life; in such mining companies as Pennsylvania Bituminous Coal, Land and Timber and Leigh Coal and Mining; and in such land enterprises as the Baring holdings in Maine and the American Land Company holdings in West Virginia.

86. The reference is to Lord Palmerston who was defeated in 1858 in a parliamentary vote on the Conspiracy Bill. The bill was introduced by Palmerston under the influence of the action of the Italian terrorist, Orsini, who attempted to assassinate Napoleon III in 1858.

87. In June, 1859, the Chinese closed the mouth of the Pei-ho and announced that any attempt on the part of the British, French or Americans to enter the river would be resisted. When the British and French endeavored to force the barriers constructed by the Chinese, a battle took place and the allied forces were repulsed. During the struggle, the American Commodore, a Southerner by the name of Tattnall, aided the British and defended his conduct on the ground that "blood was thicker than water."

88. By the Catholic Emancipation Act of 1829, Roman Catholics were admitted to all offices with the exception of a few high governmental posts. The Reform Bill of 1832 provided for a redistribution of parliamentary seats and the extension of the franchise to

the middle classes. The Corn Laws were parliamentary statutes forbidding the importation of foreign wheat unless the average price of wheat in the United Kingdom was 70s per quarter; these laws, designed to maintain relatively high grain prices, were repealed in 1846. The Ten-Hour Law of 1847 limited the labor of women and children in textile factories to ten hours a day. The war against Russia refers to the Crimean War of 1853 to 1856 when England, France and Sardinia joined Turkey in her struggle against Russia. The Conspiracy Bill, introduced in 1858 by Palmerston, was rejected by Parliament.

89. See reference note 38.

90. In 1858, Great Britain took the government of India out of the hands of the East India Company. By a parliamentary act control was transferred to a Secretary of State aided by a Council of fifteen members, eight appointed by the Crown and seven by the directors of the old company.

91. In 1858, a secret treaty was concluded between the rulers of France and Sardinia by which Victor Emanuel agreed to cede Nice and Savoy to Napoleon III in return for the latter's aid against Austria. War broke out in 1859. As a speedy victory over Austria seemed probable, the French Emperor deserted his ally. Nevertheless, he demanded Nice and Savoy and after some delay on the part of Sardinia, was given both territories (March, 1860). The Palmerston government remonstrated "warmly" against this "outrage" and even used "language which threatened war." Yet, it did nothing about the matter since it was "afraid" that Napoleon III might abrogate the recently signed Anglo-French commercial treaty whereby France had reduced her duties on all articles of British manufacture.

92. See reference note 25.

93. On January 11, 1862, Lincoln removed Cameron from his post as Secretary of War and appointed him Minister to Russia.

94. In March, 1862, Lincoln issued "General War Order, No. 3" in which McClellan was directed to take "the field at the head of the Army of the Potomac until otherwise ordered" and that he be "relieved from the command of the other military department...."

95. At the time of the *Trent* case, Yancey addressed a memorial to the British government raising the question of the effectiveness of the Northern blockade. He presented a list of over 40 ships which

had evaded capture up to August 7, 1861. A little later Mason did likewise; in his memorial he asserted that some 300 vessels had run the blockade successfully.

96. In his letter to Earl Russell, dated February 7, 1862, Mason defined quasi-inland vessels as those going "through the estuaries and sounds along the coast."

97. In 1860, Alabama, Georgia, Louisiana, Mississippi, Florida, South Carolina and Texas had a total population of 4,969,141; of these 2,312,350 or 46.5% were slaves. In two of these states, South Carolina and Mississippi, the number of slaves was greater than the combined white and free Negro population. The total population of Virginia, Tennessee, North Carolina and Arkansas was 4,134,191 in 1860; of these 1,208,758 or 29.2% were slaves.

98. As during the first American Revolution, so during the Civil War the progressive forces of the nation were aided in their struggle for freedom by European revolutionaries. Particularly conspicuous in this connection were the German revolutionary émigrés of 1848-49, bourgeois liberals like Schurz and Kapp and working-class radicals like Weydemeyer and Anneke. These men, along with a host of others like them, used the military experience they had gained during the armed uprisings in Germany to good advantage against the Confederacy by organizing and leading Union armies on the field of battle. In addition to enlisting in American recruited regiments, the "Forty-eighters" organized their own detachments. For example, the 8th German Volunteer Regiment was one of many. In this company was the one-time editor of the socialist paper, *Die Sociale Republik*, Struve, who held the rank of captain. It is estimated by one authority that about 200,000 Germans volunteered to fight on the side of the North against the reactionary slave power.

99. From a military and political viewpoint the Kentucky campaign of 1862 was of extreme importance. The Confederate line of defense, running from Columbus to Bowling Green, possessed two vital points in Tennessee, Forts Henry and Donelson. These Confederate strongholds defended two important gateways to the "deep" South, the Cumberland and Tennessee Rivers. Their capture would not only open the heart of the Confederacy to Northern penetration, but would also render untenable the Confederate position in Kentucky. Consequently these forts became the chief immediate objectives of the Union campaign and under Grant's direction were occupied. The attack upon Fort Donelson forced the abandonment of Bowling Green and Columbus and the evacuation of Nashville (Tenn.).

These Union victories were of great military significance. By opening the Tennessee River, they permitted Federal penetration into northern Alabama and especially into Georgia, thus affording the North an opportunity of driving a wedge through the Confederacy by separating the northern Atlantic from the Gulf States. Moreover, these successes meant the occupation of Kentucky, a vital Border State, and the partial recovery of Tennessee; in all, a Federal advance of over two hundred miles. Similarly the Union victories of 1862 were politically important. They showed Europe and especially England that the South was not invincible on the battlefield. Furthermore, they set at rest all doubts as to Kentucky's part in the civil conflict and thus made possible the waging of a more revolutionary war.

100. For official figures in respect to the size of the opposing armies in this and other instances, see *The War of the Rebellion: A Compilation of the Official Records of the Union and Confederate Armies.* Series I will prove especially helpful. Consisting of fifty-three volumes, it includes Union and Confederate reports of the first seizure of United States property in the Southern States and of all military operations in the field.

101. Refers to the episode of the Franco-Spanish war when Saragossa was stubbornly defended for more than two months (December, 1808, to February, 1809) against the French troops that considerably outnumbered the forces of the garrison. The other example is Moscow which was set on fire by the Russians in 1812 after it had been captured by Napoleon I.

102. During the early part of April, 1862, General Mitchell occupied Huntsville, situated mid-way between Chattanooga and Corinth.

103. The letter was sent by Mayor John T. Monroe to Farragut on April 26, 1862. Two days later the Federal naval commander replied. For both of these letters see H. Greeley, *The American Conflict* (Hartford, 1866), vol. ii, p. 95, note 17. Also consult *Battles and Leaders of the Civil War* (New York, 1887), vol. ii, pp. 95-99, for an account of Farragut's demand for the surrender of New Orleans and Mayor Monroe's melodramatic outbursts.

104. Both of these vessels were not fully completed when the battle of New Orleans began. Of the two, the *Louisiana* was the only one to see action. The *Mississippi* was set on fire by the Confederates to prevent her from falling into the hands of the Union forces.

105. For the original text of the treaty see *United States, Treaties, Conventions, International Acts, etc., 1776-1909*, compiled by W. M. Malloy (Washington, 1910), vol. i, pp. 674-87.

106. These battles were fought during Napoleon's attempted conquest of Russia in 1812.

107. In the struggle between the parties of the aristocrats and democrats, Cato the Younger (95-46 B.C.) occupied a vacillating position, declaring that he was equally grieved at the defeat of either party.

108. The reference here is to the Polish insurrection of 1831 which was put down with unexampled savagery by the generals of Nicholas I.

109. From 1815 to 1849, the Ionian Islands were under British control; in 1849, a Greek uprising occurred there which was suppressed with great cruelty by the English.

110. During the Second Punic War, the inhabitants of the town of Sagunt, an ally of Rome, stoutly resisted the siege of Hannibal, the women fighting side by side with the men.

111. See reference note 50.

112. This was done in April, 1861; slavemasters were given $300 on the average for each chattel freed. Congress appropriated $1,000,000 for this purpose.

113. In June 1862, Lincoln signed a bill declaring that "there shall be neither slavery nor involuntary servitude in any territories of the United States now existing, or which may at any time hereafter be formed, or acquired. . . ."

114. In 1780, Pennsylvania passed a law providing for the gradual emancipation of slaves by declaring that no children thereafter born in the state of slave parents shall be slaves. Such children, however, were to be "servants" until the age of twenty-eight; thereafter all claims on their services were to cease.

115. In June, 1862, a bill was passed authorizing the President to appoint diplomatic representatives to Hayti and Liberia.

116. In the resolutions referred to, the New York Chamber of Commerce declared: "Better every rebel die than one loyal soldier."

117. Joseph Weydemeyer (1818-66) was a member of the Communist League who took part in the German revolutionary movement of 1848-49. On account of his radical activities, he was forced to flee to America. In 1852, Weydemeyer published a newspaper in New York called *Die Revolution,* only one number of which was issued.

It was in this number that Marx's famous *Eighteenth Brumaire of Louis Bonaparte* first appeared. One year later, the German Communist helped found the *Arbeiterbund* (Workingmen's League). When the Civil War broke out, Weydemeyer, along with other Socialists, fought on the side of the North not only to preserve the Union but also to abolish slavery. For many years he corresponded with Marx.

118. Conscription was used to raise an army during the American Revolution as well as during the War of 1812. In the former, according to C. K. Bolton in his *Private Soldier under Washington*, a plan was adopted at one time to draft one man in every four or five, excluding those already serving, those living in seaboard or frontier towns, school teachers, students and in some cases powder-mill employees. Those wishing to avoid conscription did so by paying fines. During the War of 1812, a conscription bill was introduced in Congress over the opposition of the representatives from New England. At about the same time, New York enacted a bill to raise a conscript army.

119. In September, 1862, Lincoln adopted the step of partial slave emancipation. The rising tide of abolitionist sentiment in the North, the declining influence of the Border state slave interests, military successes in Maryland and earlier in the year in Kentucky, together with the obvious advantage of depriving the Confederacy of its labor supply, combined to make Lincoln issue a preliminary Emancipation Proclamation. The latter provided that all persons held as slaves in any state or part of a state still in rebellion on January 1, 1863, were to be free. Though limited in scope, the proclamation served as a prologue to the Thirteenth Amendment.

120. In 1862, ten Northern states gave the Opposition 35,781 votes more than the Administration, whereas two years before the Lincoln forces received a 208,066 majority in these same states. In 1862, the latter elected 67 members of the Opposition to the Congress as against 57 for the Administration, while in 1860 the Administration congressmen from these states outnumbered those of the Opposition 78 to 37.

121. Halleck was elevated to that rank on July 11, 1862, when he became military adviser to Lincoln.

122. See Halleck's letter to Stanton, October 28, 1862, in *Appleton's Annual Cyclopaedia, 1862*, pp. 162-63.

123. Refers to the victory of the Union army at Antietam, September 17, 1862. Lee, the Confederate commander, was forced to withdraw to Virginia.

124. In 1861, the *Alabama,* a Confederate war vessel, was built in England; just before she was officially launched, she was taken outside of the three-mile limit and there fitted out with munitions and armaments. The American Minister, Adams, immediately protested to the British government, condemning the transaction. For a number of years the *Alabama* preyed on Northern commerce; she was finally destroyed in 1864 by the American cruiser, *Kearsarge.* After the war, the United States, holding England responsible for the damages done, claimed and received reparations.

125. In October, 1862, Galveston (Texas) was occupied without resistance by a Union naval force consisting of four steam gunboats.

126. Marx has in mind the agitation of the Russian serfs on the eve of the "reforms" of 1861.

127. See reference note 13.

128. Refers to Rosewell Sabin Ripley, an authority on the Mexican War. His book, *The War with Mexico,* was published in 1849.

129. At the Battle of Big Bethel the inexperienced Union general, Pierce, was severely beaten by the Confederates. The Federals lost about 100 men, while the Rebels lost 8.

130. Bernstein and Willich participated in the German revolutionary movements of 1848-49. Willich fought alongside of Engels in the Baden uprising and was a member of the Communist League. He was expelled from that organization in 1852. Weber was a Berlin lawyer and an acquaintance of Marx.

131. In 1860, Lincoln received a total of 1,866,452 votes, of these 809,872 or 43.4% of his total was cast by the seven Northwestern states of Illinois, Indiana, Iowa, Minnesota, Michigan, Ohio, and Wisconsin. In the electoral college Lincoln received 180 votes of which 66 or 36.6% came from the Northwest.

132. See reference note 62.

133. Toward the close of January, 1861, the people of North Carolina voted against the calling of a convention to decide the question of secession. The vote was 47,323 to 46,672. At the same time, they voted to elect Union delegates in case a convention was held. In this election 82 Constitutional Union men and 38 Secessionists were chosen. Although the people of Arkansas decided to hold a conven-

tion by a vote of 27,412 to 15,826, they showed a distinct Union
tendency in the election of delegates to the gathering. Out of 41,553
votes cast 23,626 were given to Union representatives.

134. After Virginia passed her ordinance of secession, a convention
met at Wheeling (June-August, 1861) which set up a government
rivaling that of Richmond and which decreed the formation of a
new state. In November, a constitutional convention was held and a
new instrument of government drawn up. This was ratified by the
people in April, 1862. Toward the close of that year, Lincoln signed
a bill admitting West Virginia to the Union.

135. In February 1861, 34,794 votes were cast for the secession ordinance and 11,235 against.

136. The hostility of the North Alabama delegation to the slave
interests of the state was reflected in the fight to have the secession
ordinance submitted to the people. Davis of Huntsville declared that
North Alabama would never abide by the decision of the convention
unless the people had the opportunity to vote on the matter. Thereupon, Yancey, representing the slave power, denounced the people
of the northern section of the state as "tories, traitors and rebels."
The proposition to submit the ordinance of secession to the people
was voted down.

137. According to Greeley, "... the vote for Union and that for
Secession delegates [in Louisiana] were just about equal. As made
up by the Secessionists, they stood: For Secession 20,448; Against it,
17,296." (H. Greeley, *The American Conflict*, Hartford, 1864, vol. i, p.
348.) The convention refused to submit the act to the people.

138. Marx compares the actions of the Secessionists with the *coup
d'état* of Louis Napoleon on December 2, 1851, when Bonaparte,
relying on armed forces and with a parody of universal suffrage,
established a dictatorship.

139. For the treachery of the members of the Buchanan Cabinet see
reference note 81.

140. This was done on March 13, 1861, by a vote of 87 to 5.

141. Engels has in mind the arrests of Mason and Slidell, who were
removed from the English mail steamer, the *Trent*, by Captain
Wilkes, commander of the American warship *San Jacinto*. See reference note 28.

142. At this time, the Confederate general, Albert S. Johnston, was fighting a losing battle in Kentucky and Tennessee. His name is spelt in the same fashion as that of Joseph E. Johnston, another Confederate commander who fought in the first battle of Bull Run. Hence the interchange of personalities.

143. Napoleon fought the Russians at Eylau (1807), the Austrians at Wagram (1809), the Russians at Borodino (1812), and the combined Prussian and Russian forces at Lützen and Bautzen (1813). At Wagram, the French Emperor won a notable engagement, the others proving to be hollow victories. In the battles of Magenta and Solferino (Italian War of 1859), the decisive action of the French army brought about the defeat of the Austrian forces.

144. From the close of 1862 to the end of the Civil War, desertions in the Confederate armies mounted steadily and at times assumed the proportions of general insurrectionary movements. In 1862, there were from eight to ten thousand deserters in the mountainous districts of Alabama, many of whom banded together, killed their officers and repulsed cavalry units sent against them. Similarly western North Carolina and northern Georgia harbored roving bands of deserters. Governor Vance of North Carolina attempted to arrest them but with little success. At the same time, the commanding officer at Dahlonega threatened to send Confederate soldiers into northern Georgia to put down "an insurrectionary movement."

Throughout the following year, the number of deserters grew steadily, especially after the Vicksburg and Gettysburg defeats. The deserters, organized in groups, wandered up and down the countryside and when stopped and asked to produce their leaves of absence replied that their guns were their furloughs. In North Carolina, the officials were entirely unable to cope with the situation. Organized into bands of fifty to a hundred, deserters seized towns, held them under a sort of military occupation and called upon those still fighting to lay down their arms. In 1864, Lee attempted to bring back deserters through a general order of leniency; the response was, however, negligible. In fact, during that year, as many as 8,000 Alabamans left their regiments in Virginia and Tennessee and, according to one commandant, 5,000 returned to their homes.

145. In May 1862, the Union General Wool, upon entering Norfolk, found the dry dock blown up, the *Merrimac* completely destroyed, and two unfinished iron-clads set on fire.

146. In 1862, Chase, Secretary of the Treasury, suggested a national paper currency to help meet the mounting cost of the war. In Feb-

ruary of the same year, Congress passed a law authorizing the issue of $150,000,000 of United States notes to be accepted as legal tender for all public and private obligations except duties on imports and interest on the national debt. This act was followed by one in June and another toward the end of the year. In all, some $400,000,000 of these so-called greenbacks were issued during the war. Currency inflation brought with it higher commodity prices, gold hoarding and the disappearance of smaller coins. The latter was particularly distressing, especially in the larger cities. To relieve the situation, business houses issued brass and copper tokens, while restaurants issued "shin plasters" and meal tickets.

147. In 1863, Ferdinand Lassalle (1825-1864) organized the *Allgemeiner Deutscher Arbeiter Verein (General German Workers Union)*, the first political mass organization of the German workers, which he attempted to lead on the path of agreement with Bismarck's bourgeois-junker state. Marx and Engels subjected Lassalle's views to sharp criticism and conducted a persistent struggle against Lassalleanism. See especially the *Critique of the Gotha Programme* (1875) where Marx reveals the basic defects of the Lassallean theory.

148. During the early years of the Civil War, the Federal government attempted to discourage the enrollment of Negroes in the Union army. In 1861, Lincoln, fearful of alienating the sympathies of the Border slave interests, steadily refused to recruit colored regiments despite the remonstrances of his War Secretary, Cameron. During the following year, an even more insistent demand was made for the organization of Negro companies; a host of abolitionists, led by Frederick Douglass, demanded that the government allow Negroes to fight for the freedom of their enslaved brothers. They argued that such a procedure would demoralize Southern white regiments and stimulate slave insurrection.

Although Lincoln still hesitated, some of his radical generals did not. David Hunter, commander of the land forces on the coast of Georgia and South Carolina, organized, drilled and equipped Negro detachments. These later formed the nucleus around which General Saxton built the First South Carolina Volunteers. In the meantime, Butler organized three Negro regiments in Louisiana. From 1863 onward, when fighting was begun by the North in a revolutionary manner, Negro soldiers appeared more frequently in the Union fighting line. Recruited from Northern petty bourgeois and working class elements and from Southern fugitive and freed slaves, these Negro companies were treated in the most appalling fashion by Confederate generals who, refusing to capture Negro troops alive, allowed their men to butcher them. Yet, in spite of all atrocities, the number of

Negro soldiers constantly increased; almost 200,000 volunteered their services in the cause of freedom.

149. In June 1862, Pope was placed in command of the Army of Virginia. Toward the end of August, he was defeated at Bull Run and on September 5 was relieved of his command.

150. See reference note 119.

151. In the New York gubernatorial elections of November 1862, Horatio Seymour, Democrat, defeated General James S. Wadsworth by a majority of 10,752 votes. Throughout his campaign, Seymour criticized the administration and in his inaugural message of January 1863, opposed the restoration of the Union through revolutionary means, that is, through the abolition of slavery.

152. In 1861, the Confederate Congress empowered Jefferson Davis to call out and keep in the army for three years all white men from eighteen to thirty-five years of age, unless legally exempted. Governor Brown of Georgia, protesting the statute, refused to allow state officers to act as enrollers. In November 1862, the state legislature appointed a committee to investigate the action of the Confederate Congress. A majority of the committee reported that the Confederacy had no right to draft citizens of a state except by requisition upon the several states for their quotas.

153. Refers to Burnside's defeat at the battle of Fredericksburg, December 13-15, 1862.

154. Workers' meetings were held throughout England toward the close of December 1862. At one meeting in Manchester 6,000 were present and a resolution was passed urging Lincoln to uproot slavery completely. A similar demonstration was held in London. At this meeting the workers present requested the American President to continue his work and thereby achieve "the glorious principle on which your constitution is founded—the brotherhood, freedom and equality of all men." Lincoln, in his reply to these addresses, thanked the British proletariat for their good wishes and felt that the American people would be encouraged to know that they had the sympathy of the "true friends of freedom and humanity." (Quotations are taken from Schlüter, *Lincoln, Labor and Slavery*, New York, 1913, pp. 159, 165.)

155. In January, 1863, Hooker replaced Burnside as commander of the Army of the Potomac. For the next two months, he attempted

to make his army an efficient fighting machine by improving discipline and raising the morale of his troops. By the close of March, he had at his disposal about 125,000 men.

156. Refers to General Hooker. Toward the close of March 1863, Hooker announced to his officers that his plans were perfect and that he would have no mercy upon Lee. At the battle of Chancellorsville (May 1863), the Confederate army, though outnumbered two to one, forced Hooker to retreat. Despite this reverse, the Union commander issued an order in which he congratulated his army for its "achievements." (For his General Orders, No. 49, see *War of the Rebellion: Official Records, Army*, 1 ser., xxv, pt. 1, p. 171.)

157. One of the soubriquets of Napoleon III. It is derived from the names of the three towns from which he attempted to seize the throne, Boulogne, Strassburg, Paris.

158. The hero of an anonymous Spanish novel published in the seventeenth century. The type of hidalgo-adventurer.

159. Refers to Eleanor Marx (1855-96), the youngest daughter of Karl Marx. She became the wife of the English socialist, Edward Aveling, and took an active part in the British labor movement.

160. In May 1864, Grant crossed the Rapidan and entered the Wilderness on the march to Richmond. Lee attacked Grant on the battlefield of Chancellorsville. A bloody struggle followed and Grant, deciding that nothing could be done, retraced his steps to the Rapidan and directed his army southward.

161. Sherman occupied Atlanta in the early part of September 1864.

162. In the summer of 1864, Lincoln, desiring to attract the support of the Northern peace group in the coming presidential election, allowed negotiations to be carried on with the South. In July, Greeley met a number of Confederate "ambassadors" at Niagara Falls; since the latter were acting without any authority, the parley was soon adjourned. In the same month, Jacquess, a fighting Methodist clergyman, and Gilmore, a novelist, went to Richmond. Again the venture failed since Davis made it clear that peace could only be concluded on condition that the North recognize the independence of the South. In August, Jeremiah Black, a colleague of Stanton's in Buchanan's Cabinet, visited Toronto and conferred with Jacob Thompson, a fanatical partisan of the slave power. With both acting unofficially, little was accomplished and the negotiations soon ceased. While these

parleys were in progress, the radicals within the Republican Party bitterly condemned the actions of the administration for they fully realized that if the negotiations succeeded, their plan for unconditional emancipation and drastic punishment of the traitors was doomed.

163. Lubez was a French democrat who lived in London. He taught music and French and acted as secretary-correspondent for France in the general council of the First International. On account of intrigue and slander, Lubez was expelled from the International in 1866.

164. On the night of April 14, 1865, Booth, a fanatical partisan of the slave power, shot and killed Lincoln. In the meantime, two of his associates, Payne and Atzerodt, attempted to assassinate Johnson, the Vice-President and Seward, the Secretary of State.

165. On April 26, 1865, Johnston's army surrendered to Sherman. The terms of capitulation were similar to those extended to Lee.

166. On June 9, 1864, Johnson declared at Nashville that "the great plantations [of the traitors] must be seized and divided into small farms and sold to honest industrious men."

167. The elevation of Johnson to the presidency following the assassination of Lincoln was enthusiastically hailed by the leaders of the Radical wing of the Republican Party. They saw in the new president a man after their own heart, a vigorous opponent of "the bloated slavocracy" of the South. As such, they expected him to punish the ex-Confederate leaders, to break up their large landed estates and to guarantee Negro suffrage. Their expectations, howver, were not realized, as Johnson, wedged between a falling oligarchy (slave planters) and a rising plutocracy (industrial and financial bourgeoisie), decided to fight the latter by capitulating to the former. The result was a "reactionary holiday" the beginnings of which became apparent in May, 1865, when Johnson issued a proclamation providing for the reconstruction of seven Southern states along the lines laid down by Lincoln. During the summer and fall of 1865, all of these states, except Texas, complied with the President's request, elected state officials and sent representatives to Congress. However, in December, 1865, both houses declined to permit the newly elected members to take their seats. Under these circumstances, the battle was on with Stevens, the leader of the parliamentary Left, gradually winning over a majority of congressmen to the formulation of a Radical reconstruction program. (See J. S. Allen, *Reconstruction: the Battle for Democracy,* New York, 1937.)

168. The One Hundred Years War (1337-1453) was a struggle between France and England which finally resulted in the freeing of the western duchies and counties of France.

169. The Thirty Years War broke out in 1618 with a rebellion in Bohemia against the Hapsburg ruler of the Holy Roman Empire. Civil war in Central Europe gave Denmark, Sweden and France an opportunity to intervene. In 1648, the conflict was brought to a close by the treaties of Westphalia.

170. Refers to the period from 1740 to 1763 which was marked by a series of uninterrupted struggles. In 1740, the War of the Austrian Succession began; this conflict grew out of the desire of Frederick the Great to take Silesia from Austria. Before the war ended (1748), Prussia was joined by France, Spain and Bavaria, while Austria was allied with England. In the meantime fighting took place between the English and the French in the New World and in India. In 1754, hostilities again broke out in America; this conflict, called the French and Indian War, soon merged into a general European struggle. In the Seven Years' War (1756-1763), Prussia and England opposed Austria, France and Spain. Meanwhile, the English and the French fought for supremacy in India. The Treaty of Hubertusburg (1763), ending the European phase of the struggle, insured the triumph of Prussia over Austria, while the Treaty of Paris (1763), closing the American and Indian part of the conflict, made England the chief colonial power of the world.

BIOGRAPHICAL INDEX

ADAMS, CHARLES F. (1807-86), member of Congress, afterward minister to England (1861-68).—pp. 37, 45, 100, 134 ff., 143, 273, 279, 283.

ANNEKE, FRIEDRICH (1817-66), member of the Communist League, participated in the revolution of 1848-49, thereafter emigrated to America, fought on the side of the North during the Civil War.—pp. 247 ff.

ANDERSON, ROBERT (1805-71), Union officer, defended Fort Sumter, later fought in Kentucky as a brigadier-general, relieved of his command because of ill health.—p. 60.

ASHBURTON, ALEXANDER BARING, BARON (1774-1848), English banker and Tory politician, President of the Board of Trade.—pp. 44, 144.

BANKS, NATHANIEL P. (1816-94), Union general, Governor of Massachusetts, Congressman, president of Illinois Central Railroad.—pp. 248 ff.

BEAUREGARD, PIERRE GUSTAVE TOUTANT (1818-93), Confederate general, given charge of western theatre of war in 1862, wrote numerous papers on Civil War subjects.—pp. 60, 181, 186, 189, 198, 240 ff., 269, 272.

BENNETT, JAMES G. (1795-1872), owner and editor of the *New York Herald*.—p. 159.

BERRY, HIRAM GREGORY (1824-63), Union officer, killed in battle of Chancellorsville.—p. 188.

BIRNEY, WILLIAM (1819-1907), Union general, participated in Paris uprising of 1848, organized Negro regiments during Civil War.—p. 188.

BONAPARTE, CHARLES LOUIS NAPOLEON (1808-73), third son of Louis Bonaparte, reigned as Napoleon III, Emperor of the French (1852 to 1870).—pp. 21 ff., 40, 45, 92 ff., 114, 127, 132, 177-8, 196-7, 222, 241 ff.

BONAPARTE, NAPOLEON (1769-1821), First Consul (1799-1804), Emperor of the French (1804-14).—pp. 53, 167, 212, 261.

BRAGG, BRAXTON (1817-76), Confederate general, fought in the battle of Shiloh (1862), afterward practically acted as military adviser to Jefferson Davis.—pp. 206-7, 268.

BRECKINRIDGE, JOHN CABELL (1821-75), Vice-President of the United States (1857-61), Senator from Kentucky, Confederate general and Secretary of War.—pp. 61, 69, 77, 199, 252.

BRIGHT, JOHN (1811-89), English liberal, prominent free-trade leader, organizer of the Anti-Corn Law League, member of Parliament, sympathetic to the North during the Civil War.—pp. 119, 127.

BROWN, JOHN (1800-59), militant abolitionist, fought to make Kansas a free state, led raid on Harper's Ferry, Virginia.—pp. 11, 221.

BROWNSON, ORESTES AUGUSTUS (1803-76), editor of the *Quarterly Review*, denounced secession and urged abolition of slavery, exerted influence among the Catholic voters of New York.—p. 82.

BUCHANAN, JAMES (1791-1868), Secretary of State under Polk, Minister to England under Pierce, President of the United States (1857-61).—pp. 8, 62 ff., 77, 98, 122, 159, 164, 230.

BUELL, DON C. (1818-98), Union general, participated in western campaign, resigned from army toward the close of the war.—pp. 156, 167, 173, 207, 240, 247.

BURNSIDE, AMBROSE EVERETT (1824-81), Union general, relieved of his command as leader of the Army of the Potomac after his defeat at Fredericksburg (1862), after the war elected Governor of Rhode Island.—pp. 213, 262-3.

BUTLER, BENJAMIN (1818-93), Union general, Congressman from Massa-

GENERAL INDEX